'REALLY HELP YO ECOLOGY'

Getting nature to conrol your pests & diseases.

Plants and co-lives; their associated fauna: insects, nematodes, bacteria, fungi large & small and shared viruses

-being Volume 3 'Plant Companions and Co-lives'

paper edition Bob Flowerdew 2018

There are no 'pests and diseases' but 'co-lives' living amongst many others, and all are food for some thing else. We need to more fully understand the micro-ecology of not just the few but of the almost countless other flora and fauna inter-acting with our chosen plants. We may then reduce our 'pest & disease' problems by encouraging their natural controls, and then we also benefit from the fertility created by the process.

Also available

'REALLY HELP YOUR PLANTS'
Plants and other plants, their good and bad companions and worst weeds -being Volume 1 of 'Plant Companions and Co-lives'.

'REALLY HELP BUTTERFLIES'
Plants and Lepidoptera; the caterpillars and thus butterflies these plants support -being Volume 2 of 'Plant Companions and Co-lives'

'REALLY HELP YOUR CROPS'
Farm, orchard and horticultural crops and their associated flora and fauna including worst weeds -extracts from all 3 volumes of 'Plant Companions and Co-lives'

Dedication- to a bee, she works so hard for our honey

Contents

INTRODUCTION

Plants, both in our gardens and beyond, do not exist independently in isolation and are but one part of a huge intricate web of lives, animal and vegetable, big and small. This ecological mix involves almost all and every life on our planet and is continually in flux and evolution. Every living thing is jostling for living space and resources and needs to find its niche. In this melée some have become entwined with others, inter-dependent or actually reliant.

In nature associations have formed over time to fit local environmental conditions. Bogs, heaths, woodlands and meadows are examples of different plant communities. These are combinations of plants most suited to those conditions, and each other, and with all the other forms of life that live with and on those plants. There are lives that survive by eating certain plants, more lives that live by eating those, with further tiers up the chain of life, and also the many others who dispose of all the excreta and dead bodies, with everything eventually recycling back through the soil to the plants again.

This web of life evolved over the ages becoming more and more complex and self correcting. Whereas in our farms and gardens we cultivate only a small range of plants, many 'native' to other situations, and in a mix that would never be found in nature. Meanwhile we imagined each plant had no or but little effect on another save that of straight competition. We then dismissed most of their naturally associated life forms, their co-lives, that lived with or on them, as unwelcome intruders or worse as 'pests and diseases'. Only the bigger, prettier, co-lives were seen as 'wildlife' which needed 'encouragement'. To ensure our flowers and crops succeeded we perceived a 'need' to control some of these other plants and co-lives simply because our un-natural mix did not create the automatic checks and balances found in long standing plant communities. This attitude is coming to be realised erroneous.

Not pests & diseases but co-lives

There are no 'pests and diseases' but 'co-lives' living amongst many others, and all are food for some thing else. We need to more fully understand the micro-ecology of not just the few but of the almost countless other flora and fauna inter-acting with our chosen plants. We may then reduce our 'pest & disease' problems by encouraging their natural controls, and then we also benefit from the fertility engendered by the expanding process.

Part of the solution for the weakening of the web of life is growing more of those particular plants that enhance, improve and increase the diversity. Choosing some that sustain some 'otherwise unwanted' co-life themselves will then also increase the number and variety of the very parasites and predators most able to control it. These having increased go on to then control the same or similar 'co-life problems' on our crops.

A larger diversity of plants first increases the micro-fauna diversity and this then sustains the 'prettier and cuter' larger wild lives we love to see in our gardens. In doing so this also creates that more stable and productive mix we are after, and far more effectively than exists without such intervention.

And, in the meantime all the carnage and waste products become soil fertility to feed the plants.

This is the way nature works, one life feeds another ad infinitum. We know so little about any of the immense number of interconnections and interactions in this web of lives we are immersed within but can surely try to restore as many as we can to their original potential. Each and every life will have a significant effect on a whole chain.

It is attributed to Darwin that little changes may change much; "more old ladies in a village will lead to better crops of hay".

Old ladies often keep cats so more old ladies leads to more cats. Cats eat field mice. Thus more cats means less field mice, which destroy and take over wild bee nests. So less mice means more bees, which are necessary to pollinate clover and produce more viable seeds. Clover is a Leguminous plant providing surplus fertility to the grass so more clover means more grass and thus more hay. More old ladies, more cats, less mice, more bees, more viable seed, more clover, more grass, more hay. QED

Similar and amazing chain inter-reactions are repeated ad infinitum. "Every flea has smaller fleas...." The web of ecology is the sum of all of these. Every life has to find something to eat, and is in turn eaten, the plants feast on the remains, and also on all their excreta. The greater the number and diversity of lives the more carnage and by-products are created and the soil richens. The amount of biomass increases and in increasing variety, which produces an even more bounteous spread and the more fully and completely the plants are fed. The plants prosper oxygenating more air and fixing more Carbon, and go on to feed yet more co-lives. The base of the pyramid is all the unseen micro-life while at the top are the few larger co-lives. As the web becomes infinitely intricate the whole system supports all those co-lives we love to see- the butterflies, the birds, butterflies and bees, and us!

If we wish to hand over a functioning world to our great grandchildren we need to conserve all the species we have inherited as each is so really a vital link in that great chain, the web of life. This means we need cultivate those plants that each lives on, naturally these will mostly be native plants. Indeed any plant found to have few associated co-lives may not have long been here and is unlikely to be a native. However nature is always moving and so many imported plants, particularly evergreens, are so valuable in their way they've readily incorporated into the native web. Closely related species to a native plant may well prove as useful to some if not all co-lives. Basically and simply we need grow more plants in our gardens but especially natives!

For many decades I have gleaned old and modern literature to find references to plants and their relationships with other lives. Two important groups of 'associated co-lives' have been published as:

Volume 1 'Plants, their good and bad companions and worst weeds', notes of plant interactions with other plants.

Volume 2 'Plants and Lepidoptera', notes of which plants the caterpillars eat and thus the butterflies they support.

This, Volume 3, completes the set with the numerous other associated fauna, big and small, the multitudinous co-lives, found interacting with each plant, and which may inextricably be connected with each other, and our, survival.

The cast, in order of appearance

The following notes for each plant includes in order: inter-relationships with animals, both stock and wild, birds, many insects (other than 'benign' Lepidoptera) especially bees, with flowers being noted with particular association with a species, and co-life 'pests' or herbivorous critters: the aphids, bugs and beetles, browsers, borers and gall formers. Then come the most often found nematodes and other microscopic co-lives, bacteria (which we call 'diseases'), fungi small (more 'diseases') and larger (with notes on most commonly associated poisonous or edible 'mushrooms'), and viruses (a worryingly large and infective group of diseases we may unwittingly be aiding). And most importantly, with which other plants these co-lives are known to interact with / or spread to so we can be aware of any risks we may unknowingly fall into. I suspect most of us have little idea of the multitude of viruses threatening our crops and flowers and how wide a range of plants these can spread between.

When available I have added other pertinent notes and the mineral analysis (to determine a plants potential value for compost and green manure as well as its demands on the soil).

Key to the naming of plants and co-lives

Plant A-Z entries are alphabetical in Latin, eg. Acer followed by species under discussion eg. campestre, then common name(s) in capitals eg. FIELD MAPLE. Thus Acer campestre, FIELD MAPLE .

Where A-Z entries are not individual plants but are important or generic terms, these are in plain capitals thus MINERAL ACCUMULATORS.

Co-lives are referred to in the text by their English common name and only if needed to prevent confusion does the Latin follow, but without the intervening comma as used with plant names.

Where alternative common or Latin names are derived from older reference books, and recognised as such, these are entered spaced with / as in Galium aparine, GOOSE-GRASS / CLEAVER

Common names of other plants and co-lives embedded in the text are entered without initial capitals unless especially important to the case in question. For readability in the text where ever possible the common names are used, their specific Latin name will be found in the glossary.

Latin names are always started with a capital. Some annoying confusion occurs as Latin names keep being changed, this adding a huge level of complexity. Thus after a most recent, still commonly accepted name may follow a string of older or newer genus and species names, eg. Another gall-midge Mikiola fagi / Hormomyia / Cecidomyia / tornetalla causes smooth waxy pouch galls

My profuse apologies for the inelegant, indigestible chain this has created in places.

Although great effort has been made to determine the exact species and variety under discussion many notes have necessarily been gleaned from rather old literature where a then-common common-name was used. So occasionally there will be 'wrong' or mis-identifications. Most probably this will be the substitution of a widespread species or variety in place of an originally local one employing the same or similar name (eg. Old references to 'Chamomile' are often suspect and misnomer).

Also bear in mind that although any particular genus and species may be noted as having a certain association there is a strong probability that other species in the same genus will have the same or similar associations which so far have gone unrecorded.

Please accept my apologies for any errors, and let me know so the next edition can be improved.

Abies alba / pectinata, EUROPEAN SILVER FIR

Most species grow up to 1,200ft above sea level, a few to 2,200ft.

Branches develop Witches-broom distortion much like bird nests with upright twigs and dropping needles caused by a galling-fungus Melampsorella caryophyllacearum / Aecidium / Peridernium elatinum, this moves to alternate hosts of chickweeds Cerastium and Stellaria and other Caryophyllaceae.

Another fungus Calyptospora goeppertiana / Melampsorella attacks seedlings, this has it's other stage on Vaccinium species.

Abutilon

The plants that first revealed how variegation could be caused by a virus infection.

Prone to Hollyhock rust Puccinia malvacearum, a widespread fungal co-life this invades many hosts and spreads to common mallows, tree mallows, hollyhocks and Sidalcea, it infests the leaves and petioles forming yellow to brown pustules on the undersides also causing swelling and distortion.

Abutilon theophrasti, VELVETLEAF

All parts have potentially useful fungicidal properties.

Acacia

Tropical species source of the edible gum Arabic Many species in warm countries have hollow thorns, exude nectar and support myriads of tiny ants, often Pseudomyrma bicolour, which then protect the plants from other insects.

Acanthus, BEAR'S BREECHES

Flowers much favoured by bumble bees.

Acer, MAPLES

Mostly robust species however the ornamental Japanese maples dislike full sun and windy conditions, require shelter, dappled shade and plenty of damp leaf mould to thrive.

Most other maples are tough trees and hedgerow shrubs. Maple leaves are reputed to have a preservative action when used as packing for roots or apples in store indicating antifungal and/or antibacterial influence.

Acer campestre, FIELD / COMMON MAPLE

Leaf-blades are attacked by acarine gall-mites Eriophyes macrochelus / Aceria macrochela / Phytoptus macrochelus / moniezi / Erineum purpurescens / Cephaloneon solitarium, causing small, globular, slightly downy, greenish to orange, red or brown pimples, up to as many as 100 per leaf, usually on upper surface in the angle between veins.

Another gall-mite Aceria macrochela / heteronyx causes bark galls. Eriophyes macrorhynchus / similar parallel names to above species, also causes leaf galls, these come in greater numbers, up to 1,000 per leaf mostly on upper surface, small pimples, greenish yellow to red or purple, commonly found on lower branches and on hedgerow specimens, also attacks sycamores.

Acer pseudo-platanus, SYCAMORE

Which despite interesting leaf galls are effectively large
weeds! Seldom found higher than 1,500ft above sea level.
Sap has been boiled down for sugar and made into wine.
Their leaves have hidden pockets, domatia, underneath a
fringe of hairs at the forks of the ribs which provide
shelter for mites who help control 'hostile' fungi and
bacteria by eating them.
Leaf-blades attacked by acarine gall-mite Eriophyes
megalonyx causing pouches on underside of hairy
blotches of light brown while on top surface each appears
green, yellow or reddy brown.
Sycamores also suffer from E. macrorhynchus as found on
common maple, see above.
Roundish black blotches on leaves are remarkably
common but do little apparent harm.

Acer saccharum, SUGAR MAPLE

Maple syrup is concentrated sap collected from this
maple, most prolific during hot spring after hard winter.
Sap is reduced to the syrup or further to the sugar, or
made into wine, similar has been made from other Acers.

Achillea millefolium, YARROW

Accumulates Calcium, Copper, Magnesium, Nitrogen, Phosphorus, Sodium and Potassium. Another analysis gives reduction of dry matter to a crude ash 9.61% containing N 2.3%, P 0.93%, K 3.15%, Ca 3.84% and Na 1.17%.

Thought beneficial to grazing animals and increases overall fodder value when grown with Hungarian Grazing Rye, Lolium perenne.

Long flowering blooms rich in nectar attract hoverflies, bumble bees, ladybirds and predatory wasps, visited by at least 87 different insect species: 6 butterflies and moths, 30 species bee, 21 species Diptera flies and 30 others.

The buds are galled by Dipteron gall-midge Rhopalomyia / Hormonyia / Cecidomyia / millefolii / achillae which cause up to half a dozen galls near ground level in the axils of the leaves, each up to a third of an inch across green, yellow, red or brown.

The leaf is galled by a nematode eelworm Anguillulina / Tylenchus millefolii forming spindle shaped swellings on the rachis and globular swellings on the pinnae, glossy and greenish to brown, hollow though each full with eelworms.

Actinidia deliciosa, KIWI

Plants naturally dioecious and so need at least one male to every seven females, though some new garden forms are self fertile.

Very vigorous climbers though can be spur pruned and espalier trained where space is available.

Fruits contain enzyme that prevents setting of jellies unless first cooked.

Fruits also contain a fungicidal protein that controls Grey mould Botrytis cinerea.

ACTINOMYCETES

Bacterial organisms found in soil, may help or retard other organisms and plants. Of 796 isolates extracted from actinomycetes 60 caused growth inhibition greater than 30% in plants tested, 70 stimulated growth of alga by more than 20%, 6 caused dry matter increases in corn, soybeans, cucumbers, tomatoes and sorghum while 9 decreased dry weight produced of flax, soybeans, corn and cucumbers.

ADRENIDEA bees

These allegedly smell of garlic (odd but too curious a fact to leave out).

Aegopodium podagraria, GROUND ELDER / GOUTWEED / BISHOPWEED et al.

Edible as spinach though not recommended as it's not very nice.
Reputed to cure gout.
Blooms visited by at least 104 species of insect: 0 Lepidoptera, 15 species bee, 34 species Diptera flies and 55 others.

Aesculus hippocastanum, HORSE CHESTNUT

Seldom found above 800ft line.
Nuts are poisonous to us containing many saponins, and slugs will avoid crossing ground up horse chestnuts.
The trunks, stumps and large branches, dead and alive, support a semi-circular bracket fungus Polyporus / Polyporellus squamosus, brown scales with white edible flesh, smelling of cucumber, this grows quickly can reach many pounds in weight, harms trees causing the wood to decay with timber White rot, also spreads to beech, lime, poplar, willow and walnut.

Ageratum

Introduced flowers mostly from new World and foliage apparently contains substances toxic to caterpillars.

Agropyron repens, COUCH GRASS / WITCH / TWITCH / QUACK GRASS et al.

Common tough invasive grass, disappears from regularly cut sward.
Edible roots have been dried, ground, baked and eaten during famines.
Decaying roots encourage Fusarium culmorum which may then cause Foot rot and stunting in barley crops.
Stems galled by Hymenopteran gall-wasp Aulacidea hieracii / Aylax / sabaudi / graminis / Cynips which over-winter in the gall.
The inflorescence stalk is attacked by Dipteron chloropid Chlorops taeniopus Gout fly / Ribbon-footed corn-fly which lays eggs on the leaves or stalks, the larvae move into the shoots which thicken and form cigar shaped galls, the flowers fail and the fly after hatching moves to an alternate host, often barley.

Agrostis canina, BENT GRASS

This in particular, though most other grasses as well, over-winters Reed-mace fungus Epichloe typhina.

Agrostis stolonifera, FIORIN

Eaten readily by cows, horses and sheep.

Agrostis vulgaris, FINE BENT / COMMON BENT

Found on poor dry sandy soils, eaten by Welsh sheep but not so readily by cattle.

AIR & AIR MOVEMENT

Necessary for plants in several ways. Air only contains a small amount of carbon dioxide which can be used up in bright sunshine in less than a half hour, thus no air movement means cessation of growth. Stagnant air also encourages problems especially moulds.
Hedges and windbreaks clean air of dust and many chemicals.

Under cover house plants clean our air; the spider plant, Chlorophytum, is well known and usefully removes benzene as do Pelargoniums and rubber plants, the spider plant also removes trichloroethylene, but to get rid of toluene you need Kalanchoes. However it seems the micro-organisms in the pot of compost are even better at doing so!

Ajuga reptans, BUGLE

Extract repels weevils, and Cabbage White caterpillars are most discouraged by it's taste compared to other (unspecified) repellent plants tested.
The inflorescence and terminal leaves are attacked by acarine gall-mite Eriophyes / Phytoptus ajugae turning red and purple streaked, swollen, distorted and covered in whitish hairs.

ALGAE

Some of the most important life forms usually going unnoticed, a tremendous source of food for other living organisms especially in wet or marine conditions. They are destroyed by most herbicides and many pesticides but their loss is not heeded until detrimental side effects appear. Lichens are symbiotic relationship of algae and fungi, neither can survive as well alone as together, a visible result of a common process that goes on in nature all the time.

ALLELOPATHY

A word first used by Molisch in 1937 for the biochemical interactions by which plants and micro-organisms affect other plants and micro-organisms by the addition of chemicals to the environment through root, leaf, flower, fruit and stem exudations and emission of volatile compounds while alive or as breakdown products after. On the other hand plant competition as such is usually through the abstraction of compounds, or light or water, from the environment.

Allelopathic compounds may be used by plants to prevent the competition of different plants, or often of more of the same. Many plants make the soil unsuitable for their same species for some time until such compounds have been broken down. The compounds involved frequently inhibit germination, then growth, particularly of seedlings, these effects generally become less pernicious as the seedlings age. These chemical residues are a very good reason for practicing rotation. Often these compounds work by altering the populations of soil micro-organisms and especially those mycorrhizal ones living on the roots of other plants. On the plus side allelopathic effects may be helpful for weed or disease control when applied to a farm or garden situation. However despite increasing interest in such compounds we have so far rather overlooked how certain preceding crops can inadvertently reduce, or improve, the performance of a following crop.

Alliums

The Onion family, related to the lilies these usually form bulbs and many are used for culinary purposes: onions, leeks, shallots, garlic and chives.

These have a strong smell helping hide other plants from pests, and as most accumulate Sulphur also often have fungicidal effects. Chives are often grown under roses for this purpose and hide the bare lower stems into the bargain.

Reputed to repel moles -you should be so lucky.

Allium ascalonicum, SHALLOTS

Plantains should not be allowed nearby as these support Shallot aphids Myzus ascalonius (which also move onto strawberries).

Allium cepa, ONIONS

Do not press the sets into place as this damages their basal plate; instead make a raised mound of soil around the set holding it there till it's rooted, this also helps prevent worms from moving them around. And DO NOT bend their necks down to 'help ripening' as this actually lets in rots, particularly Neck rot, which appears later especially if the crop is stored in poor conditions.

When mature onions are swelling and ripening it's beneficial to let weeds grow up amongst them as this takes up spare moisture and nutrients particularly Nitrogen and so the bulbs will keep better.

Onions or their extracts may deter Colorado beetles. Onion extracts have proved efficacious at preventing the hatching of many insect eggs.

Onion Fly Delia / Hylemyia antiqua attacks seedlings but plants from sets are older and tougher so often escape damage. The eggs are laid on the neck of the bulb, the maggots hatch in a week and destroy the roots causing flagging and yellowing then pupate in the soil, there may be up to three generations in a year with the last over-wintering as pupae in the soil.

Allium crops suffer from Pea eelworm nematode when their leaves swell and distort, and their bulbs crack and rot.

In cool wet years onion and shallot leaves will yellow and die or simply look awful with a light greyish felt of Downy mildew Perenospora destructor, this often comes in on the sets; never plant any that are soft or suspicious.

Neck rot Botrytis alii appears during storage, a grey mould on the outside with brown rotting inside, the fungus gets in through damage especially any when the leaves are withering.

Onion Smut Urocystis cepulae is a notifiable disease, it starts with greyish blackish spots and streaks on the leaves of seedlings which then twist and distort and black spores ooze from under bulb scales, may attack other Alliums as well.

Bright orange spots are Onion Rust Puccinia porri which rarely does much damage to older plants but kills seedlings, this is more of a common problem with leeks and chives.

If plants wilt without obvious damage, with yellowing and die back, and leaves then come away when pulled but there are no maggots eating the roots, and if there is a white mould covering the base with black dots then it is the dreaded White Rot Sclerotium cepivorum. Once this gets in (do not use cheap or culinary quality shallots and garlic for sets) it is impossible to be rid of and the ground needs resting for a decade from all Alliums. Burn every infected plant and the soil around it. This can spread sideways in the soil over five yards in a year, much further if accidentally carried on boots or implements, beware introducing it on the roots of 'gifted' plants (of any genus as it is carried on the soil).

Allium porrum, LEEKS

Leeks intermixed with carrots decrease attacks of their Carrot Root flies.

Can help hide Brassicas from pigeons.

Onion rust Puccinia porri bothers leeks more than it does most onions and causes yellow or reddish spots and streaks which kill leaves and stunt plants.

White Tip Phytophthora porri causes ends of leaves to wither and turn white, the leaf margins may distort and water soaked areas form with loss of vigour and crop.

Allium sativum, GARLIC

The most pungent of the onion family and a most effective accumulator of Sulphur which may explain its very ancient reputation as a fungicide. It has strong bactericidal and fungicidal effects and is considered excellent for improving our health.

Plant cloves in the autumn for bigger yields than spring plantings, and never put them too deep.

Garlic emulsion kills aphids and onion flies, it has also been used against codling moths, snails, root maggots, Japanese beetles, carrot root fly and even peach leaf curl. The cloves put in with stored grain discourage weevils.

Allium schoenoprasum, CHIVES

Often grown (en masse not singly) with other plants to reduce fungal diseases, particularly blackspot on roses and scab on apples, but be patient as this may take three years to show effect.

These and their extracts discourage aphids from chrysanthemums, sunflowers and tomatoes and benefit carrots.

Chive sprays have been used against both Downy and Powdery mildew on cucumbers and gooseberries.

Aloe vera

Common house plant contains a slimy clear sap in the jelly like pith, this is good for healing skin problems especially burns and scalds and may be used as a wound dressing for trees and shrubs in dry conditions. This jelly is sort of edible as well as medicinal.

The yellow outer-skin sap is bitter enough when applied to other plants to prevent rabbit damage, and has been used to deter other pests from eating fruit and other plant parts.

Aloe vera planted near trees such as Citrus said to deter termites and ants from them and is thought to also prevent disease.

Alnus glutinosa, ALDER

Small damp loving tree good for reinforcing banks of streams.

Seldom found above 1,600ft line.

Buds and leaves are sticky and once used as flea and insect traps.

Alders suffer several acarine gall-mite attacks to their leaves. Eriophyes / Erineum / nalepai / axillare / Phytoptus alnicola, make pouch galls, ovalish yellow, orange, purple and red, sticking up from top surface and full of russet hairs in pockets underneath. Eriophyes brevitarsus / Phytopus / Phyllerium / Erineum alneum, makes bigger glossy blister like pouches, sometimes of whole leaf, greeny yellow to reddish brown, with tawny hairs underneath. E. laevis inangulis / Phytoptus / Cephalonean pustulatum, causes numerous pimple like galls on upper surface, also green through yellow and orange to purple and brown, up to 400 per leaf, and hairy inside.

Leaf is also galled by Dipteron gall-midge Dasyneura alni which curls the leaf edges upwards, and swollen, which then turns from green to russet.

Alnus incana, GREY ALDER

The rootlets may be galled by fungal slime infestation that sticks them together into numerous short clubs of reddish brown, this especially common when roots are standing in water.

Alopecuris pratensis, MEADOW FOX-TAIL

Sheep and horses enjoy eating this grass but cows do not.

Alpinia

Garden flowers, may carry Bean Yellow mosaic; dark and yellow patches with bright yellow spots which then spreads to many other Legumes: Cajanus, Canavalia, Cassia, Cicer, Cladrastis, Crotolaria, Dolichos, Glycine, Hedysarum, Lathyrus, Lens, Lupinus, Medicago, Melilotus, Phaseolus, Pisum, Robinia, Trifolium, Trigonella, Vicia, and Vigna, and also Chenopodium, Gladiolus, Freesia, Babiana, Sparaxis, and Tritonia.

Althaea / Alcea rosea, HOLLYHOCK

Boiled leaves are edible if so desperate.
The bird-dropping-like slug of the Lily beetle Lilloceris lilli, a bright reddy orange rather smart looking beastie, may destroy the leaves though more common on lilies, also spreads to lily of the valley, Hostas, Solomons seal, and even potato and tobacco.
Extremely prone to the rust disease (the fig leaf form less so) Hollyhock rust, Puccinia malvacearum, which infests many hosts though does not alternate between them at different stages. Be warned this will spread to common mallows, tree mallows, Abutilons and Sidalcea. In all of these it infests the leaves and petioles forming yellow to brown pustules on the undersides often causing swelling and distortion and lack of vigour.

Alyssum

Often suffers Flea beetle damage, see Flea beetles.
Also conceals slugs and snails underneath mats of foliage.

Alyssum bertolonii, MADWORT

Accumulates Nickel up to ten percent of dry weight of ash.

Amaranthus, GRAIN AMARANTH

Edible highly nutritious semi-tropical annuals, leaves often used as salading or spinach with the seeds eaten in many ways.
Needs hot summers to do well in UK.
Host plant to ground beetles.

Ambrosia artemesifolia, RAGWEED

An American weed, host to parasites of Strawberry leaf roller and Oriental fruit moth.
It may discourage flea beetles.

Ammophila arenaria, MARRAM-GRASS

Planted to bind loose soil especially sand-dunes
Attacked by Hymenopteran chalcid Eurytoma which cause
a shortening and imbricating in the leaves making cigar
shaped galls which the adults quit in midsummer.

Anagallis arvensis, SCARLET PIMPERNEL

Once considered edible but now thought poisonous.
Prefers a lime deficient soil yet accumulates Calcium.
Flowers have no honey, these open at 7am and close 2-3pm.

Anagallis foemina / caerulea

A rarer blue flowered form preferring lime rich soil,
flowers close at 3pm.

Anchusa azurea, ALKANET

Flowers rich in nectar, very attractive to humble and
bumblebees.

Anchusa officinalis, BUGLOSS

Young leaves once eaten as spinach.

Androsace

Very prone to Red Spider mite, this often found overwintering on ivies nearby.

Anemone

Share with Aquilegia a Stalk and Bulb rot Sclerotinia sclerotiorum that rots and withers the stems.
Also get Stem rot Sclerotinia tuberosa that attacks the stem with small spots then rots the bulbs making them waxy, and in spring these develop small brown cluster cup fungal fruits.
Share a fungal disease with plums so do not plant these nearby.

Anemone nemorosa, WOOD ANEMONE

Leaf blade and petioles become swollen and coloured yellow to purple by fungus Crowfoot smut Urocystis / Polycistis pompholygodes, the petiole spirals and the skin eventually splits as black powdery spores are emitted, this smut often spread from creeping buttercup.

Anethum graveolens, DILL

Plant and its extracts repel aphids and spider mites.
Blooms visited by 46 species of insect: 0 butterflies or
moths, 6 species bee, 15 species Diptera flies and 25
others.

Angelica sylvestris, WILD ANGELICA

Blooms visited by 30 species of insect: 1 Lepidoptera, 2
species bee, 11 species Diptera flies and 16 others.

Anthemis cotula, STINKING MAYWEED

Often confused with similar weeds so see also Matricaria
entry.
The odour can be used to repel rodents and fleas,
beekeepers use smell to keep bees off their skin.
Said to warm up their flower heads to aid pollinators.

Anthemis nobilis, CHAMOMILE, ROMAN CHAMOMILE

Often confused with other similar plants so see also
Matricaria and Chrysanthemum entries. This is perennial
and sweet scented.

If you really enjoy hand weeding then a seat or lawn can be made from Roman chamomile, but use the creeping variety Treneague propagated from root cuttings.
The tea from dried flowers, usually the double, is therapeutic.

Anthemis tinctoria, OX-EYE / YELLOW CHAMOMILE

Flowers rich in nectar, attract humble and bumblebees.

ANTHOCORID bugs

These are flattish red bugs useful for eating red spider mites, aphids and caterpillars.
Prefer to live on glossy leaved Brussel sprouts to matt ones.

Anthoxanthum odoratum, SWEET-SCENTED VERNAL GRASS

Eaten but not readily by cows, horses and sheep.

Anthriscus cerefolium, CHERVIL

Annual edible herb, likes shade, needs moisture and loathes transplanting.
Deters aphids from nearby lettuces.

Anthriscus sylvestris, WILD CHERVIL

Blooms recorded as visited by 73 species of insect: 0 Lepidoptera, 5 species bee, 26 species Diptera flies and 42 others.

ANTIBIOTICS

These are naturally occurring compounds produced as defense mechanisms by many fungi against bacteria and other organisms. Some such as penicillin have proved useful as medicines though may well cause long term problems and side effects.
Plants extract these from the soil; lettuce and tomatoes especially so, used as raw materials but may still be present when plants consumed. More are created in poor over-worked soils, less in humus rich ones in good heart. Often help or hinder plants by altering the populations of other soil microorganisms especially mycorrhizal ones.

Antirrhinum majus, SNAPDRAGON

Flowers exclude most insects except humble and smaller bees.
In trials bees preferred yellower to whiter flowers.
Rather prone to aphids.
Leaf spot Septoria antirrhinum causes brown and white spots.
Older garden varieties prone to Rust Puccinia antirrhinum, starts with rusty brown patches under leaves, proceeds and can cause plant to wither and die.
May be infected by Clover Yellow Vein virus causing yellow mosaic, necrosis and wilting which can spread to most Legumes: Cajanus, Canavalia, Cassia, Cicer, Crotolaria, Dolichos, Glycine, Hedysarum, Lathyrus, Lens, Lupinus, Medicago, Melilotus, Phaseolus, Trifolium, Trigonella, Vicia, and Vigna, and also Atriplex, Chenopodium, Coriandrum, Cucurbita, Gladiolus, Gomphrena, Nicotiana, Nicandra, Papaver, Petunia, Proboscidea, Rubus, Spinacia, Tetragonia and Viola.

ANTS

In the UK it's said black ants do not sting but may bite, red ants sting and bite, neither cause serious injuries to most people.

These uproot seedlings and even larger plants with their burrowing, and often cover leaves and even whole plants with spoil. Though annoying this pulverised soil aids other plants especially as it contains much immediate and potential plant food in the form of finely divided organic material.

Their common annoyance is their arrival in the house or store.

Strewing the mint family especially spearmint or pennyroyal may repel them. Growing mints or tansy near their entrance point may similarly help. Non drying sticky bands are very effective preventatives on fruit tree trunks. Barriers of powdered starch, ashes, talcum powder and so on can also prevent them getting to something

Standing pot and container plants and their saucers, on supports, in water in bigger saucers to form a moat, keeps them off.

A traditional preventative was a barrier of soot in hempseed oil. You can buy a parasitic nematode, Steinernema feltiae, which is watered onto their nest site and can be used anytime the soil is moist and above 12°C (54 -55°F).

Several species of woodlice live in ant nests; Lucasius myrmecophilus, L. pallidus, L. tardas and L. pauper. One wood louse Platyarthrus hoffmanseggi, is associated with ants all over Europe. It has been living in their nests so long it has evolved to an eyeless white form found only in ants nests.

Mites Antennophorus ublmannni scavenge and steal in the nests of Lasius mixtus, L. niger and L. flavus.

The fly Microdon mutabilis also has its larvae live in the nests likewise scavenging wastes and excrement.

The Round-backed millipede Blanjulus guttulatus is often found in ant nests of Formica rufa and Lasius fuliginosus.

The yellow beetle Claviger testaceus is found in nests of the Yellow ant Lasius flavus.

Another beetle Atemeles emarginatus is found in nests of Formica fusca, Myrmica laevinodis, M. ruginodis and M. scabrinodis.

Rose chafers Cetonia aurata and C. floricola are found in F. rufa nests feeding on nesting material.

Rove beetles Lomechusa strumosa and Dinarda dentata are found in nests of the slave-making Blood-red ants Formica sanguinea. (Interestingly Lomechusa suffers from littler mites Leolaps myrmecophilus, which fortunately the Dinarda likes to eat.) Myremedonia funesta is found in Black ant Lasius fuliginosus galleries in rotting stumps and posts, ant-like in appearance it is said to smell of formic acid and so goes unnoticed.

Ants also sustain a pretty moth Myrmecozella ochracella whose larvae feed on nest material of Formica rufa and F. pratensis. Another tiny moth Brachmia gerronella has often been found in Lasius fuliginosus nests.

Long standing worldwide has been the observation that ants have a special relationship with 'Blue' Lepidoptera caterpillars. 60 plus species in 29 genera of Lycaenidae are known to be attended by ants. These caterpillars have a gland on the eleventh ring that oozes 'nectar' which the ants consume and in return the ants keep away parasites such as Ichneumon wasps. This has been observed with Long-tailed Blue Lampides boeticus, Chalkhill Blue Agriades coridon, and the American Celastrina pseudargiolus (very similar to our Holly Blue Celastrina argiolus).

The rare Large Blue Lycaena arion larvae feed on wild thyme then are thought to move into ants nests to complete their last stage protected and possibly even fed by the ants.

Ants are attracted to the honeydews secreted by aphids and scale, these vary in strength and quantity; Lime tree aphids give nineteen drops a day, maple aphids forty eight. Ants milk, protect and move aphids to better feeding, and over-winter aphids and eggs in their nests. They also do the same for other pests such as scale insects, leaf-hoppers, possibly whiteflies and probably mealy-bugs. The scale Lecanopsis formicarium is found in nests of Lasius niger.

Ants have long been known to protect black bean aphids from Lacewing larvae and also protect aphids and scale from ladybird and hoverfly as well as Lacewing larvae but they apparently fail to stop Diaeretus parasitic wasps from laying their eggs.

Ants may predate other pests; Chinese citrus growers have long used them to control caterpillars, and ants may be pollinating or patrolling plants unbeknown to us. Many plants exchange 'nectar' exuded from glands for 'protection' notably vetches and cherries. Many plants, more of them tropical than temperate, create hollow chambers for ants; Acacia sphaerocephala, A. fistulosa, Cecropia, bamboo, Kibara, Myristica, Randia, Tachigalia, Humboldtia, Cordia, Polygonum, Pterocladon, Pterocarpon, Bombax, Tococo and Clerodendron.

ANT-APHIS

Forda formicaria grey aphids are found in nests of many ants; especially of Yellow ant Lasius flavus, Big Wood ant Formica rufra, F. rubra and Myrmica spp. Forda viridana are found in Lasius flavius and Formica fuliginosa nests. Wood ant nests may house another aphid Lacnus formicophilus. In the US a root aphid Aphis maidi-radicis is tended by ants who move them between fox-tail grass, smartweed and ragweed and onto maize.

APHIDS / APHIS / PLANT BUGS / PLANT LICE / DOLPHIN

Able to reproduce extremely quickly as females give birth to exact replicas without sex only mating after autumn migration. Generally considered a plague these often do more apparent than real harm though admittedly sucking sap and spreading virus diseases, however they can often just be taking surplus nutrients without affecting growth by much overall. Even the curling and shrivelling of leaves especially of tip growth may have the same result as good summer pruning. For many plants, redcurrants and sweet cherries in particular, withering the tips causes young buds lower down to convert to fruit buds instead of staying vegetative. There are many different aphids, some are specific to a few plants while others are less particular.

Chives discourage aphids on many plants especially Chrysanthemums, sunflowers and tomatoes. Nasturtiums although themselves attacked may keep broccoli clear. Woolly aphids on apple trees are discouraged by nasturtiums grown underneath, though this may take several years to be effective.

Glossy as opposed to matt leaved Brussel's sprouts suffer less from cabbage aphids but often get more peach-potato aphids.

Brushing your greenhouse plants with a feather, especially such as tomatoes, aubergines and melons, (gently, 20 times, twice daily from soon after emergence) significantly reduces future aphid populations.

Ladybirds and hoverflies are the best controls so use attractant plants like Limnanthes douglassii, buckwheat and Convolvolus tricolour.

The parasitic midge Aphididoletes aphidimyza is a good control for aphids under cover and works if the temperature is at least 10°C (50°F).

Aphids under cover can also be controlled with a minute wasp Aphidius spp. and/or by ladybirds and Lacewings both of which are now commercially supplied.

Almost indistinguishable but usually a bit smaller are Psyllids and Leaf-hoppers. Psyllids much resemble small aphids, these and the similar Leaf-hoppers are tiny yellowish active insects which attack leaves leaving bleached areas and dropping honeydew much the same as aphids or thrips. These are especially damaging to greenhouse flowers such as Calceolarias, Fuschias, Pelargoniums, Primulas, Salvias and Verbenas.

-Aphis Brassicae CABBAGE GREEN FLY

Causes serious damage to cabbage family.

-Aphis granaria / avenae CORN APHID / DOLPHIN / PLANT-LOUSE

A major problem for cereal crops also infests most grasses.

-Aphis rumicis BLACK FLY / DOLPHIN

Similar co-life infesting most Vicia beans. Now renamed Myzus.

Apios tuberosa, GROUNDNUT

Leguminous, scented, edible roots, dreadfully prone to Red spider mite.

Apium graveolens, CELERY

Edible but tough and bitter unless you have rich constantly moist soil, perhaps grow celeriac instead as celery is a very difficult crop. It must never dry out, is prone to bolting, suffers badly from slugs, and also needs blanching. Self blanching types are barely so and I find tougher textured.

Celery seed is a remarkably good and much under-used condiment.

If left to flower celery attracts many beneficial insects especially predatory wasps.

Foliage may be attacked by Celery & Parsnip fly Tephritis / Trypeta onopordinis this conflated with Celery fly Philophylla heraclei, which lays on the underside of the leaves and raises tunnels and blisters inside the leaf blade in which the maggots feed, finally leaving to pupate in the soil and overwinter, before then they may breed up to three generations in a year.

One of the many sub-races of microscopic Stem eelworm nematodes Ditylenchus dipsaci causes thickening of the leaf bases and crown with loss of vigour.

Celery may suffer Root rot Phoma apiicola causing worst case plants to fall off at ground level, this is seed borne.

Soft rot Bacterium carotovorum sometimes gets in through damage and then the inside just moulds away. Celery Leaf Spot / Celery Rust Septoria apii is serious once introduced, on seed or by debris, small yellow brown spots spread from outer to inner leaves then all over with a totally debilitated if not dead plant. Can be discouraged from starting with a tea made from stinging nettles and equisetum.

Apium graveolens rapaceum, CELERIAC

Near identical to celery but with swollen edible root not stalk thus different co-lives interact. Easier to grow well than celery, but still needs constant moisture, remove lowest leaves and any surface roots to make the crown swell.

Soft rot sometimes gets in through other damage and then the inside moulds away.

Rust and leaf spot diseases are serious once introduced (often on seed).

Aquilegia, COLUMBINE

Badly attacked by Red Spider mites in hotter sites and under cover, can be used as trap plants to pull them off more important crops.

Attacks by Leaf miners are less in soils rich in organic material.

Fungal disease, Stalk and Bulb rot Sclerotinia sclerotiorum which is more often found with bulbs and corms can sometimes causes Aquilegias to fail.

These often get fungal Leaf spots from Ascochyta / Coleosporium / Marssoniona spp. with blackish blue, ashen, or even yellow spots.

Recent strain of Downy mildew causes yellow patches on leaves, white fluffy underneath, reddy brown marks on flower stems with distortion, worse in damp conditions.

Arabis caucasica, GARDEN ARABIS

Roots are galled by brown headed white larvae of Coleopteran weevil Ceuthorrhynchus pleurostigma / assimilis / sulcicollis a.k.a. 'Turnip and cabbage gall weevil' which forms marble sized swellings on the roots, may seriously harm growth in young small plants and older ones may also suffer as larval exit holes allow in other infections. This can be widespread in an area as also invades turnips, cabbages, swedes, wild radish and charlock.

In poor conditions leaves may get shiny white patches of White rust Cystopus candidus.

Brownish or greyish white powdery patches are Grey mould Peronospora parasitica.

Co-host of Arabis mosaic virus which invades strawberries.

Arachis, PEANUT / GROUNDNUT

Leguminous tender crop, oil rich seed.
Many people violently allergic to this crop.
Wild birds avoid eating the red skin of the seed/nut, it
would be prudent for us to do so as well although small
pieces are often left in commercial mixes.
May carry Peanut Mottle virus; necrosis and wilting, this
can seriously damage bean crops.

Arctium lappa, BURDOCK

Edible root, Japanese varieties bred for consumption are
tenderer.
Flowerheads host Tephritid gall-flies / Dipteron fruit-fly;
Tephritis bardanae.
The stems and roots feed weevils Apion carduorum and A.
onopordi.
Roots support Aphis Protrama radices, Trama troglodytes
and DysAphis spp.
The leaves and stem support Aphis Capitophorus eleagni
which alternate onto sea buckthorn Hippophae
rhamnoides.

Arctium vulgare, WOOD BURDOCK

Seed heads are galled by Tephritid gall flies / Dipteron fruit-fly Tephritis bardanae / Trypeta which swell the seeds and turn them brown and useless, each head may contain up to a dozen galled seeds each with several larvae.

Aristolochia clematitis, BIRTHWORT

European species, many more in S. America, most give off a carrion smell to attract flies, these pass down tube of flower getting any pollen scraped off by stigmas, held until later when anthers distribute their pollen and downward pointing 'holding' hairs wither allowing flies to escape to next bloom.

Armeria maritime, THRIFT

Flowers rich in nectar especially attract humble and bumble bees.

ARMILLARIA ROOT ROT / HONEY FUNGUS

A. mellea is a much feared fungus which decimates trees and shrubs especially Rosaceae, the boot-lace like strands found on the roots carry honey coloured mushrooms with brown scales in dense clusters in autumn. The fungus 'hunts' new victims and usually gets in through any slight wound at or below ground level. The 'roots' may travel many yards in search of new victims.
It is now thought thick mulches of willow bark around threatened plants can prevent or reduce attacks.

Armoracia rusticana, HORSERADISH

Edible root, especially good grated with garlic, chilli, mustard and cider vinegar to make a warming sauce!
The leaf spine bruised and retted for a fornight or so self bleaches into good twine.
In US extracts used against Blister beetles and Colorado beetles.
The tea has been used against Brown Rot in apples.
The roots may be attacked by Black rot Pseudomonas campestris, the same as attacks turnips and seakale, if cut the roots show blackened rings, the foliage is often also seen to suffer in vigour.
The foliage also gets White Blister from glistening white pustules of Cystopus candidus more commonly found on Brassicas.

Leaf Spots are most likely Pale Leaf Spot caused by fungus Ramularia armoraciae with whitish spots which may lose their centres becoming shot-holed.

Artemesia abrotanum,

SOUTHERNWOOD

Odd scent of lemony/pine discourages moths and insects both fresh and when dried.
This's not so universally disliked by other plants as wormwood so can be used as pest deterrent particularly near Brassicas and carrots.

Artemesia absinthum / princeps,

WORMWOOD

Wormwood was used in the legendary drink Absinthe reputed to turn people mad (and blind), of course the huge amounts of alcohol consumed together with it had no responsibility......
It is strongest of the family and detested by other plants. Do not even put wormwood on compost heaps as it will slow the composting process considerably.
Wormwood supplies nectar for bees and hoverflies and the smell discourages many pests including cats and dogs.

Artemesia vulgaris, MUGWORT

Common roadside weed with family exudates that retard other plants and a smell that repels insects.
Mugwort seed is liked by hens, it may help control their lice and worms.

Arum maculatum, LORDS & LADIES / CUCKOO PINT

Roots once commercial source of starch for stiffening ruffs, caused considerable uncomfortable skin reactions. These roots are sort of edible in desperation if toxic chemicals are destroyed by boiling.
Poisonous berries, following flowers useful for early spring insects, mostly small flies and midges attracted by carrion smell, these pass down tube of flower leaving any pollen they brought on female flowers which develop first, held until later when male flowers mature to dust them with more pollen then downward pointing 'holding' hairs and spathe wither and allow flies to escape to next bloom.

The rod like spadix in the orchid like spathe generates considerable warmth helping pollinators who visit them. Also warmth makes scents more volatile and thus reach patrolling insects telling them of comfort station nearby. Anyway the plant burns off starch to warm itself, giving off large amounts of carbon dioxide at the same time and can raise their spathe's temperature by at least twenty and apparently up to sixty degrees Fahrenheit! Noticed since 1777 various experimenters have since found many other species give off heat. Arum cordifolium raises the temperature by nearly seventy degrees (sic)! Closely related Caladiums and Colocasias also shown to raise their temperature by twenty to fifty degrees. Philodendrons can apparently become too hot to hold according to one old report. Other plants warm up their flower heads including Cistus, Anthemis and Onopordum, even water lilies.

Arundo phragmites, COMMON REED

Alternate host for the Mealy Peach aphid Hyalopterus amygdali so should not be allowed near peach and almond trees.

Asclepias, MILKWEEDS

Flowers very rich in nectar, this has been made into sugar, young shoots and seed pods were once eaten after boiling though plant should be considered poisonous.

Asparagus officinalis, ASPARAGUS

Originally of maritime regions, traditionally grown in vineyards of Beaujolais as this likes conditions under grapes, and berries said to distract birds though I do not observe this to be so.

Dioecious with male and female plants, the females produce fewer thicker spears which become the ferny top growth carrying red berries. The males produce more crop by weight but in smaller spears as the fern only has to support tiny male flowers.

Tomato foliage smells can hide it from asparagus beetle, while a root secretion from asparagus kills Trichodorus, a nematode that attacks tomato roots.

Asparagus Beetle Crioceris asparagi larvae cause serious damage, many tiny greyish grubs chomp the foliage down to twiggy stems, the adult is rather dapper in black with orange markings.

Reddy orange blisters on the stems and leaves browning before autumn is Asparagus rust Puccinia asparagi, this overwinters as black streaks on the withered stems and reappears as rusty powder on the summer fern.

A rusty, brownish or purplish colour to the roots and crown which then die away indicate fungal Violet root rot / Copper-web Helicobasidium purpureum which also attacks beet, carrot, parsnip, potatoes, clover, alfalfa, and several weeds.

Asphodeline lutea, ASPHODEL

Roasted roots are edible, and were once esteemed.

Asters, MICHAELMAS DAISY

Flowers rich in nectar and pollen and reliably late
blooming for autumn insects.
Succumbs to Wilt Verticillium vilmorinii where shoots
weaken with yellow mottled leaves withering then dying
away.
Stem rot Fusarium spp. is common with the leaves and
flowers wilting and hanging, they turn yellow and die
while the bottom of the stem turns black.
Several virus diseases have also reduced this once popular
plant to a weed of railway cuttings.
(Asters, though I suspect it's the the Callistephus China
asters, share an aphid Brachycaudis helichrysi with
plums.)

Astragalus

Warm country species were source of gum Tragacanth
and the roots of several species were once eaten.
These are one of the few plants known to accumulate
Selenium a scarce yet necessary element, and it is
Leguminous so probably should be grown just for fertility
enrichment if nothing else.

Atriplex, ORACHE

Unusual edible spinach, and a vegetable come weed.
May be infected by Clover Yellow Vein virus; yellow
mosaic, necrosis and wilting which spreads among most
other Legumes: Cajanus, Canavalia, Cassia, Cicer,
Crotolaria, Dolichos, Glycine, Hedysarum, Lathyrus, Lens,
Lupinus, Medicago, Melilotus, Phaseolus, Trifolium,
Trigonella, Vicia and Vigna, and also Antirrhinum,
Chenopodium, Coriandrum, Cucurbita, Gladiolus,
Gomphrena, Nicotiana, Nicandra, Papaver, Petunia,
Proboscidea, Rubus, Spinacia, Tetragonia and Viola.

Atriplex hastate, HASTATE ORACHE

Leaves are roll-galled by Homopteran aphid SemiAphis
atriplicis, this thickens and rolls edges to midrib, narrow
leaves becoming sickle shaped (which then may be
confused with galls caused by mite Eriophyes galii),
turning yellow to light brown, infested leaves fall and
blow about spreading the aphids to new food supplies,
also galls Common Orache and Chenopodium album.

Aucuba japonica, SPOTTED LAUREL

Shade tolerant evergreen.
Sometimes suffers conspicuous White scale on either or
both upper and lower leaf surfaces.

AUTO-INTOXICATION

Redundant term for how plants use allelopathic exudations to prevent not only alien seeds germinating but their own as well, eg. rice litter gives off phytotoxic residues that inhibit the next sowing until well rotted away. Growing different crops over a rotation helps avoid this.

AUXINS

Plant growth hormones, may be used to help plants interact, these also cause plants to grow towards or away from light, against or with gravity, may speed up or retard rooting and flower formation and may be used by plants to 'warn' others of pest attacks. Related chemicals from other sources including animal by-products and synthetics may also affect plants in similar ways.

Avena eliator, TALL OAT GRASS

Does best on clay, disliked by cows, sheep and especially by horses.

Avena flavescens, YELLOW OAT GRASS

Eaten by sheep and cows, yields have been doubled by application of calcerous manure.

Avena sativa, OATS

A cereal and weed often found in with other cereals. Oats reduce to 4% ashes which themselves contain 21% potash and very little soda, 10% lime, 8% magnesia, 4% iron oxide, 0.4% manganese oxide, 51% phosphoric acid, negligible sulphuric acid, 4% silica and 0.6% chlorine.
Oats make a good mixed fodder crop for stock at two to one with vetches or beans, best if sown after the beans have germinated.
These and occasionally other grains were sown in the bottom of planting holes for trees, whether for the heat of germination, nutrients or by-products is not known. Mouldy oats aid peach trees but oat root secretions may be unfriendly to apricots.
Of 3,000 oat varieties tested 25 produced an exudate that inhibited Cruciferous weeds.
The Frit fly Oscinis frit has eggs laid in spring which hatch to tiny legless larvae which eat into the growing point and the plant is stunted even killed, leaves are stunted and crops suffer, there can be up to three generations in a year, then larvae overwinter in grasses, also attacks maize.

The Stem Eelworm Tylenchus devastatrix of clover has alternate host of oats and especially of the old tulip-rooted oats, so not wise to follow or precede oats with clovers.

In soils containing much Penicillium griseofulvum the plants abstract the antibiotic griseofulvin and become seriously retarded.

Azalea, see also Ericaceae and Rhododendrons.

Well known for needing lime free soil, larger leaved forms generally prefer shade, the smaller leaved preferring more sun.

Under cover plants often attacked by Leaf Miner moths Gracilaria azaleella causing leaves to brown and drop as if scorched, often worst in the winter months the leaves may be distorted and folded around the cocoons.

White Fly Trialeurodes vaporariorum, possibly conflated with Dialeurodes chittendeni, causes the leaves to pale, go yellow, and greenish flattened scales will be found, there may also be a sooty mould covering other leaves with a black felt.

Similar damage with chocolate spotting on the underside of leaves could be Rhododendron bug Stephanitis rhododendri.

Thrips Heliothrips haemorrhoidalis cause leaves to have pale yellowish patches which may go brown or bleached with brown specks underneath.

Azaleas often suffer Vine weevils eating their roots and leaves.

Bud Blast causes buds to fall off confirmed by little black dots on their surface.

Two fungal Basidiomycetes of Rhododendrons also harm Azaleas; Exobasidium vaccinii and E. rhododendri, cause galls on the underside of the leaf which become powdery with spores.

Leaves and buds are damaged by fungal attacks of Exobasidium japonicum with swollen buds, pinkish in colour with white bloom.

Babiana

Bulbous garden flower, this may bring in Bean Yellow mosaic; dark and yellow patches with bright yellow spots, which can spread to many Leguminous plants: Cajanus, Canavalia, Cassia, Cicer, Cladrastis, Crotolaria, Dolichos, Glycine, Hedysarum, Lathyrus, Lens, Lupinus, Medicago, Melilotus, Phaseolus, Pisum, Robinia, Trifolium, Trigonella, Vicia, Vigna, and also Alpinia, Chenopodium, Gladiolus, Freesia, Sparaxis and Tritonia.

BACILLUS thuringiensis

A naturally occurring disease of caterpillars, produced and sold commercially, used against caterpillars on cabbages and related Brassicas. In US used against tobacco bud and boll-worms.
(A traditional remedy for larvae of any form was to sprinkle the soil from under the worst infestation over the others, which would undoubtedly spread this or another disease from any grub already suffering.)

Barbarea vulgaris, WINTERCRESS / YELLOW ROCKET

Edible. Useful for hen feed.
Shoot apex galled by Dipteron gall-midge Dasyneura sisymbrii / Cecidomyia barbarea, this arrests normal growth causing glossy swellings and lumps, often cream, pink or reddish, worst in floral parts, serious infestations can form what look much like small raspberries, often infests other Cruciferae such as hedge mustard, creeping yellow cress, cabbage, charlock and wild radish.

BEE plants

Lists of plants that provide bees either nectar or pollen are commonplace however not all plants are bee friendly. Bumble bees have reportedly been killed by toxins in nectar of red chestnut, some species of lime, particularly the non-native pendant silver lime and large-leaved lime, and have been reported as stunned by those of laburnum. Rhododendron, Azalea and other (often Ericaceous) plant nectars concentrated in honey have allegedly poisoned people, apparently even whole armies succumbed during Classical times.
Rape / colza and other Brassica nectars make a white honey that sets so hard it cannot be easily utilised by the bees, especially when copious water is not available.

Begonias

Leaves have been used as food (they're not very nice). Attacked by eelworm nematodes causing brown spots and blackened areas, these spread to ferns, Coleus, Gloxinias, orchids and Salvias.

Bellis perennis, DAISY

Accumulates Calcium and Magnesium.

Not edible though leaves have been used as spinach in times of famine and the petals are sometimes employed for their novelty by over-enthusiastic chefs.
The flowers open at sunrise and close at sunset thus Days eye.
Host to Stem eelworm Tylenchus devastatrix.

Berberis

This genus, especially our native wild BARBERRY, B. vulgaris, have edible berries which need jellying with much sugar then are delicious.
The leaves are galled by Black rust of wheat fungi Puccinia graminis forming yellow brown spots and orange cluster-cups underneath, as Berberis hosts this Wheat rust over-winter so it should not be grown near cereal fields.

Beta vulgaris, BEET / RED BEET / BEETROOT / LEAF BEAT / PERPETUAL SPINACH / SWISS CHARD / SUGAR BEET

Originating from maritime regions these need trace elements more than most crops and thrive on seaweed products.

Good mineral accumulators up to one quarter of leaf ash content is Magnesium.

Any shortage of Manganese especially in dry conditions may cause yellowing and poor growth.

If soil is deficient in Boron these may develop Heart rot with a brown centre as leaves wilt and turn black.

The most troublesome co-lives by far are birds eating seeds, seedlings and younger leaves.

If beets start to bolt and form flower stems those should be pulled to stop them encouraging others.

Beet frequently bothered by Black aphids, Flea beetles and the Pea eelworm nematode.

The Mangold fly Pegomyia hyoscyami / betae has small whitish larvae which tunnel and blister the leaves which drop early, the larvae pupate in the soil and emerge three weeks later giving three generations in a year.

Leaves may be eaten by Beet Carrion Beetle Silpha opaca which also consumes dead animals and general garbage.

Soil bacteria Enterobacter, Klebsiella, Citrobacter, Flavobacterium, Achromobacter, Arthrobacter and Pseudomonas reduce germination and seriously hinder growth and increase infection by root colonizing fungi.

Leaf spots Cercospora beticola cause brown spots with purple borders grey in middle which become small holes.

Heart rot mentioned above causes the leaves to turn black and die back, crown first then outer leaves, then the root rots, remember this may be induced by Boron deficiency.

If the root and or stem below the seed leaves turns black and dies first it was more likely Black Leg Phoma betae, Pythium aphamidermatum and Corticum solani, several diseases with similar symptoms, and all are seed borne. Rough patches are just common Scab and do little harm. Downy mildew Personospora farinosa causes younger leaves to thicken with a greyish mat on the underside, then to yellow, brown and blacken with loss of growth, this is spread both on the seed and on debris and litter. The underground parts get attacked by fungus Urophlyctis leproides which galls the flesh into large swellings.

Beets and chards are attacked by same Violet root rot that kills asparagus and carrots.

Rhizomania is a new disease of sugar beet increasingly rendering East Anglian fields unproductive, the roots proliferate ridiculously but work ineffectively.

Virus Yellows is also more common in farming with sugar beet than in garden beets, it's spread by aphids Myzus persicae and Aphis fabae, the leaves develop patches of yellow turning orangey red, mostly on the edges, the leaves then become brittle and break up on handling, the growth is poor and so are resultant crops.

Beet Curly Top virus is spread by leaf-hoppers and also invades Cucurbits, beans, tomatoes and many other plants.

Beet Pseudo-Yellows virus, spread by whiteflies, also invades Cucurbits and many other plants.

Beet Western Yellows virus, spread by aphids, also invades many other plants especially lettuce.

Garden-beet mosaic also attacks spinach.

Betula alba, BIRCH

One of the most frost resistant deciduous trees though seldom found above 2,500ft line.

The twigs make excellent besom brooms, the spring sap was once used for making wine though too weak to profitably make sugar.

The peeling bark, acidic ph 3.2-5.0, is impregnated with resin that has insecticidal properties and is gathered for nest building by birds, and is also useful dried as fire-lighting tinder.

The roots give off secretions that accelerate composting so trees may be useful screens for manure heaps or compost bins.

Birches are strongly associated with the classic fairy tale red-with-white-spots toadstool Fly agaric, Agaricus muscarius / muscaria once used as a fly killer (dried mushrooms soaked in milk which is then placed somewhere to avoid the cat!). A. regalis is similarly poisonous and has a liver coloured cap. Both are also found under spruce.

Several Boletus fungi are found on birch roots especially the edible and tasty Boletus / Leccinum / Krombholzia scaber / scabrum / scabra with grey brown cap, a whitish flesh with excellent flavour when fresh though this blackens with age or cooking. The edible Boletus / Leccinum / Krombholzia aurantiacus / aurantiacum / aurantiaca with a red orange cap, greyish pink flesh, is also found on aspen as well as birch. Another is the edible and tasty Boletus / Leccinum / Krombholzia versipellis / rufescens / testaceoscabrum which has a reddish brown cap, greyish violet pink flesh.

But the brown toadstool Paxillus involutus once eaten but now known poisonous is common, on litter and deadwood, brown with yellowish flesh, and the similar P. atrotomentosus is not actually poisonous but not very nice.

Pluteus cervinus, edible, grows on stumps and rotting wood, it has a light to dark grey or brownish cap and streaked stipe, the gills start white then go pink with red spores, also found on oaks, hornbeams and beeches. Cortinarius / Telamonia armillatus / armillata, edible but unpalatable, has a brick red to reddy brownish cap, yellow to brown gills and brown stipe with faint red stripes, found in mossy birch litter in acid soil.

Betula pendula, SILVER BIRCH, and B. pubescens, HAIRY BIRCH

Bud and leaf galls are caused by acarine gall-mites Eriophyes lionotus / Phytoptus / Cephaloneon betulineum / Phyllerium tortuosum / Erineum, which cause typical nodular galls filled with hairs eventually turning reddish. Branches and trunk get Witches-broom caused by fungus ascomycete Taphrina betulina / Exoascus betulinus / turgida swelling the base of the 'broom' which puts out masses of twiggy growths, up to a yard across. Witches-brooms may also be caused by fungi Puccinia and Melampsorella.

Bidens pilosa & B. bipinnata

New World weeds may carry Bidens Mottle virus which can spread to lettuce and endive so beware garden flower versions.

Bilderdykia / Polygonum convolvulus, BLACK BINDWEED

Pernicious weed and host to Stem eelworm Tylenchus devastatrix.

BIODYNAMIC

A method of gardening and farming using organic principles allied to careful consideration of human, plant and animal interactions and their symbiosis with the environment. Several specific preparations are utilised, astrological timing may be considered important as is companion planting.

BIRDS

Friends and foes, in general it's better to attract as many as possible and then provide protection for fruit etc. Providing water is important, food and shelter also. Evergreens, conifers and thick hedges most useful, and plentiful nest boxes advisable.

Birds peck fruit such as apples and pears selectively thus Lord Lambourne and Cox's Orange Pippin are much more heavily damaged than Laxton's Fortune and Worcester Pearmain, Conference pears get four times more damage than Williams'.

BLACK FLY / DOLPHIN, Aphis rumicis

see APHID one of several varieties of aphids especially damaging to broad bean, cherry and globe artichoke.

BOMBUS hortorum

The longest tongued UK bumble bee with 15mm, honey bee has only 6mm.

Borago officinalis, BORAGE

One of the best bee plants.
Edible in moderation as spinach.
A good accumulator of minerals for compost it makes an excellent liquid feed better than comfrey as richer in Magnesium and at some stages of growth also richer in Nitrogen.
Used to discourage attacks of Japanese beetles and tomato hornworms.

Botrytis cinerea, GREY MOULD

Most of a problem when growth is slow in cold damp low light with stagnant air.
This mould has been prevented on Cyclamen by spraying leaves with fungus Ulocladium atrum.
Kiwi fruits contain a fungicidal protein that may inhibit it, as can the urea in fresh urine, the fresh squeezed juice of cauliflower leaves, thyme oil and oregano oil.
Freshly made water soluble extracts from good garden compost also inhibit it remarkably well.

Brassicas

The cabbage family are highly bred and very specialised needing rich soil with plenty of lime. In acid soils they become prey to Club root, see below, and also to Whiptail where the leaves become reduced to straps or whips and the growing point may be lost, this is a deficiency not a disease, cured by adding seaweed products or Molybdenum salts to the soil.

Most Brassicas especially cabbage and cauliflower also need Magnesium or leaves become pale, marbled with a purplish hue.

(Sometimes Brassicas suffer similar looking frost damage, resembles disease with whitish patches going brown with the leaves dying.)

Under-sowing Brassicas with clover or bird's foot trefoil reduces aphid infestations without harming yields.

Interplanting Brassicas with French beans significantly reduce pest levels on both.

Brassicas may inadvertently support colonies of spiders, earwigs, wood lice and other critters to little or no detriment and often to advantage as these predate each other, process material or act as pollinators. Slugs and snails are another matter.

Young plants may be damaged or destroyed by cutworms, wireworms and cockchafers, see Cutworms & ground caterpillars.

The Turnip sawfly Athalia rosae is a major pest on the continent, especially to turnips and oilseed rape and could re-invade the UK.

Far worse is Cabbage root fly Erioischia Brassicae / Delia / Anthomyia radicum, this eats the roots of all Brassicas, the females consume nectar of Cow parsley Anthriscus sylvestris so are most prevalent when this is flowering, the Brassica plants turn reddish purple once attacked. These flies can be lured to traps containing Swede root juice as bait. Interplanting lettuce, clover or Tagetes marigolds reduces infestations. Carefully fitted collars of felt or similar at ground level stop the fly climbing down the stem to the soil and prevent her laying eggs, there are two or more generations a year. Heavy attacks of aphids deter this fly and apparently the Garden Pebble moth caterpillar Evergestis forficalis exudes a deterrent chemical in its frass. Rove and Ground beetles also help control the root fly by eating the eggs and the Rove Aleochara Bilineata eats large numbers of the pupae. However the major parasite is a small wasp Idiomorpha rapae which lays eggs in the pupae which the larvae then feed on from inside.

The Radish Fly Anthomyia floralis, also damages roots and lower stalk, especially of turnips, may also lay in exposed fresh dung.

Most Brassicas suffer from Cabbage Fly Anthomyia Brassicae which is also known as Snowy Fly / Cabbage Powdered-Wing / Cabbage Whitefly Aleurodes Brassicae / proletella / cheledonii (and also very often wrongly confused with the glasshouse whitefly Trialeurodes vaporariorum which is sometimes found outdoors on other crops). The tiny larvae, in huge numbers, have a serious effect depriving the plants of sap and exuding honeydew which then coats leaves and becomes infested with Sooty mould which 'mess up' the plants, and as the complete life cycle is only a fortnight there can be up to ten generations a year.

Flea beetles Phyllotreta atra, P. nemorum, P. undulate and other spp. are small, black or yellow striped, eat the young leaves and cause serious loss of young plants, deterred by damper conditions or presence of tomato foliage (the adults are the problem, the larvae live in the soil on plant roots doing little harm).

The Swede midge Contarinia nasturtii attacks all Brassicas despite the name, the grubs are small creamy and found on the leaf stalks of plants that have gone Blind, ie the central growing point is destroyed and the plant becomes useless, the wounds may also allow diseases to infect as well.

Mealy Cabbage Aphis Brevicoryne Brassicae is blueish grey, usually on underside of leaves, damages growth and 'messes up' the plants, these overwinter as eggs on the stems. May be parasitised by tiny Chalcid wasps Aphidius spp. which lay an egg in each aphid which the larva eats before emerging leaving the now empty light brown skin through a small round hole.

The Peach potato aphid Myzus persicae, Shallot Aphis M. ascalonicus, Onion thrips Thrips tabaci, Cabbage thrips Thrips angusticeps, Brassica shield bug Eurydema oleracea, and the common flower bug Anthocoris nemorum may all be found but seldom doing serious damage.

Various leaf and stem miners may also be present: Cabbage Leaf miner Phytomyza rufipes, Phytomyza horticola, and the Cabbage Stem weevil Ceutorrhynchus quadridens live in most Brassicas especially spring sown crops.

A Coleopteran weevil, Cabbage / Turnip Gall Weevil, Ceuthorrhynchus pleurostigma / sulcicollis / assimilis a.k.a. 'Turnip and Cabbage gall weevil' has brown headed white grubs which form marble sized swellings on the roots of all Brassicas, may seriously harm growth in young small plants and older ones and the larval exit holes allow in other infections. This can be widespread in an area as it also attacks Arabis, turnips, cabbages, Swedes, wild radish and charlock. The damage is often confused with that of Club Root, see below, however cutting open galls reveals maggots and not a stinking slimy mess.

The Cabbage Stem Flea beetle Psylliodes chrysocephala grubs tunnel into the stems of young plants causing them to fail, particularly bothering cauliflowers.

Turnip Stem weevil C. contractus is found in the stem, veins and midribs.

Turnip Mud beetle Helophorus spp. larvae may be found in winter mining the stems.

Mustard / Watercress beetle Phaedon cochleariae larvae may be found in summer.

Pollen beetles Meligethes spp. are more of a problem for oilseed rape and for those growing Brassicas for seed, they may be lured onto yellow coloured sticky traps. Likewise the Rape Winter Stem weevil Ceutorhynchus picitarsis is only a major problem on over-wintering rape crops.

The Cabbage Seed weevil Ceutorhynchus assimilis female feeds on pollen first then eats the seeds in the seedpod and finally lays eggs which hatch inside and eat even more seeds. Worse, the damaged pods allow the Brassica Pod midge Dasyneura Brassicae to lay it's eggs and their larvae cause the pod to become bladder-like and spill any surviving seeds.

The shoot apex may be galled by Dipteron gall-midge Dasyneura sisymbrii / Cecidomyia barbarea, this arrests normal growth causing glossy swellings and lumps, often cream, pink or reddish, worst in floral parts, serious infestations can form what look much like small raspberries, often infests other Cruciferae such as hedge mustard, creeping yellow cress, charlock and wild radish. All these co-lives are inter-active, when all small white butterfly eggs and caterpillars were removed from a stand of collards the numbers of flea beetles Phyllotreta Cruciferae increased, when these were removed another flea beetle Phyllotreta striolata increased.

Wasps predate caterpillars, particularly the Small White. Cabbage white (sic) caterpillars are most discouraged by taste of Bugle, Ajuga reptans, extract.

Brassicas, and Nasturtiums, are seriously damaged by larvae of the Large Cabbage White Pieris Brassicae, which has black markings on creamy white wings, these lay yellow eggs in clusters of thirty to a hundred, caterpillars start greyish green but may become bright green with black markings or bluish green with three lines yellow and black spots when mature, they quit the plants to pupate nearby, the butterflies are deterred by tomatoes, thyme and by fake eggs or crushed eggs. Parasitised by small black braconid wasp Apanteles glomeratus, this lays eggs in caterpillars which eventually form up to thirty yellow cocoons around the poor critter having eaten it from the inside. However these are themselves parasitized by hyper-parasites, an even smaller metallic green wasp Tetrastichus galactopus and an Ichneumon wasp Lysibia nana.

Apantales cocoons may be conflated with small yellow silky cocoons containing pupae of the Ichneumon fly Microgaster glomeratus who lays about sixty eggs in a Large White caterpillar parasitising it. Another Ichneumon Fly Pteromalus Brassicae lays up to two hundred and fifty eggs on the newly formed chrysalis the larvae parasitizing it.

As these caterpillars mostly damage the outer leaves they can do more harm to such as kales (which they seldom touch) and Portugese cabbage, Trouve conchuda, while with cabbage, cauliflower and broccolis the heads may escape almost unscathed, though growing less if the leaf area removed was significant.

These caterpillars can be controlled with Bacillus thuriengiensis, found naturally in the soil or available commercially.

Also causing much damage are the similar Small White or Turnip Moth Artogeia / Pieris rapae, eggs laid singly becoming velvet green caterpillars with three yellow lines and NO black spots, and the Green Veined White P. napi, eggs laid singly, grub velvet green with a row of red to yellow breathing holes on sides. These both do much damage to the heads of cabbage, cauliflowers, broccolli as they eat into the middle. More of these caterpillars will be found on plants growing on their own than on those in stands of many. For other Lepidoptera caterpillars see volume 2. Really Help Butterflies.

Damping Off from Rhizoctonia solani kills small Brassica seedlings which wilt and die the stem collapsing at about ground level. Similar symptoms occur with Ascochyta spp. and Pythium spp. The spores live in the soil and attacks are worst with overcrowded plants in high humidity and with stagnant air.

Sawdust, even 1%, added to soils makes Brassica seedlings more susceptible to Pythium damping off.

Black Rot, Pseudomonas / Xanthomonas campestris bacterial invasion causes yellowing leaves with blackened veins, when cut stems show black dots in a ring, seen in warm wet years, mostly attacks cabbage and cauliflower may also spread to turnip, Swede and seakale, often introduced on the seed but also soil borne.

Soft Rot, Bacterium carotovorum, slimy rotting, also attacks carrot, turnip, Swede celery etc. often worst after plants frosted or over-fed.

Downy mildew Peronospora parasitica is most often found on seedlings, especially cauliflowers, raised under cover or in overcrowded high humidity conditions, soil borne this causes yellowing of the leaves with downy patches underneath, may kill seedlings or weaken them, also attacks the curds of cauliflowers and broccolis and can be pernicious on Brussel's sprouts.

Grey Mould, Botrytis cinerea, the only too well known grey fluffy fungal mould is worst in humid conditions and under cover.

Brassicas are exceedingly prone to slime fungal attacks of Clubroot disease / Finger & toe / Anbury, Plasmodiophora Brassicae, causing distorted swollen roots which rot inside and smell vile. If you do not have this in your soil NEVER bring in any Brassica plants or soil from infected allotments. Do without as once present this disease is almost incurable. Exudates and extracts from peppermint, summer savory and thyme can reduce infections of Clubroot fungus, rhubarb has only a small effect, frequent short term green manuring with mustard may reduce infestation. Also attacks and lives on Cruciferous weeds such as shepherds purse and charlock. Club root is much worse in wet heavy acid soils and less severe in lime containing ones.

Black Leg / Black Stem / Canker Phoma lingam fungal attack, spots on leaves, brownish purple to black cankers on stems at base cause roots to wilt and die, also attacks Swedes, usually seed borne.

Leaf Spots / Ring Spots Mycosphaerella brassicola, brown spots with green border or rings, fungal attack on lower leaves, most often found in wetter counties and on broccolis, more of an appearance problem than actual damage.

White Blister Cystopis candidus fungal attacks cause glistening white blisters in spots or rings, often found on over-crowded plants especially Brussels sprouts, also attacks radish, turnips etc. and Cruciferous weeds.

Ringspot virus causes small spots which start off pale green, may also cause distorted leaves and yellowing, also attacks stocks, wallflowers, sweet rocket and Arabis where it may affect flowers as well.

Cauliflower mosaic virus causes the veins to stand out with the leaf blade between a yellowed or paler green, vigour is lost, this is spread by aphids Brevicoryne Brassicae and Myzus persicae, hosted by several weeds especially related Cruciferae.

Turnip mosaic virus, also spread by aphids, also invades most Cruciferous plants and lettuce.

Brassica juncea / alba / nigra / campestris, BROWN MUSTARD

(see also Sinapsis)
What is often sold as salad mustard may be the cheaper oilseed rape, true mustard is not as hardy and is killed by hard frosts.

It makes a good cover crop leaving soil in fine condition and can be used to attract many pests off Brassicas, then dug in or composted.

Gertrud Franck maintains that although mustard is a Brassica this is botanical classification rather than a close family relationship and that mustard can be used frequently as a green manure without any affect on rotations. This is controversial as most books on disease state mustard suffers from Club Root, the most feared disease of Brassicas. However, if the mustard does not live for long and is incorporated or composted well before the disease can produce a new crop of spores, there is unlikely to be a problem. This may then also help control nematodes.

Brassica chinensis, CHINESE GREENS / CHINESE CABBAGE / PAK CHOI

These need rich soil with almost bog conditions and sowing after midsummer to succeed, avidly eaten by flea beetle, slugs and aphids, so make good sacrificial and trap crops.

In the USA used as sacrificials for maize crops as it attracts their corn worms.

Brassica napus / rapa napoBrassica, SWEDE

Very similar to turnip but orange fleshed, prone to 'Crown gall' which has many points of similarity to cancer tumours in animals as it spreads forming tumours elsewhere than original site, caused by bacterium Agrobacterium / Bacillus / Phytomonas / Pseudomonas tumefaciens, which spreads to nearly twenty families of herbaceous and some woody plants.
Like cabbages and many Cruciferous weeds Swedes suffer slime-fungus attacks to their roots by Plasmodiophora Brassicae, the dreaded Club Root which forms finger like galls on the side branching roots.

Brassica napus oleifera, RAPE or COLZA

Annual crop very much like mustard but which it should not be confused with. In UK oilseed rape is usually derived from Swede rape, in Canada and Scandinavia from Turnip rape.
Grown for oil it gives about three tons of rough dry matter per acre containing about three to four hundred pounds of oil and over a quarter ton of mineral ash.
It makes a good green manure / cover crop over-winter if not close in rotation with other Brassicas.

Brassica oleracea / botrytis cymosa, BROCCOLIS

Winter cauliflowers are usually broccolis as these are hardier than true cauliflowers.

These are highly bred and require very rich conditions and heavy soil to form the swollen and immature lateral and terminal flower buds. The shape and texture of these heads makes pest problems more detrimental than for say cabbage where damaged outer leaves can be discarded.

Brassica oleracea gemmifera, BRUSSELS SPROUTS

One of the hardier Brassicas, they have the family tendencies with a liking for really firm soil, in windy areas tie the matured plants at the top to make stable tripods. White Blister Cystopis candidus fungal attacks cause glistening white blisters in spots or rings, is often found on over-crowded plants, also attacks radish, turnips etc. and Cruciferous weeds.

Brassica oleracea / capitata, CABBAGE

A cabbage is a terminal bud and to get it to swell without opening is a marvel of controlling nature. Constant unchecked growth in rich moist conditions is required. There are red versions (rubra) as well as white (alba) and the Savoys (sabauda) which have crinkly leaves and are hardier than the others.

Ash contains 0.4% Potassium, 0.15% Phosphorus and 0.2% Calcium, and the plants need plenty of Magnesium or leaves pale and mottle and go purplish.

Most important, as with all Brassica family, is liming, rotation and avoid importing anything potentially carrying Club Root disease.

One old companion plan was to plant wormwood or southernwood with cabbages to drive away the white butterflies. It worked but the leaf exudations poisoned the soil and lowered yields significantly.

Cabbages especially suffer from the Cabbage moth Mamestra Brassicae whose fat brown caterpillars eat the inside of the heart causing far more damage than other caterpillars which consume mostly outer leaves, the eggs are laid singly so hard to find though the grub's greenish brown frass is easily spotted.

Brassica oleracea botrytis botrytis, CAULIFLOWER

These are cauliflowers if they head up in the warmer months but the over-wintering ones are botanically broccolis.

The part we eat is an enormous multiple flowered head suspended in the bud stage. Any check or damage will lead to 'button' heads.

There are red and green cauliflowers and dwarf ones that take less space, these all require rich moist soil to do well, and as these are so highly bred sowing dates are critical! Break and bend outer leaves over ripening heads to prevent white curds from yellowing.

Acid soils especially those lacking in trace elements may cause cauliflowers especially, and some other Brassicas, to develop thin spindly leaves called Whiptail, easily cured with seaweed sprays, Molybdenum salts and liming.

The Cabbage Stem Flea beetle Psylliodes chrysocephala grubs tunnel into the stems of young plants causing them to fail.

Brassica oleraceae, COLLARDS

These are primitive cabbage plants grown for their small loose heads. Smaller but tougher than cabbages they're easier to grow especially in hot conditions though then often suffer from Flea beetles.

Brassica oleraceae, KALES

Another Brassica prone to the same pests and diseases but tougher than most and very hardy, will survive most UK winters.
Chopped fine and deep fried this is too often sold as 'seaweed' by perfidious chefs.

Brassica oleraceae, KOHLRABI

A tough pest and disease resistant crop much like a turnip but easier and not as hot, should be more widely grown especially as it can store well.

Brassica rapa rapa TURNIPS

Not Swedes, Turnips are smaller, whiter, quicker to crop and hotter to taste.
May develop a brown centre to the root if the soil is deficient in Boron.
Many co-lives are named Turnip this or that as they were first noticed on turnips but interact with most Brassicas so their entries are with the respective species.
Flea beetles Phyllotreta spp. are often an especial problem best cleared by waving sticky flypaper close above the seedlings.

Cabbage root fly Erioischia Brassicae / Delia / Anthomyia radicum, eats the roots of all Brassicas, but as it tunnels through the swollen edible part of a turnip becomes more of a problem and sometimes does the same with Swedes, the females consume nectar of Cow parsley Anthriscus sylvestris so are most prevalent when this is flowering, the leaves often turn reddish purple if plant is attacked. These flies can be lured to traps containing Swede root juice as bait. Interplanting lettuce, clover or Tagetes marigolds reduces infestations. Heavy attacks of aphids deter this fly and oddly the Garden Pebble moth caterpillar Evergestis forficalis apparently exudes a deterrent chemical in its frass. Rove and Ground beetles also control the fly by eating the eggs.

Sometimes the Turnip Gall weevil makes lumpy swellings which disclose a whitish legless grub, this may be confused with Clubroot if the maggot is not seen.

Turnips suffer from Soft rot where some damage allows disease in to rot the heart out.

Radish scab Streptomyces scabies makes scabby patches on the skin but seldom does serious harm, attacks may be reduced by mixing grass clippings or other rich organic material into the soil when sowing or planting.

Black Leg / Black Stem / Canker Phoma lingam is a fungal attack, spots on leaves, brownish purple to black cankers on stems at base cause roots to wilt and die, also attacks Swedes, usually seed borne.

Brassica sinapis, see Sinapis, CHARLOCK.

Bryonia, BRYONY

Consider poisonous though young shoots and or tuberous roots were once eaten after boiling or baking which destroyed toxin.

Apparently the sole blooms known visited by Andrena florae bees.

Perfidious weeds as these are alternate hosts for Bryonia mottle virus, spread by aphids, which badly affects Cucurbits in many countries.

Bryony is also thought alternate host of Spinach Blight / Cucumber Yellow Mottle mosaic virus.

Buddleia / Buddleija davidi, BUTTERFLY BUSH

Legendary for attracting butterflies, and good for bees, also a self-seeding weed and very invasive which since WWII has populated almost every waste ground and railway track-side in the UK.

Buddleia globosa

This form does not self seed aggressively like B. davidii so should be grown more widely.

BUTTERFLIES

Well, to some only the most garish butterflies will please, small drab ones and most MOTHS sadly do not. Yet all perform the same task and their appearance may delight your close attention with a hand lens.
These are often specific pollinators for specific flowers closely adapted over countless ages, even smelling remarkably similar with many they visit.
Probably the most widespread butterfly attractant flowers are thistles, field scabious and red clover. Of course few of their nasty grubby caterpillars are ever welcome anywhere, however these are all part of the great scheme.....

Buxus, BOX

Well known for harbouring snails which are probably grazing the algae on the box leaves.
The terminal bud is swollen by the Box Cabbage gall an Homopteran Psyllid to a small 'cabbage' an inch or so across and this may also cause some swelling, yellowing and distortion in leaves below.

Cajanus cajan, PIGEON PEA

A Leguminous perennial crop grown in many semi-tropical countries.

May carry Bean Yellow mosaic; dark and yellow patches with bright yellow spots which also infects many other Leguminous plants: Cajanus, Canavalia, Cassia, Cicer, Cladrastis, Crotolaria, Dolichos, Glycine, Hedysarum, Lathyrus, Lens, Lupinus, Medicago, Melilotus, Phaseolus, Pisum, Robinia, Trifolium, Trigonella, Vicia and Vigna, and also Alpinia, Chenopodium, Gladiolus, Freesia, Babiana, Sparaxis and Tritonia.

Also carries Clover Yellow Vein virus; yellow mosaic, necrosis and wilting which infects most other Legumes as with previous virus, and also Antirrhinum, Atriplex, Chenopodium, Coriandrum, Cucurbita, Gladiolus, Gomphrena, Nicotiana, Nicandra, Papaver, Petunia, Proboscidea, Rubus, Spinacia, Tetragonia and Viola.

Calceolaria

Not very hardy garden flowers and house plants.

Green or greenish brown aphids Macrosiphum solani can be a problem as these spread to Arums, tomatoes, carnations and lettuce, especially under cover.

Leaf-hoppers Erythroneura pallidifrons, pale yellow or white, eighth inch long, active insects do some damage causing bleached areas, also spread to Fuschias, Geraniums, Primulas, Salvias, and Verbenas.

CALCIFUGES

Mostly belonging to Ericacae and a few other families these plants cannot prosper in soil with free lime. Chelated Iron and seaweed extracts can help, as will increasing the acidity of the soil by incorporating plentiful organic matter.

CALCIUM, LIME / CHALK

One of the most important plant nutrients for many crops but poison to Ericaceae and calcifuge lime haters.
When a change to the soil ph is required apply calcified seaweed or dolomitic limestone instead of plain lime / chalk which may lack trace elements.
Lime although needed by most vegetables especially Brassicas will encourage scab on potatoes though organic material included in the soil when planting the sets will counteract this.
Lime is essential for the larger and most useful earthworms.
Lime is especially accumulated by buckwheat, lupin and melon.

Plants that will grow in limey soil are legion as most need lime or are indifferent. Problems with chalky soils are usually more due to their tendency to be a thin layer short of organic material and thus hot and dry. Most plants will show chlorosis and other signs of progressive mineral deficiency in very alkaline soils.

Calendula officinalis, POT MARIGOLD

Old garden flower beneficial to many insects and plants, often bothered by slugs though self seeds so prolifically this is rarely a problem.
Supposedly repels dogs from their vicinity.
Fresh and dried the petals are used as flavouring, seasoning and medicinally.
Sprays of the extract have been used against asparagus beetles and tomato hornworms.

Callistephus hortensis / chinensis, CHINA ASTER

Often prey to Cutworm damage being razored off at ground level when planted out, see Cutworms.
Brachycaudus helichrysi aphids from plum trees fly to these asters which may then be stunted seriously.
Yellow red dusty patches on the underside of the leaves are the mould Coleosporium campanulae.

Calluna vulgaris, LING

An Ericaceous acid lover, good nectar producer, excellent for bees.

Caltha palustris, MARSH MARIGOLDS

Poisonous, flowers rich in nectar and pollen, attract bees and bumblebees.

Caltharanthus roseus, MADAGASCAR PRIMROSE

Famous for it's medicinal properties, applications of dried powdered leaves dramatically reduce soil infestations of root knot nematodes.

Camellia

A fungal disease Pestalozzia guepini attacks the leaves causing silvery white irregular blotches with tiny black specks.

Campanula

These are recorded as the only flowers visited by Halictoides bees.
May suffer from a Stem and Root rot Sclerotinia sclerotiorum that more usually bothers bulbous plants and Aquilegias.

Campanula lactiflora, MILKY BELLFLOWER

Flowers rich in nectar and pollen attract most bees.

Campanula rapunculoides, CREEPING CAMPANULA

The flowers are attacked by Coleopteran weevil Miarus campanulae / campanulata which causes the ovary to swell into a gall, often lopsided, containing one or two larvae. The same also bothers the Harebell C. rotundiflora.

CAMPHOR

A plant resin with a very strong smell frequently found in tropical trees, good at discouraging insect attacks this unfortunately taints food crops.

Canavalia, HORSE BEAN

Leguminous Asian weed and crop plant, may carry Bean Yellow mosaic; dark and yellow patches with bright yellow spots which spreads to many other Leguminous plants: Cajanus, Cassia, Cicer, Cladrastis, Crotolaria, Dolichos, Glycine, Hedysarum, Lathyrus, Lens, Lupinus, Medicago, Melilotus, Phaseolus, Pisum, Robinia, Trifolium, Trigonella, Vicia and Vigna, and also Alpinia, Chenopodium, Gladiolus, Freesia, Babiana, Sparaxis and Tritonia.
Also carries Clover Yellow Vein virus; yellow mosaic, necrosis and wilting which spreads to most other Legumes as with prior virus and also Antirrhinum, Atriplex, Chenopodium, Coriandrum, Cucurbita, Gladiolus, Gomphrena, Nicotiana, Nicandra, Papaver, Petunia, Proboscidea, Rubus, Spinacia, Tetragonia and Viola.

Cannabis sativa, HEMP

Has bactericidal qualities and may be fungicidal as reputed to help prevent potato blight.

Hemp was once planted extensively to deter cabbage white butterflies.

It's also a good green manure as it creates intense shade excluding other plants, and reduces to fibrous residues once ploughed under.

Not practical at present as currently unlawful to cultivate this in most countries.

CANOPY PERIOD

This is the time during which any tree or shrub is in full leaf. The shorter the period the less competition there is underneath for other plants. Those that come into leaf late are more 'garden friendly' than those that leaf early if their total periods are the same, as early leaf fall is of little benefit when most plants are fading anyway. Ash has one of the shortest periods.

Capsella bursa-pastoris, SHEPHERD'S PURSE

Edible. This will germinate even in winter months. Accumulates Calcium.

Host for many plant pests especially Cabbage Root Fly Phorbia Brassicae and of nematodes that attack many crop and ornamental plants in particular Stem eelworm Tylenchus devastatrix.

Also harbours diseases over-winter especially Lettuce Mosaic and Cabbage Black Ringspot viruses, Brassica Clubroot, and Cabbage White Rust Cystopus candidus. May suffer Albugo / Cystopus spp. phycomycetes fungal attacks also called White mould / White Blister / Blister Rust, causing blistering galls erupting with white powdery spores, worse in a wet season, spread by aphids, often mixed with Peronospora parasitica moulds, also spreads to other Cruciferae such as Coronopus and Erysium spp.

CAPSID BUGS

Often green, some quite pretty like the related Shield bug, these all do much damage typically including distortion of young growth, but they also control tortrix and other caterpillars, red spider mites, aphids and leaf-hoppers. The problems often do not show till long after the pest has attacked and gone, it is the after affects of it's feeding that show with distorted growth and damaged fruits. You rarely spot capsids, though you may come across the very similar Froghopper Philaenua spumarius because it sits in it's own froth of Cuckoo Spit, this rarely becomes a problem except perhaps on Coreopsis, Geums, lavender, Phlox and Solidago and other plants where it may cause shoots to wilt. Infestations of the closely related Tarnished bugs often cause damage to leaves, shoots and blooms and most commonly on Dahlias, Delphiniums and Zinnias.

Capsicum, HOT / SWEET / BELL PEPPERS

Tender plants that although prone to aphids themselves are the source of hot chilli pepper made from the dried fruit and seeds and effective at discouraging many pests. Mammals feel the burning sensation caused by capsaicin however birds apparently do not taste it.

Over thirty viruses are known to cause losses including Potato virus, Tobacco Etch virus, Pepper Mottle virus, Pepper Veinal Mottle virus, all spread by aphids. Tobacco mosaic and Cucumber mosaic virus are amongst the worst.

Carduus, THISTLES

Often alternate hosts for Black fly Aphis rumicis.

Flowerheads host Tephritid gall flies; Acanthiophilus helianthi and Tephritis hyoscyami.

Flowerheads also sustain Lepidoptera caterpillars (which may also eat gall fly larvae as well) Phycitodes binaevella, Eucosma cana and Myelois cribrella.

Flowerheads also sustain gall midges: Dasineura spp., Clinodiplosis spp. and Lestodiplosis spp.

The stems are the preferred home of the agromyzid stem-borer Melanagromyza aeneoventris.

The stems also sustain stem boring caterpillars Epiblema scutulana and Agapeta hamana.

The stems and the roots sustain the weevil Apion carduorum.

The stems support Aphis Dactynotus / Uroleucon cirsii.

The leaves support the rather polyphagous Aphis Myzus persicae which often alternates onto Prunus persica.

All parts support Aphis Brachycaudus helichrysi and B. cardui which alternate on Prunus domestica.

The leaves and stems support Aphis Capitophorus carduinus and C. eleagni which alternate onto Hippophae rhamnoides.

One aphid, the carrot-willow aphid transmits the Carrot Motley Dwarf virus which turns the outer leaves red with yellow mottling on the inner ones.

The Celery eelworm causes thickening of the leaf bases and weak growth.

Several Tortoise beetles mine the leaves: Psylliodes chalcomera, Sphaeroderma rubidium, S. testaceum, Cassida rubignosa and C.vibex

Carduus acanthoides

The blooms recorded visited by 44 different insect species: 4 butterflies and moths, 32 species bee, 3 species Diptera flies and 5 others, another reference says of every hundred visitors to the flowers 58 are bees, 27 butterflies and moths and 12 flies.

Flowerheads host Tephritid gall flies: Tephritis hyoscyami, Terellia serratulae and T. winthemi.

Carduus arvensis, CREEPING THISTLE

These blooms recorded visited by 88 insect species. Gets attacked by Puccinia suavolens Thistle rust which turns the entire head into one huge gall.

Carduus crispus, WELTED THISTLE

Flowerheads host Tephritid gall flies Terellia serratulae.

Carduus lanceolatus, SPEAR THISTLE

The blooms recorded visited by 12 unspecified insect species.

Carduus nutans, MUSK / NODDING THISTLE

Flowerheads host Tephritid gall flies: Tephritis hyoscyami, Terellia serratulae, gall forming Urophora solstitialis and the weevil Rhinocyllus conicus (successfully introduced as biological control in North America).
Psylliodes chalcomera Tortoise beetle larvae mine the leaves.

Carduus palustris, MARSH THISTLE

The blooms visited by 22 unspecified insect species.

Carex, SEDGES

These are alternate hosts for Gooseberry-leaf cluster-cups
Puccinea hieraci.

Carpenteria

This flowering shrub may be attcked by reddish brown
oval Peach scale which spreads to Cotoneaster, Escallonia,
Lonicera and flowering and fruiting currants.

Carpinus betulus, HORNBEAM

Branches and trunk invaded by fungus ascomycete
Taphrina / Exoascus carpini causes 'witches-broom'
similar to those on birch but usually stubbier.
Leaf-blade galled by acarine gall-mite Eriophyes
pulchellum / Phytoptus tenellus, which cause smooth
shiny roughly triangular swellings on the upper surface.
Midribs are galled by Dipteron gall-midge Zygobia carpini
which cause severe swellings, spindle shaped galls up to
an inch or more long paler than the leaf which may
coalesce and can cause considerable distortion of the leaf.

The large brown bracket fungi of Peziza arvernensis is found amongst fallen leaves, distinguished by fine warts on the spores.

Dead branches often support Tremella mesenterica fungus with a brain like appearance, bright yellow while moist.

The litter grows the highly poisonous Boletus satanus with a light grey to brown cap, pale blue flesh, most often found on calcerous soils.

Even worse is the Death Cap Amanita phalloides, usually greenish but sometimes white, with white gills, the flesh is sweet and pleasing to the taste so easily eaten in error with dire results, also found under oaks.

Pluteus cervinus, edible, grows on stumps and rotting wood, it has a light to dark grey or brownish cap and streaked stipe, the gills start white then go pink with red spores, also found on oak, birch and beech.

More common in the warmer parts of the continent than in the UK is the highly poisonous Entoloma / Rhodophyllus sinuatum / lividum / sinuatus, this has pale greyish cap, pink to orangish gills and pink spores, it likes calcareous soil and is also found under oaks and beeches.

Carum carvi, CARAWAY

Deep rooted and difficult to establish.
Blossoms have been recorded as visited by 55 species of insect: 1 Lepidoptera, 9 species bee, 21 species Diptera flies and 24 others.

Cassia obtusifolia, SICKLEPOD

This and C. sophera, another warm climate weed may become infected by Bean Yellow mosaic; dark and yellow patches with bright yellow spots which spreads to many other Leguminous plants and also Alpinia, Chenopodium, Gladiolus, Freesia, Babiana, Sparaxis and Tritonia.
Also carries Clover Yellow Vein virus; yellow mosaic, necrosis and wilting which spreads to most other Legumes as for prior virus, and also Antirrhinum, Atriplex, Chenopodium, Coriandrum, Cucurbita, Gladiolus, Gomphrena, Nicotiana, Nicandra, Papaver, Petunia, Proboscidea, Rubus, Spinacia, Tetragonia and Viola.

Castanea sativa, SWEET CHESTNUT

Seldom found growing beyond 800ft above sea level. The leaves of this have been used to make a spray against beet moths (sic).

CATCH CROP

Growing a quick crop like radish, lettuce or spinach before a slower growing plant needs all the space. For example many Brassicas and most tender plants such as tomatoes, sweet corn or courgettes are planted in their final position in May. Catch crops can use the ground till then. Others can follow the early potatoes or the Japanese onions as soon as cleared in July. Catch crops may be fitted in between the main rotation crops only if they are not too closely related to them and do not exhaust the soil or build up pests and diseases.

CATERPILLARS / MAGGOTS / GRUBS / WORMS

These are often conflated, probably as all do much the same damage, that is bits go missing from leaves, shoots and fruits. And although the majority of such co-lives are not serious pests there are very few which are 'useful'. Some are beautiful, and many of the butterflies and moths they become even more so, yet most are undoubtedly not very plant friendly. Many other co-lives have a maggot or grub stage but the Lepidoptera outnumber them in species, these are dealt with in detail in Volume 2 Really Help Butterflies.

Common serious offenders are the Tortrix Moth family who wriggle backwards if tapped on the head, these tie leaf tips and ends together to make tents. The Angle Shades moth who looks like a crumpled leaf does a devastating job on most plants with it's small olive brown or greenish caterpillars which are often found eating the flowers or leaves near the flower buds.

There are some commercially available controls such as one for Brassica caterpillars; Bacillus thuriengiensis, which you merely water or sprinkle on your cabbages, if they ingest it they die, it is naturally occurring and found in the soil, and does not affect us.

Many caterpillar, maggot, worm and grub attacks can be prevented by growing your crops under nets or fleeces to exclude the adults flying or clambering in. Under cover the ventilation and doors can be fitted with mesh screens. A few species have adults who can't fly and have to climb the trunk or walls; these can be easily excluded with little more than non-setting sticky bands or tape.

Whereas generally we think of caterpillars as leaf eaters other 'maggots', 'worms' and various 'grubs' inhabit the insides of fruits and storage organs. Their protected position there makes them harder to tackle. Some have specific controls which catch them at different stages and nature's natural balance can be moved in our favour particularly with companion plants encouraging more predators and parasites.

The true Worms do little damage. The casts of the big Lugworms may cause problems on the turf but the drainage and aeration caused should be seen as the greater benefit. (Their casts are worth gathering for adding to pot plant composts.) But worms also annoy by dragging over and damaging onion and shallot sets and leek plants by their leaves. The sets need the wee dead bit of leaf removing before they are put out. The leek plants need to have enough of the longer leaf tips cut away so the remainder stands proud and does not drag on the soil. The onion and shallot sets can be held firmly in place with a small surrounding mound of fine soil or sharp sand brushed away later.

Ceanothus, CALIFORNIAN LILAC

These are excellent bee plants with large masses of blue flowers.
They're prone to frost damage which may resemble a disease.
May be infested with Mussel scale as found on Malus and Pyrus.

Centaurea cyanus, CORNFLOWER

Flowers provide bees with nectar even during very dry weather.
Analysis of dry matter: Crude ash 8.12%, N 2.3%, P 0.78%, K 1.94%, Ca 3.13,% and Na 1.07%.

Host to Stem Eelworm Tylenchus devastatrix.

Centaurea jacea / nigra, KNAPWEED

The flowers are reported visited by at least 48 different insect species: 13 butterflies and moths, 28 species bee, 6 species Diptera flies and 1 other, another reference says of every hundred visitors to the flowers 58 are bees, 27 butterflies and moths and 12 flies.

In SE Europe the knapweeds, and some other Compositae, have Chafer beetles attacking their flowerheads, thus the plants exude 'nectar' from the scales of the capitulum which attracts ants who then repay by keeping off the chafers.

Flowerheads also host Tephritid gall flies: Acanthiophilus helianthi, Chaetostomella cylindrica and Urophora jaceana (this often parasitised by Eurytoma tibialis / curta).

The stems and roots sustain the weevil Apion onopordi and the stem boring caterpillar Epiblema scutulana.

Cassida vibex Tortoise beetles mine the leaves.

Shoots and stems are attacked inside by Hymenopteran gall-wasp Phanacis centaureae / Aylax showing as wrinkled succulent greenish swellings usually about half to three quarters of an inch sometimes longer, the larvae pupate within to emerge the next spring, this also attacks other Centaurea species.

Flowerheads also sustain Eucosma cana Lepidoptera caterpillars (which conveniently eat many gall fly larvae as well).

Centaurea diffusa, DIFFUSE KNAPWEED

This and C. maculosa are pernicious weeds in North America now partly controlled by the introduction of Urophora affinis, U. quadrifasciata and U. stylata Tephritid gall flies.

Centaurea scabiosa, GREATER KNAPWEED

The blooms reported visited by 21 unspecified insect species.
This and C. nigra LESSER KNAPWEED, have their stems galled by Hymenopteran Knapweed gall-wasp Iscolus scabiosae / Aylax centaureae / Diastrophus scabiosa which makes a large gall sometimes up to nearly three inches long.
Iscolus fitchi wasps gall the base of the stems and I. jaceae and I. rogenhoferi gall the Centaurea fruits, while the seed head is galled by Dipteron fruit-fly Euroibia solstitialis / Urophora / Trypeta which causes seeds to swell to an oval mass over a third of an inch long, part smooth and part with tufted grey hairs.

Centranthus, FALSE VALERIAN

Easy garden plant useful for dry and rocky places with red to pink flowers beloved by butterflies.

CEREALS

Wheat, barley, oats and rye, and debatably rice and maize / corn.
With their relations the many grasses and sugar cane these sustain most of the world's population directly or as animal feed. See Grasses to which they are closely related for general associations. Particularly bothered by Corn Aphis / Dolphin / Plant-louse Aphis granaria / avenae.

Chaemaecyparis, CYPRESS

Mulches of this shown to slow growth of Hydrangeas, Spirea and Viburnum, probably due to leaching of phenolic allelopathic chemicals; which same make their wood resistant to decay.

Chaerophyllum temulum, ROUGH CHERVIL

Blossoms recorded visited by 23 species of insect: 1 bee, 10 species Diptera flies and 12 other.

CHAFER BUGS

Chafers are whitish grubs with a brown head. These grubs have six small legs and destroy roots and tubers. They come in several sorts from those about the same size as, to those three times larger than vine weevil grubs which they sort of resemble. The adult Chafers are lustrous beetles which may also seriously destroy foliage and flowers.

Melolantha vulgaris, Phyllopertha horticola and Cetonia aurata attack mostly the roots of grasses. However these may bother any plants during the first years after converting turfed areas to vegetable bed or flower border, and also in beds weedy with grasses. The symptoms are sick weak plants, and your lawn and turf suffers poor patches of yellowing growth which birds, foxes and badgers all tear up to get at the grubs. Chafers can be controlled by watering on the parasitic nematode Heterorhabditis megidis when the soil is wet and warmer than 12°C (54°F).

Cheiranthus cheiri, WALLFLOWERS

Be warned plants of these, and the soil on their roots can bring Clubroot disease into your garden, see Clubroot entry.

Chenopodium album, FAT HEN / WHITE GOOSEFOOT

Edible weed, the young shoots were once eaten much like asparagus.
Very rich in Nitrogen, Calcium, Iron, Phosphorus, Potassium, Sulphur, and in vitamins C & A.
Seeds known to remain viable up to 1,700 years.
Of benefit to Cucurbits and many flowers when used as a sacrificial attracting leaf miners.
Host for plant pests over-winter especially Black bean aphid and Peach-potato aphid, Myzus persiceae, which also attack lettuces and other crops.
May also harbour Mangold Fly Pegomyia betae.
 Fat Hen is often source of nematodes that bother many crops and ornamental plants.
Leaves are roll-galled by Homopteran aphid SemiAphis atriplicis, this thickens and rolls edges to midrib, on narrow leaves becoming sickle shaped (then may be confused with galls caused by mite Eriophyes galii), turning yellow to light brown, infested leaves fall and blow about spreading the aphids to new food supplies, also spreads to Atriplex spp.

Dipteron Pegomyia chenopodii cause galls in the leaves which they mine and this makes the surfaces bulge. Over-winters fungal Peronospora effusa that spreads to spinach.

May carry Lettuce Mosaic and Cabbage Black Ringspot viruses. Chenopodiums may be infected by Bean Yellow mosaic; dark and yellow patches with bright yellow spots, this spreads to many other Leguminous plants and also Alpinia, Gladiolus, Freesia, Babiana, Sparaxis and Tritonia. May also carry Clover Yellow Vein virus; yellow mosaic, necrosis and wilting which spreads to most Legumes and also Antirrhinum, Atriplex, Coriandrum, Cucurbita, Gladiolus, Gomphrena, Nicotiana, Nicandra, Papaver, Petunia, Proboscidea, Rubus, Spinacia, Tetragonia and Viola.

Chenopodium ambrosoides

Was once used medicinally.

Chenopodium bonus-henricus, GOOD KING HENRY

This little known delicacy has succulent young shoots eaten in the manner of asparagus.

Chenopodium urbicum, UPRIGHT GOOSEFOOT

Dipteron Pegomyia chenopodii cause galls in the leaves as they mine and make the surfaces bulge.

CHICKENS

Good companion in the orchard where they eat pests and spread fertility, very easy to look after, bantam varieties give more beaks and eyes per pound of bird fed and are thus more efficient but require better fencing.
Their manure is powerful compost fuel.

Chrysanthemum

Many species use exudations against pests and diseases; C. cinerariafolium and C. roseum flowers have been powdered for thousands of years for use as insect killer. The commercial version, Pyrethrum, was used in massive amounts on account of it's low toxicity to mammals.
Earwigs get in the flowers and damage shoots.
More common in the US Midges Diarthronomyia chrysanthemi cause conical one eighth of an inch long galls with larvae inside on most parts, notifiable in the UK as considered a serious threat.

Often have Aphid Macrosiphoniella sanborni, black or blackish red, which cause much damage and distortion. Leaf-curling aphids from plums may also do some damage.

Capsid bug Bishop bug / fly / Tarnished plant bug Lygus pratensis twists and distorts leaves, dwarfs and deforms flowers and causes galls on stems. L. pabulinus the common Green Capsid bug of currants does similar damage.

Leaf miners Phytomyza atricornis cause yellow whitish lines in the leaves, this same species attacks Cinerarias and sow thistles.

An eelworm nematode that attacks Chrysanthemums may spread to Asters, Dahlias, Delphiniums, Rudbeckias and Verbenas.

Chrysanthemums may get Mildew Oidium chrysanthemi as white powdery patches on top or bottom surface of the leaf.

Dark brown patches on the upper leaf surfaces is the Leaf spot Septoria chrysanthemi, the leaves curl up and drop. Reddish rust Puccinia chrysanthemi appears on the underside of leaves, worst in dry seasons.

Chrysanthemum coccineum

Exudates from this are effective at killing nematodes.

Chrysanthemum coronarium, Chinese MARIGOLD

The shoots get invaded by bacterium Corynebacterium fascians, causes fasciation, stems become broad, flattened and ribbed, splayed and curved, this spreads to jasmine, plantains, dogwood, Cotoneaster, Euphorbias, Forsythia, Hibiscus, holly and Inula.

Chrysanthemum leucanthemum, OX EYE DAISY

Closely related to tansy both have been used to repel pests.
Attracts 72 different insect species with it's long flowering period: 5 butterflies and moths, 12 species bee, 28 species Diptera flies and 27 others.
Flowers may be attacked by acarine gall-mite causing proliferation, phyllody and even a second capitulum.

Chrysanthemum parthenium, FEVERFEW

A common garden plant that self seeds with a vengeance though the yellow form is very cheerful in shade and sun. The strong scent hides many plants from pests.

Some use the double flowered version medicinally against migraine.

Cicer arietinum, GRAM / CHICKPEA

Warm climate Legume crop.
May carry Bean Yellow mosaic; dark and yellow patches with bright yellow spots, this spreads to many other Leguminous plants and also Alpinia, Chenopodium, Gladiolus, Freesia, Babiana, Sparaxis and Tritonia.
Also carries Clover Yellow Vein virus; yellow mosaic, necrosis and wilting which spreads to most other Legumes, and also Antirrhinum, Atriplex, Chenopodium, Coriandrum, Cucurbita, Gladiolus, Gomphrena, Nicotiana, Nicandra, Papaver, Petunia, Proboscidea, Rubus, Spinacia, Tetragonia and Viola.
Often infected by Bean Curly Dwarf mosaic; mosaic, stunting and rugosity, this spreads to other Phaseolus species, soybean, pea, lentil, broad bean, mung bean and Leguminous weeds.
Thrips tabaci and Frankliniella occidentalis convey the Tobacco Streak virus / Bean Red Node; red nodes, necrosis and red spots, also seed borne this also spreads to alfalfa, fenugreek, Datura, sweet clover, soybean, Nicotiana, most beans and other plants.

Cichorium intybus, CHICORY / SUCCORY

Pretty wild flower and the garden forms have edible roots and leaves.
Accumulates Iron, Magnesium and some Potassium.

Cineraria, DUSTY MILLER

Garden foliage plant which may repel rabbits but not hardy in UK.
Leaf miner Phytomyza atricornis may cause some damage and moves between carnations, sow thistles and Chrysanthemums.

Cirsium arvense THISTLES

Unwanted companions in most gardens but can be hand weeded with a daisy grubber.
Accumulate Potassium, Calcium, Copper and Iron, really should be encouraged as their penetrating roots bring up minerals from deep down.
Their blooms are visited by 88 different insect species: 7 butterflies and moths, 32 species bee, 24 species Diptera flies and 25 others.

Thistles harbour Mangold Fly Pegomyia betae, Celery Fly Acidia heraclei, Ghost / Otter Moth Hepialus lapuli, Aphis rumicis Black fly and in the US Colorado beetle Doryphora decemlineata.

Foliage and other parts eaten by Thistle Lacebug Tingis ampliata and T. cardui.

Leaves are mined by Pegomya steini, Cnephasia spp., Agonopterix spp., Scrobipalpa acuminatella, Phytomyza cirsii, Sphaeroderma rubidium and S. testaceum.

Flowerheads host Tephritid gall flies: Acanthiophilus helianthi, Chaetostomella cylindrica, Tephritis cometa, Terrellia ruficauda, Xyphosia miliaria.

The stems are attacked by Dipteron fruit-fly / Tephritid gall fly Euribia / Trypeta / Urophora cardui causing galls up to an inch long near the top of the stem, which become woody as they change from yellowish green to brown.

The stems also attacked by agromyzid stem-borer Melanagromyza aeneoventris.

Flowerheads sustain gall midges: Dasineura spp., Clinodiplosis spp. and Lestodiplosis spp.

Flowerheads stems and roots sustain the weevils Apion carduorum, A. onopordi, Rhinocyllus conicus, Larinus planus, Lixus algirus, Phyllobius spp., Tanymecus palliatus, Ceutorhynchus litura.

Near sandy coasts roots are often galled by weevil larvae of Cleonis piger.

The crown rosette hosts C. trimaculatus and Trichosirocalus horridus.

The stems sustain stem boring caterpillars Epiblema asineura, Agapeta hamana, Aethes cnicana and Nyelois cribrella.

Roots support Aphis Protrama radices, Trama troglodytes and DysAphis spp.

The leaves support polyphagous Aphis Macrosiphum euphorbiae which alternates on Rosa spp. and Myzus persicae which alternates on Prunus persica.

Stem and leaves support Aphis fabae group of polyphagous aphids which alternate living on Euonymous europaeus, Aulacorthum solani, Dactynotus / Uroleucon cirsii, Capitophorus carduinus and C. eleagni which alternates on Hippophae rhamnoides.

All parts support Aphis Brachycaudus helichrysi and B. cardui which alternate on Prunus domestica. The stems support Aphis Dactynotus / Uroleucon aenus.

Several Tortoise beetles mine the leaves: Cassida rubignosa, C.vibex, C. viridis, Lema cyanella, Oulema melanopa, O. lichenis, Galeruca tanaceti, Crepidodera ferruginea, C. transversa and Longitarsus luridus. Predatory soldier beetles, ladybirds and reddish brown Cotinicara gibbosa beetles are also commonly found on thistles.

Cirsium dissectum

The flowerheads host Tephritid gall flies Terrellia ruficauda.

Cirsium eriophorum

The stems sustain stem boring caterpillar Myelois cribrella.

Cirsium helenioides

Flowerheads host Tephritid gall flies Tephritis conura,

Cirsium palustre

Flowerheads host Tephritid gall flies Tephritis cometa, Terrellia ruficauda (forms a gall) and Xyphosia miliaria. The leaves and stems support Aphis Dactynotus / Uroleucon cirsii,

Cirsium vulgare

Stem and leaves support Aphis Capitophorus carduinus. Flowerheads host Tephritid gall flies Terrellia serratulae and Urophora stylata which are parasitised inside by Eurytoma tibialis and Tetrastichus daira, and from outside by Pteromalus / Habrocytus elevates, Torymus chloromerus / cyanimus and Eurytoma robusta, and predated by Palloptera spp. and Lestodiplosis spp.
The stems and roots sustain the weevils Apion carduorum and A. onopordi.

The stems sustain stem boring caterpillar Myelois cribrella.

The leaves sustain caterpillars of Agonopterix arenella and agromyzid leaf miners Phytomyza cirsii.

Flowerheads also sustain Lepidoptera caterpillars (which may also eat gall fly larvae as well) Eucosma cana, Homoeosoma nebulella and Phycitodes binaevella.

Citrullus lanatus, WATERMELON

This require different conditions to melons, even more heat and a less rich compost, and no more than one fruit per plant.

If soil temperature drops below about 70°F roots may simply rot away.

Pollen from sweetcorn and maize seriously inhibits growth and prevents successful fruiting.

These suffer most of the co-lives that also visit melons and cucumbers.

Like melons these are very susceptible to Red Spider mite.

Watermelon Mosaic / Papaya Ringspot virus is not seen in UK but elsewhere causes severe stunting, mosaic, shoe string leaf laminae, and distorted knobbly discoloured fruits. It may also attack any Cucurbit, most Legumes and is a serious problem for beans.

Cistus

One of the plants known to warm up their flower heads to aid pollinators.

Citrus

Not hardy in Northern Europe but easy to over-winter and move outside for summer in tubs, the flowers have exquisite scent.
Empty peels make good slug traps and dried are effective firelighters.
Peel extracts have been used for sprays against fall armyworms and bollworms.
Commonly attacked by just about everything, especially Aphids, Scale and Red Spider mites (even having their own special variety).

Cladrastis, YELLOW WOOD

Small Leguminous ornamental tree.
May be infected by Bean Yellow mosaic; dark and yellow patches with bright yellow spots which spreads to many other Leguminous plants and also Alpinia, Chenopodium, Gladiolus, Freesia, Babiana, Sparaxis and Tritonia.

Also carries Clover Yellow Vein virus; yellow mosaic, necrosis and wilting which spreads to most other Legumes as with prior virus and also Antirrhinum, Atriplex, Chenopodium, Coriandrum, Cucurbita, Gladiolus, Gomphrena, Nicotiana, Nicandra, Papaver, Petunia, Proboscidea, Rubus, Spinacia, Tetragonia and Viola.

Clematis

Mostly climbers though some are herbaceous species, generally need cool moist root runs so benefit from mulch, ground cover and prefer limey soil.
C. montana, C. armandii and C. flammula have scent, the majority do not. All are good hosts to insects and provide shelter for birds.
Prone to sudden death called Clematis wilt, though similar death is caused by wood lice and slugs girdling the new shoots.

Clematis recta

Produces no nectar but blooms are visited by insects for pollen.

Clematis vitalba, TRAVELLER'S JOY

The fluffy seed heads are good for bird nesting material.

CLUBROOT / FINGER & TOE, / ANBURY

A serious disease caused by Plasmodiophora Brassicae. Much feared and highly virulent problem of cabbage tribe, introduced in soil or on infected plants. It causes foul smelling swellings on roots and ruins yields.
Clubroot affects all Brassicas and the related wallflowers, stocks and candytuft.
It is harboured by plants other than Brassicas such as docks, nasturtiums and many grasses though doing little damage to these. Slight protection is afforded by rhubarb in planting holes and more from heavy liming beforehand. Exudates from peppermint, summer savory and thyme may significantly reduce infestations of clubroot fungus. If you do not yet have this disease in your soil NEVER bring in Brassica plants especially from doubtful sources. If you must buy susceptible plants choose container grown ones in sterile composts.

COBALT

Micronutrient element not apparently required by plants but needed by Leguminous plants' nitrogen fixing organisms, worms and most larger animals. Soils in some places lacking in Cobalt produce apparently normal fodder crops but these cannot adequately supply full animal nutrition without mineral or seaweed supplements.

Colchicum autumnale, NAKED LADIES

The flowers appear without leaves in autumn, secrete
much nectar and are useful for late pollinators.
Plant is toxic and contains chromosome affecting chemical
colchicine used medicinally and to induce polyploidic
growth (doubles or more the chromosomes) causing more
vigour in treated plants.

Coleus

Tender decorative foliage plant.
Attacked by Eelworm nematodes causing brown spots and
blackened areas, which also attack ferns, Begonias,
Gloxinias, orchids and Salvias.

COLORADO BEETLE

Doryphora decemlineata, a major pest in the US rarely
seen in Europe, resembles a yellow and black ladybird.
Thornapple and possibly black nightshade are poisonous
to these beetles and will help keep them away from
potatoes, tomatoes and other Solanaceae.

COMPOSITAE

Daisy family, one of largest groups of flowering plants, many have inhibitory root secretions and most are good at repelling pests while providing for beneficial insects. Many such as Shasta daisies cause other cut flowers sharing the same water to wilt.

COMPOST

Sowing composts are most often made from sharp sand, peat, leaf mould, sterilised loam and little nutrient. They are best sterilised to stop seedlings damping off or being out competed by weeds.

Potting composts are similar but have increased nutrient levels as growing plants are more robust. They do not need to be sterile for most uses but freedom from weed seeds is a distinct advantage.

Garden compost is not sterile and the less so the better, it is a mixture of as many materials as possible rotted down together. It contains an unimaginable number of different bacteria, fungi, protozoa and other forms of life in the process of killing and eating each other and everything about them. These then feed the plants with their by-products and dead bodies and their offspring inoculate the soil increasing its activity. Various plants speed up composting especially stinging nettles and birches. Most herbs are beneficial but not the wormwood family or conifers which retard composting. Any weeds can be composted and those that accumulate minerals the more so. Weeds in seed or those that may reroot should be wilted for several days in the sun before composting, or just rotted in buckets of water. Otherwise seed bearing weeds should be put in really 'cooking' heaps. Always in short supply, sieved garden compost is good to incorporate in planting holes. Mix it well with the soil. It can be used as potting compost when mixed with peat and or leaf mould and or molehill soil and or rich loam. Important point; water soluble extracts of compost inhibit Grey mould, Damping off and Tomato wilt!

COMPOST STIMULATORS

Herbs recommended by Rudolph Steiner to encourage microorganisms to thrive are: stinging nettle, dandelion, oak bark, yarrow, chamomile and valerian. These can be obtained ready prepared from BioDynamic suppliers. The Maye E. Bruce compost stimulator uses similar recipe with honey. These work but I find are no more effective than a few shovels of poultry manure! More important is mixing in air and enough moisture with sufficient bulk to heat up.

CONIFERS

Mostly evergreens these give off secretions that inhibit composting and prevent many plants from germinating, particularly wheat.
To protect young conifers from squirrels interplant with tree onions.
The dense growth of some conifers makes them good winter quarters for many forms of life and so at least some should be in most gardens.

Convallaria majalis, LILY OF THE VALLEY

The flowers are nectar less but hive bees collect the pollen.

The bird-dropping-like slug of the Lily beetle Lilloceris lilli, a bright reddy orange rather smart looking beastie, destroys the leaves and also eats lilies, hollyhocks, Hostas, Solomons seal, potatoes and tobacco.
Never under-plant or follow Paeonies with Convallaria as they share the disease Botrytis paeoniae which browns the leaves which then drop off.

Convolvulus, BINDWEEDS

Thee are mostly pernicious weeds but beautiful, if you can't learn to live with them, move or resign yourself to eternal weeding.
The blooms are full of nectar, good for humble bees.

Convolvulus arvensis, FIELD / LESSER BINDWEED

The blooms close in wet weather and at night

Convolvulus sepium, GREATER BINDWEED

The huge trumpet shaped blooms stay open in wet weather but close at night.

Convolvulus tricolour

A hardy annual unlike rest of family, flowers resemble petunias but easier to grow, an excellent hoverfly attractant.

Coreopsis

One of the prettier Compositae, repels many pests while blooms attract many pollinators.

Coriandrum sativum, CORIANDER

The seeds are added to bread and baked dishes. The leaf is used in salsas and savoury dishes.
It repels aphids and has been used as a spray against spider mites. It attracts bees.
May carry Clover Yellow Vein virus; yellow mosaic, necrosis and wilting which spreads to most Legumes and also Antirrhinum, Atriplex, Chenopodium, Cucurbita, Gladiolus, Gomphrena, Nicotiana, Nicandra, Papaver, Petunia, Proboscidea, Rubus, Spinacia, Tetragonia and Viola.

Cornus sanguinea, CORNEL / DOGWOOD

Flowers more visited by flies than bees.
Leaf-blade attacked by Dipteron gall-midge Craneiobia corni, forming unusual pouch galls in shape of small bottle, base pushing up through upperside and neck protruding down underneath, yellow, pink to purple in colour.
Shoots get invaded by bacterium Corynebacterium fascians which causes fasciation, stems become broad, flattened and ribbed, splayed and curved, this spreads to jasmine, plantains, Chrysanthemums, Cotoneaster, Euphorbias, Forsythia, Hibiscus, holly and Inula.

Coronopus squamatus, SWINE CRESS

This suffers from White mould / White Blister / Blister Rust Albugo / Cystopus spp. phycomycetes fungal attacks causing blistering galls erupting with white powdery spores, worse in a wet season, spread by aphids, often mixed up with Peronospora parasitica moulds, this also spreads to other Cruciferae such as Capsella and Erysium.

Corylus avellana, HAZEL / COB / FILBERT

The cultivated forms such as Cosford cob or Webb's prize cob produce bigger nuts than the wild yet sustain as many forms of wildlife. They're beneficial in hedges and pastures for fodder and as fly deterrents. The proliferation of shoots around the base should be kept trimmed back. They make excellent windbreaks.
Plenty of pollen but no nectar as wind pollinated.
May be host for the semi-parasitic plant Toothwort Lathraea squanaria.
Various critters munch their leaves, others leave empty shells of the nuts but the ONLY serious problem for the grower is Squirrels. Interestingly if you simply pick the hanging or fallen nuts the percentage with dead or rotten nuts inside the shell is much higher than that of buried nuts- ie. the squirrels only take and bury good ones. I mulch heavily then after leaf fall I rake deeply around the trees recovering many of their hidden nuts.
Empty shells with a wee hole had the kernel eaten by the larvae of the brown Nut Weevil Balininus nucum.
Hazels may get Nut scale which is similar to Peach scale except the base of each is widened just above the junction, which spreads to elms, pears, hawthorns and Pyracantha.

The buds can suffer Big Bud where buds swell and distort without opening, all three; leaf-bud, flower bud and catkin bud galls are caused by these acarine gall-mites Eriophyes avellanae / Calycophthora / Phytoptus / Acarus pseudogallarum. These are predated by a midge Arthrocnodax coryligallarum, and a Chalcid Tetrastichus eriophyes and are most vulnerable as the new generation move to new buds in late spring early summer.
Another mite Eriophyes vermiformis may also be found crinkling the leaf.
The litter underneath grows the highly poisonous Boletus satanus with a light grey to brown cap, pale blue flesh, most often found on calcerous soils.
The giant edible puffball Calvatia gigantea is often found in hazel and elder copses.

Cosmos

Another of the prettier Compositae, allegedly repels pests while the decorative flowers attract many other insects.

Cotoneaster

These useful semi-evergreens are excellent bee plants and the red berries feed the birds.
They may suffer Mussel scale as found on Malus and Pyrus. May also be attacked by reddish brown oval Peach scale which spreads to Carpentaria, Escallonia, Lonicera, fruiting and flowering currants.

Shoots get invaded by bacterium Corynebacterium fascians, this causes fasciation, stems become broad, flattened and ribbed, splayed and curved, this spreads to jasmine, plantains, Chrysanthemums, dogwood, Euphorbias, Forsythia, Hibiscus, holly and Inula.

COWS

Cows select plants they prefer but pick up bad food habits just like us. Clear their pasture of ragweed, bracken, larkspur and other poisonous weeds. Hedge garlic, wild garlic and similar strong flavoured plants will taint their milk.

Crambe maritima, SEAKALE

Decorative and edible UK native of seashores, the spring shoots were once popular blanched as a crop.
Soft rot Bacterium carotovorum which spreads to carrots, celery and other roots, worse in wet conditions causes stems and other parts to go soft, wet and slimy.
Black Rot, Pseudomonas / Xanthomonas campestris is a bacterial invasion which causes yellowing leaves with blackened veins, cut stems show black dots in a ring, seen most in warm wet years, often attacks cabbage and cauliflower may spread to turnip and Swede, introduced on the seed but also soil borne.
Downy mildew Peronospora parasitica can attack seakale much as it does the Brassicas.

May also get Violet Root rot, see carrots Daucus, and worst of all it may get Clubroot, see entry

---

Crataegus oxycantha, QUICKTHORN / HAWTHORN

This makes one of the best, and quickest hedges. It benefits wildlife more than most others, and makes attractive flowering trees, especially the dark red varieties.

May get Nut scale similar to Peach scale except base of each is widened just above the junction, this spreads to elms, pears, hawthorns and Pyracantha.

The leaves are attacked by acarine gall-mites Eriophyes goniothorax typicus / Phytopus / Erineum clandestinum / oxycanthae; leaf edges are curled down into a rolled spike filled with dense hairs.

Leaf-blade gets leaf blistering caused by acarine gall-mite Eriophyes / Phytoptus / Typhlodromus, small swellings on both sides of leaf, yellowish green to red and purple, brown at maturity, unless it is a very heavy infestation it does little damage to established trees but can weaken poor ones.

The leaf-blade is also galled by Homopteran aphid Rhodalosiphum crataegellum / Aphis crataegi, brightly coloured small pouch gall up to an inch or so, yellow, pink or russet and often blotchy, usually found in shadier parts of plant, after the aphids move to herbaceous plants in summer old gall pouches are often moved into by mites, thrips, earwigs, millipedes, caterpillars, ants, spiders and chelifers. The same aphid is sometimes predated by Elm Gall bug Anthocoris gallarum-ulmi which also often attacks aphid Eriosoma ulmi in its galls on elm.
The terminal leaves of hawthorns are attacked by Dipteron gall-midge Dasyneura / Perrisia / Cecidomyia crataegi which form a rosette gall, deformed, thickened, reddened, leaves further down stem usually also affected and deformed.
Host to Diamond Back moth parasites (sic).
Juniper rust fungi Gymmnosporangium clavariaeforme / Rostelia lacerata moves onto hawthorn where it forms orange to brownish cluster-cups on stems and leaves which then suffer early death making these bad neighbours.

Crocus

One of the first tasks each year is to tie black cotton on sticks to stop birds eating the crocus flowers, though the whole plant disappearing is probably because the bulbs were eaten by rodents especially voles.

Crotalaria pallida

A Leguminous Asian weed this may carry Bean Yellow mosaic; dark and yellow patches with bright yellow spots which spreads to many other Leguminous plants and also Alpinia, Chenopodium, Gladiolus, Freesia, Babiana, Sparaxis and Tritonia.
Also carries Clover Yellow Vein virus; yellow mosaic, necrosis and wilting which spreads to most other Legumes and also Antirrhinum, Atriplex, Chenopodium, Coriandrum, Cucurbita, Gladiolus, Gomphrena, Nicotiana, Nicandra, Papaver, Petunia, Proboscidea, Rubus, Spinacia, Tetragonia and Viola.

CRUCIFERAE

Includes plants of the Brassica / cabbage family and many weeds and most are prone to similar co-lives.

CRYSTALLIZATION

A method used by Pfeiffer to determine companion effects between plants; evaporating extracts with copper chloride and examining the pattern formed.

Cucurbits see also Citrullus.

All this family are tender, have edible fruits and need warm moist rich conditions.

Most of the following co-lives will have a go at almost any Cucurbit but have been listed under those they visit most. All are plagued by Red Spider mites in hot dry conditions and Grey mould Botrytis cinerea in cold damp conditions. These share a common virus Cucumber mosaic, spread by more than 60 aphid species, this invades more than 800 plant species, often first noticed on the fruits which become distorted, mottled and stunted, leaves become smaller, mosaiced and malformed. This may plague many weeds and crops including pepper, tomato and even blackcurrants, it is known to be spread on the seeds of at least 19 different plant species.

Many other viruses damage Cucurbits world-wide, most are spread by aphids, the name often indicating an alternative host: Bryonia mottle, Clover Yellow Vein virus; yellow mosaic, necrosis and wilting which spreads to most Legumes and also Antirrhinum, Atriplex, Chenopodium, Coriandrum, Gladiolus, Gomphrena, Nicotiana, Nicandra, Papaver, Petunia, Proboscidea, Rubus, Spinacia, Tetragonia and Viola.

Also: Muskmelon vein necrosis, Papaya ringspot-w, Telfairia mosaic (also on seed), Watermelon mosaic, Watermelon mosaic Morocco, Zucchini yellow fleck and Zucchini yellow mosaic (also on seed).

Whiteflies spread: Beet Pseudo-yellows, Cucumber Vein Yellowing, Cucumber Yellows, Lettuce Infectious Yellows, Melon Leaf Curl (also invades Phaseolus beans), Squash Leaf Curl and Watermelon Curly Mottle (also invades Legumes).

Beetles spread: Melon Rugose, Squash mosaic (also on seed) and Wild Cucumber mosaic.

Nematodes spread: Tobacco Ringspot (also on seed) and Tomato Ringspot.

Thrips spread Tomato Spotted Wilt.

Leaf-hoppers spread Beet Curly Top.

Fungi (on the outside of the zoospores of chytrid fungus Olpidium radicale / cucurbitacearum) spread Cucumber Necrosis and Melon Necrotic Spot (also spread on seed).

Unknown vectors spread: Cucumber Green Mottle (also on seed), Cucumber Leaf-spot (also on seed), Cucumber Pale Fruit viroid and Ournia Melon virus.

Cucumis melo, MELON

Accumulates considerable Calcium in the leaves.
These are subject to the usual undercover culprits: Aphids, Whitefly, Woodlice, Thrips, and they're very susceptible to Red Spider mite so moist conditions are essential.

Leaf-hoppers Erythroneura pallidifrons bleach leaves (so does sun scorch) so look for the little yellow pests underneath the leaves.

Melons are prone to Neck rot / Canker Bacterium carotovorum where the stem rots where it emerges from the compost then the whole plant wilts and dies. This is prevented by keeping the neck dry, this usually by growing the plant out of the top of a raised mound, even when in a pot.

Cucumis sativus, CUCUMBER

Bitter fruits of indoor varieties are caused by pollination so all male flowers (no wee fruit behind bloom) must be removed. Outdoor / Ridge cucumbers conversely do need pollination.

These may attract whitefly off tomatoes.

Stinging nettle tea helps prevent them getting Downy mildew and extracts of garlic and field horsetail control Powdery mildew on cucumbers if used early, and often.

Extremely palatable to Red Spider mite, as these climb upwards some relief can be had by training plants down strings not up (grow them in big pots set up high on shelves).

Cucumbers can be attacked (at night) by millipedes.

Fungus gnats, white legless maggots up to half inch long eat the roots especially in dry conditions.

Similar looking Symphalids Scutigerella immaculata may eat the roots at ground level causing corky patches and letting in rots.

Cucumbers are subject to Root Knot eelworm nematode Heterodera radicicol which may stunt growth to point of wilt and makes galls on the roots.

Cucumbers suffer Neck rot / Canker Bacterium carotovorum where the stem emerges from the roots, though more of a problem with melons it's worth planting cucumbers on a mound, even in a pot, and keeping the neck dry to prevent this.

If the top dies from dead or decaying damage further up the stem then it is probably Gummy Stem blight Mycosphaerella melonis, this gets in through damage causing a spreading rot dotted with small black fruiting bodies.

In cold soil cucumbers get Verticillium wilt, in warm soil Fusarium wilt, both result in wilting, yellowing and dessication, the former often shows a stain in the cut stem. Otherwise the symptoms are rather similar to Red Spider mite and may be misdiagnosed either way.

Mildew Erysiphe cichoracearum can cover the younger growths with a powdery coating that can indicate poor ventilation.

Gummosis Cladosporium cucumerinum is promoted in the cold and wet, it appears on the leaves as small light brown odd shaped spots, these damage growth, but worse are the small soft sunken discoloured, then grey and oozing, spots on the young fruits, which enlarge as they become covered in a thick layer of fungal mycelium and sporulating tissue, then the fruit distorts, cracks and decays.

Blotch Cercospora melonia used to be prevalent but modern varieties are resistant and no longer get the pale water soaked blotches withering the leaves.

Leaf spot / Anthracnose Colletotrichum lagenarium with pale red or green spots can be fatal though better humidity and temperature control and good prompt hygiene removing infected material can halt attacks, this survives on litter and debris.

If the leaves mottle, pucker, wrinkle or distort or have yellow mottling then they have a virus, the commonest being Cucumber Mosaic virus or the harder-to-spot Green Mottle virus which is a transitory light mottle to the leaves as they enlarge, both seriously impede growth and fruiting. Both are spread by aphids Myzus persicae but Green Mottle is also often transmitted on tools etc.

Cucurbita maxima, WINTER SQUASHES / PUMPKINS

These need immense fertility and copious water to get really big. Pick fully ripe with a short length of stem to aid storage.

Cucurbita pepo, MARROW / ZUCCHINNI / COURGETTE / SUMMER SQUASH

These are the same plant bred to produce different fruits.

Seeds, flowers and fruits are edible and during Victorian times some ate the foliage as a spinach (not recommended).

Mildew Erysiphe cichoracearum can cover the younger growths with a powdery coating, this may indicate poor ventilation or water stress.

Cuscuta, DODDERS

These are vicious parasites which spread amongst varied plants with suckers and orange threads. One plant of C. trifolii, Clover dodder, can kill thirty square yards of clover in a season. Also spreads to vetches, lupins, potatoes, beet, carrots, fennel and aniseed.

-C. campestris attacks tomato plants and carrots.

-C. epithymum attacks furze, thyme, ling and heaths.

-C. epilinum attacks flax, hemp and camelina.

-C. europaea is found on vetches and nettles, also attacks hops, hemp, vetches, potatoes and sugar beet.

-C. gronovii attacks Lucerne and other Legumes, potatoes, beet and chicory.

CUTWORMS & GROUND CATERPILLARS

These eat roots and much worse they cut off seedlings at ground level.

Cut-worms are usually dingy brown, dirty grey with blackish spots. Yellowish greenish grey ones with black or greenish stripes are soil living caterpillars Euxoa segetum, E. exclamationis and Graphiphora pronuba, which often decimate young seedlings and small plants. These all do most damage from mid to late summer and on into autumn and survive in pupal form from late winter into spring. As they are nocturnal visiting the surface at night they are easiest to detect with a torch.

Causing similar damage are Swift moth root eating caterpillar grubs. Whitish with a red head they look similar to vine weevil grubs and may be found eating almost any herbaceous or bulbous plants.

Cyclamen, SOWBREADS

These were once common enough to feed pigs.
The spherical seed pods are borne on unique neat spiral springs.
Few co-lives bother Cyclamen other than Vine weevils Otiorhynchus sulcatus.

Cyclamen purpurascens

Slugs and snails have been shown to avoid the crushed tubers and will not cross a barrier made of them.
Botrytis cinerea the dreaded Grey mould has been prevented on Cyclamen by spraying the leaves with water extracts from the fungus Ulocladium atrum.

Cynara, GLOBE ARTICHOKE & CARDOON

The flowers are much loved by humble bees.
Aphids often coat the tender tips and just under the flowerbuds.
These may be attacked by Cassida rubignosa leaf mining beetle larvae and Apion carduorum and A. onopordi stem boring weevils.

Cynosurus cristatus, CRESTED DOG'S-TAIL GRASS

This is eaten by deer and South-down sheep but not readily by Welsh sheep.

Cytisus see Sarothamnus

Dactylis glomerata, COCK'S-FOOT GRASS

This is eaten by cattle, horses and sheep.

Dahlias

Originally introduced as a potential food crop, the tubers are sort of edible, but not nice.

Blooms have been observed attracting a very wide range of insects, and also believed to intoxicate bees.

Dahlias are prone to earwig damage especially the flowers.

Eelworm nematodes can build up if Dahlias are grown for long without rotation, though allegedly some may be handicapped by Dahlias.

Cauliflower like growths amongst the roots at the stalk base are Crown gall Bacterium tumefaciens.

Suddenly flagging plants may have Wilt Verticillium dahliae, thought to be co-hosted with raspberries where it causes Blue Stripe disease.

Yellowish green spots turning greyish brown are the fungal Leaf spot Entyloma dahliae, this overwinters on debris, supports and dead leaves.

Mottled or distorted plants will probably have Mosaic virus.

DAMPING-OFF

Fungal and or bacterial infections that cause small seedlings to die. Caused by non-sterile sowing compost or infected water. Use only boiled or clean water on vulnerable seedlings. Trichoderma virides the predatory fungus has been shown to prevent infection when added to 'dirty' water. Some protection may be given by sprays of diluted seaweed solution.

Daphne

The whole family resent any pruning, are poisonous, and miffy but have the most exquisitely scented flowers. Often difficult to establish needing a well drained humus rich soil, the most reliable is D. odora aureomarginata. Aphids are an insidious problem as they go unnoticed but spread viruses later shown with distorted or mottled leaves and Sudden Death.

Datura, THORNAPPLES

Poisonous.
These accumulate Phosphorus to one third of their mineral content.
The leaves have been used to smoke bees and medicinally for asthma.

In US extracts used to repel Japanese and Colorado beetles.

An alternative host for Tomato mosaic virus, spread by aphids, on tools, in soil and on seed, this may reduce yields by a quarter, also invades tobacco.

Thrips tabaci and Frankliniella occidentalis spread Tobacco Streak virus / Bean Red Node; red nodes, necrosis and red spots, also seed borne this spreads to alfalfa, chickpea, fenugreek, sweet clover, soybean, Nicotiana, most beans and many other plants.

Daucus carota, CARROT, wild and cultivated

Do not overfeed or use fresh manure or organic material as these cause poor flavour and forked roots.

Poor germination often occurs if heavy rain follows sowing.

Heavy soil (carrots prefer a light soil) may be improved the year before sowing them with a green manuring of flax or soya beans.

Wild carrots (in herbage presumably) are said to increase milk yield and flavour of sheep and cows.

If left to flower carrots attract hoverflies and beneficial wasps and are recorded as visited by 61 species of insect: 2 butterflies and moths, 8 species bee, 19 species Diptera flies and 32 other.

Plagued by Carrot Root fly Psila rosae whose small white larvae tunnel around the carrot roots, two or three generations a year ruin most sowings, overwinters as pupae in soil or as larvae in roots if frost free. The fly finds carrots by smell, allegedly from up to seven miles away, numerous herbs and strong smelling remedies have been used with some success mostly from onions, leeks and salsify but best preventative is crop rotation, and a physical barrier of fleece to stop the fly laying it's eggs by the seedlings. This spreads to celery, parsley, parsnips and also most related umbelliferous plants and weeds such as Cow Parsley

The Aphis Capitophorus eleagni alternates between sea buckthorn and carrots, possiby conflated with the greyish white Carrot aphid SemiAphis dauci found on the foliage causing poor growth and deformed leaves. Another, the greenish Carrot-Willow aphid Cavariella aegopodii does likewise, and also transmits the Carrot Motley Dwarf virus.

The Celery eelworm causes thickening of the leaf bases and weak growth.

The flowerhead of the wild species may be attacked by Dipteron gall-midge Kiefferia / Schizomyia / Asphondylia / Cecidomyia pimpinellae which causes the walls to thicken and the ovary to swell considerably, going greenish yellow to purple or brown, but as carrots are seldom left to flower this does not often get seen in gardens.

Leaves are attacked by Common Flat-Body Moth Depressaria cicutella.

The seeds are consumed by Purple Carrot-seed Moth D. depressella, which are predated by Odyneri solitary wasps.

The flowers and seeds eaten by Carrot-blossom Moth D. daucella, which last may be lured onto parsnips which they prefer.

Soft Rot, Bacterium carotovorum, makes stored roots soften and rot away, damage to roots allows this to get in so only store perfect specimens.

Black Rot, Alternaria radicina, causes black sunken patches in store.

Violet Root Rot, Helicobasidium purpureum, causes violet purplish threads to grow over roots, worse in wet soils with un-rotted organic material, may spread to many other crops including asparagus, beet, seakale, clover and alfalfa.

Sclerotinia Rot, caused by S. sclerotiorum, gets in through damage, often near crown, white fluffy rots appear then the tissues mummify and form black sclerotia, burn all affected roots before it spreads to mangolds, Dahlias and artichokes which it rots in store and to potatoes, tomatoes and lettuces which it attacks in growth.

Carrot Motley Dwarf virus spread by Carrot-Willow Aphis turns the outer leaves red with yellow mottling on inner ones.

Delphinium ajacis, LARKSPUR

The wild annual delphinium is highly poisonous as are most related species including garden forms.

The flower spur is so deep only Bombus hortorum bee can reach the nectar.

Garden Delphiniums are notoriously slug prone.

Weak or sickly plants may have an eelworm infestation or Swift moth Hepialus spp. white root eating caterpillars at work.

Bacterial Spot Bacterium delphinii causes black irregular spots all over plant and infects seeds which will carry it over.

Mildew Erysiphe polygoni causes flour like white dust all over, the leaves and buds dry up and die.

Also sometimes gets Stalk and Bulb rot, see Aquilegias.

DERRIS / ROTENONE

Plant extract (from a S. American tree) that breaks down rapidly, deadly to fish, used as a dust or spray it was allowed under most organic systems when other methods had failed.

Dianthus, PINKS & CARNATIONS

Their flowers are usually accessible only to long tongued Lepidoptera.

Roots subject to massive attacks of grey aphid Forda formicaria often tended by yellow ants Lasius flavius.

Aphids Myzus persicae mottle the leaves yellow. Green or greenish brown Aphids Macrosiphum solani can be a problem as these spread to Arums, tomatoes, Calceolarias and lettuce, especially under cover.

Red Spider mites cause foliage to go yellowy brown and look dusty.

Pale yellowed leaves covered in minute black flecks are caused by Thrips tabaci which also distort and speckle the flowers.

Carnation Tortrix moths Tortrix pronubana roll leaves together, may also enter flowerbuds to eat out the middle.

Powdery mildew Oidium spp. damages both leaves and flowers.

Leaf rot Heteropatella dianthi is particular to border carnations where the base of the leaves rots so they die off.

Die Back and Wilt are due to Fusarium spp.

Leaf mould Heteosporium echinulatum causes pale grey spots an eighth inch across on leaves, these turn brown with olive spores.

Leaf spot Septoria dianthi causes light brown patches, some with dark spots, on leaves and stems, the leaves hang down and sometimes curve lengthways.

Leaf spot Macrosporium dianthi causes elongated or round spots on leaves later covered in black tufty growth, then die.

Rust Uromyces dianthi / caryophyllinus is often a problem appearing as reddish brown spots or yellow brown cushions, starts on lower leaves and leaves yellow, curl and die.

Root rot Rhizoctonia solani attacks roots, causes brown rot and plant yellow and wilts during day.

Dianthus barbatus, SWEET WILLIAM and others

Reddish brown spots on the underside of the leaves will be Rust Puccinia lychnidearum.

DIATOMACEOUS EARTHS

Finely ground rock dusts, especially abrasive silicas, applied dry, get into joints of insects and damage, choke and even kill them. These may kill smaller slugs and snails on the surface but will not harm earthworms and soil life once mixed into the soil. Do not inhale the dust yourself!

Dictamnus albus

Probably the original burning bush, gives off so much volatile oil (including benzene) that it can catch fire but this is so brief the plant usually escapes damage.

Digitalis purpurea, FOXGLOVE

Poisonous.
Accumulates Iron, Calcium, Silica and Manganese.
Apparently slugs detest foxglove leaves and will not cross them if they are laid around crops
Almost exclusively fertilised by humble bees.
A tea made from the leaves may be used to keep cut flowers fresh.
Sometimes attacked by caterpillars that bore down the stems causing wilting.

Diplotaxis muralis, STINKWEED

As name suggests this has unpleasant smell of hydrogen sulphide.
Small yellow flowers have scent and are visited by Apidae bees.

Dipsacus pilosus and D. sylvestris, TEAZELS

Flowers feed many insects and seed heads feed the birds.
The joints where the leaves meet the stem form a cup that traps water making it available to insects, birds and other small critters.

Dolichos

Legume bean crop of warmer climates.
Often carry Bean Yellow mosaic virus; dark and yellow
patches with bright yellow spots which spreads to many
other Leguminous plants and also Alpinia, Chenopodium,
Gladiolus, Freesia, Babiana, Sparaxis and Tritonia.
And carries Clover Yellow Vein virus; yellow mosaic,
necrosis and wilting which spreads to most other Legumes
and also Antirrhinum, Atriplex, Chenopodium,
Coriandrum, Cucurbita, Gladiolus, Gomphrena, Nicotiana,
Nicandra, Papaver, Petunia, Proboscidea, Rubus, Spinacia,
Tetragonia and Viola.

DROUGHT indicators

Some plants wilt before others and these will then give
you warning that the situation is critical. Hydrangeas,
Phlox, Daturas and Astilbes are amongst the first to flag.

DUN-BAR moth Cosmia trapezina

This eats foliage of many trees but later instars usefully
eat larvae of other pests including other Lepidoptera.

Dryopteris filix-mas, MALE FERN / PRICKLY BUCKLER FERN

Fronds are galled by tiny grey flies, Dipteron muscids Chirosia parvicornis, causing them to appear knotted.

EARWIGS

These may do some damage to such as show Chrysanthemums and Dahlias but are valuable predators of aphids and woolly aphids, pear suckers, mussel scale and codling moth.

They can be encouraged with rolled up bundles of dry twigs hung in dry places near or on plants needing protection. They can be trapped in small tubes stuck on top of canes, or the traditional pot of hay. Likewise winding corrugated cardboard around a cane or stick makes an excellent trap, and one that's easily emptied

Echium vulgare, VIPER'S BUGLOSS

The flowers observed visited by at least 67 different species of insect, and are the sole blooms known visited by Osmia adunca and Osmia caementaria bees.

EELWORMS see NEMATODES.

ELECTRICITY

In Japan they found ac voltages applied to seeds and seedlings made them move faster.... wouldn't you?

Elaeagnus

Tough, mostly evergreen shrubs remarkably prone to Sudden Death syndrome from no apparent cause.

Epilobium angustifolium, ROSE BAY WILLOW-HERB

Accumulates Cobalt.
Invasive weed, nice purple pink flowers so originally introduced as garden plant, allegedly wind spread seeds carried along railway tracks to colonise burned ground. Blooms visited by many insects.

Epipactis, HELLEBORINES

Orchids pollinated exclusively by wasps.

Equisetum arvense, HORSETAIL

Often wrongly called marestail.
An ancient plant and pernicious weed, once dried for 'sandpaper' and pan scourers.
Very high Silica content, also accumulates Cobalt, Iron and Magnesium.
The powdered, dried plant is made into a spray with fungicidal properties that also makes plants grow tougher cell walls more resistant to attack.

ERICACEA

These are lime haters, see calcifuges.
These inhibit most other plants eventually covering large areas, often die in lime based soils and thrive in humus rich acid soil.
Most of family prone to white powdery coatings of Mildew Oidium spp.

Erica cinerea, BELL HEATHER

This produces tasty dark nectar for lovely honey.

Erysium cheiranthoides, TREACLE MUSTARD

Suffers from White mould / White Blister / Blister rust Albugo / Cystopus spp. phycomycetes fungal attacks causing blistering galls erupting with white powdery spores, worse in a wet season, spread by aphids, often mixed with Peronospora parasitica moulds, also spreads to other Cruciferae such as Capsella and Coronopus

Erythraea centaurium, CENTAURY

Blooms contain no discernible nectar yet oddly are frequently visited by butterflies.

Escallonia

These may be infested by reddish brown oval Peach scale which spreads to Cotoneaster, Escallonia, Lonicera and fruiting and flowering currants.

ETHYLENE

This gas is given off by many plants and ripening fruits. It causes other fruits to ripen prematurely and can affect germination and growth. Particularly given off by dandelions and bananas these can be put in plastic bags with under-ripe fruit to bring them on.
Because of this do not store early and late ripening fruits together or mix fruits and vegetables in store.
When seedlings are stroked gently they start to give off ethylene, production increases up to thirty fold in half an hour after stroking. This restricts growth in a favourable way making for sturdier plants with shorter lengths between leaf joints. This may be one mechanism that makes a tendril grasp and encircle an object it touches.

Eucalyptus

A large number of tree species well known for their scented oil which can be used as an insect repellent.
Be careful; wood is brittle and large branches fly off.

Eucryphia

These trees support a benign fungus, Gliocladium, which produces volatile compounds that control Pythium and Verticillium diseases. Similarly some rain forest leaves shown to have bacteria which produce an anti fungal agent effective against damping off diseases such as Pythium and even potato blight.

Euonymous europaeus, SPINDLE

The flowers especially attract Diptera flies and Hymenoptera.
The tree is winter host of broad bean black aphids Aphis fabae group of polyphagous aphids which alternate living on Cirsium spp. amongst others.

Eupatorium adenophorum and E. riparium

The presence of these weeds reduces number and variety of soil microlife especially of bacteria.

Eupatorium cannabinum, HEMP AGRIMONY

The blooms visited by 18 different insect species: 9 butterflies and moths, 2 species bee, 6 species Diptera flies and 1 other.
Alternate host for Leaf-hopper Eupteryx aurata shared with hogweed, mint, stinging nettles and ragwort.

Euphorbia

Poisonous, irritant genus with very nasty burning sap. Shoots invaded by bacterium Corynebacterium fascians which causes fasciation, stems become broad, flattened and ribbed, splayed and curved, this spreads to jasmine, plantains, Chrysanthemums, dogwood, Cotoneaster, Forsythia, Hibiscus, holly and Inula.
Whiteflies Bemesia tabaci transmit Euphorbia mosaic virus; necrotic lesions and distortion, also infects lentil, soybean and other Legumes.

Euphorbia helioscopia, SUN SPURGE

A pernicious little weed which accumulates Boron.

Euphorbia lathyrus CAPER SPURGE

This and E. lactea are among the many plants people use hoping to drive away moles. Unfortunately this remedy rarely works but does spread itself for free quite quickly and is unpleasant to weed because of their very irritant poisonous sap once used to remove warts.

Euphorbia splendens

An extract from this killed slugs and snails.

Fagopyrum esculentum, BUCKWHEAT

Calcium and phosphate accumulator and useful green manure.
Secretes plentiful nectar, one of the best bee and hoverfly attractants, and said to make beautiful wax but poor honey.
Seed much loved by pheasants and hens.

Fagus sylvatica, BEECH

These make big trees! Seldom found above 1,200ft line. Improve the fertility of soil but tend to shade out all underneath.

Beech mast or seed is valuable to wildlife, now thought not edible as such though once pressed gives oil rated as good as olive.

The leaves were traditionally considered one of the best for mattresses.

Beech leaves are galled by three acarine gall-mites Eriophyes spp.

E. nervisequus causing what are termed Filzgalls which are hard to spot being felted hairs on the upper surface of the leaf running in the grooves of the veins, first these are whitish then turning brown as they mature.

E. stenopis typicus forms Roll galls forming tubes on the upper surface, hairy on the inside, glossy to start with and green turning brown later.

E. macrorhynchus ferruginus forms shallow rust red pouches between the main veins and shiny broad bands of club-shaped hairs.

The leaves are also galled by Homopteran aphids PhyllAphis fagi which congregate on the underside, they cover themselves with woolly fibres much like woolly aphids on apples, the leaves develop curled edges and tiny swellings between the veins on the upper side while the leaf fades to light brown.

Dipteron gall-midges Hartigiola annulipes / Oligotrophus / Cecidomyia piligera / polymorpha form pouches of yellow cylinders covered in white hairs sticking out of the upper side which turn reddy brown and drop off when mature, there may be up to fifty per leaf.

Another gall-midge Mikiola fagi / Hormomyia / Cecidomyia / tornetalla causes smooth waxy pouch galls on the leaf upper side which are yellow green turning red to purplish brown and up to half an inch long in such numbers it's often hard to find unaffected leaves. Both these last two galls fall off in autumn providing over-wintering quarters for hibernation.

Large brown bracket fungi of Peziza arvernensis are found amongst the fallen leaves, distinguished by fine warts on the spores.

Exidia plana / glandulosa is a black protuberant convoluted fungus commonly found on stumps and dead wood.

The trunks, stumps and large branches, dead and alive, support a semi-circular bracket fungus Polyporus / Polyporellus squamosus, brown scales with white edible flesh smelling of cucumber, this grows quickly can reach many pounds in weight but harms trees causing the wood to decay with timber White rot, also grows on horse chestnut, lime, poplar, willow and walnut.

The litter grows the very tasty edible Boletus aestivalis / edulis / reticulatus with a light brown cap, sweet white flesh, most often found on calcerous soils and also under oaks.

Pluteus cervinus, edible, grows on stumps and rotting wood, a light to dark grey or brownish cap and streaked stipe, the gills start white then go pink with red spores, also found on oak, birch and hornbeam.

More common in the warmer parts of the continent than in the UK is the highly poisonous Entoloma / Rhodophyllus sinuatum / lividum / sinuatus, this has pale greyish cap, pink to orange gills and pink spores, it likes calcareous soil and is also found under oaks and hornbeams.

Fallopia / Reynoutria japonica,

JAPANESE KNOTWEED

This feared weed accumulates Zinc and Cadmium.
The shoots have long been eaten in the East.
It is difficult to eradicate when established however an extract of the leaves has been shown to control powdery mildew infestations on many crop plants.

FARMYARD MANURE

This is usually from cows with a mix of straw, urine and faeces, on average containing three quarters water, and only a small percentage of actual N, P & K. However the bacterial load, animal hormones and by products, and mineral content all make this invaluable to plants, perhaps more than we yet know. It should never be applied fresh but only after it has been well rotted, preferably for many months.

Other animal manures (pig, sheep, goat etc.) are similarly valuable and need rotting likewise. Chicken and bird manure are even stronger and these can kill plants if not first composted.

FERNS

Ferns can be killed rather easily by excess fertility.
Mealy bugs Pseudococcus citri cause much damage under glass, less outdoors.
Thrips causes bleached areas on the fronds speckled with black, the tiny insects are blackish or yellowish.
Ferns have a Fern Mite Tarsonemus tepidariorum, this especially bothers Asplenium bulbiferum, causes distortion, swelling, deformation and tiny brown spots on the fronds.
Eelworm nematodes cause brown spots and blackened areas on the fronds, may spread to Begonias, Coleus, Gloxinias, orchids and Salvias. Fascinatingly the old boys found these pests can be removed with hot water treatment of the plants immersing them at 110 degrees Fahrenheit for twenty minutes before cooling and repotting.

FERTILISER (or Fertilizer)

The choice is yours; soluble chemical salts that are cheap in cash terms but destroy micro-life and damage the environment or natural ones that sustain them. The more important factors for improved growth are really air, light & water!

Festuca duriuscula, HARD FESCUE GRASS

This is eaten readily by most cows, horses and sheep.

Festuca ovina, SHEEP'S FESCUE-GRASS

This is also eaten readily by cows, horses and sheep.

Festuca pratensis MEADOW FESCUE-GRASS

Also liked by cows, horses and sheep.

Ficus, FIGS

These are surprisingly hardy tough plants.

Avoid the milky sap of figs which can irritate and has been used to treat warts.

Few co-lives visit figs save Birds and Wasps eating the ripening fruits. On hot walls and under cover Red Spider Mite may be troublesome.

The fruits must be thinned, and most important, all fruits and fruitlets still on outdoor figs in early winter must be removed. This will allow the next set of embryo figs to develop in spring and crop in summer, thin these so those left will attain a good size and remove all others that appear after. With unbelievable care la Quintayne in France forcing potted figs achieved three crops a year and that was several centuries ago!

In UK we have varieties that produce ripe figs without pollination and which are therefore seedless. However original wild fig trees as in Mediterranean and Bible need the aid of a small Chalcid wasp, these trees produce four types of flower, male, female, dummy female and gall-flowers in three batches of figs. (The spring dummy female bearing figs have sterile female flowers and may ripen into inferior seedless fruits.) The male flower bearing figs swell at the same time in early spring, a hole in the end lets in female wasps which lay eggs in the gall-flowers deep inside, the brood hatches, males first which fertilise the females then die, these females leave through the hole which is now lined by pollen bearing male flowers. They have wings and fly to the next batch of summer swelling figs whose holes allow them in, inside are only normal female flowers which are shaped to prevent the wasps laying eggs. However the wasps pollinate these figs in the process. The third or autumn batch of figs then swell, their holes open and allow female wasps in where they find only gall-flowers in which they can lay their eggs. These autumn figs house and feed the gall wasps which then emerge in spring to start the cycle again. Years of cultivation has produced strains which have all female fruit bearing trees and separate goat-fig trees which carry the male and gall-flowers. The first figs to swell are dummy female ones on the fruit bearing trees which seldom come to much and figs on the goat fig trees which have male and gall-flowers and are laid in by the over-wintered wasps emerging form the old gall-flower figs. The new eggs and larvae grow then pupate and emerge in time for the summer swelling figs, which are all normal females on the fruit bearing trees, these get pollinated and make the most important crop. Then in autumn the third batch of figs swell, normal flowering ones on the fruit bearers and gall-flower ones on the goat-fig trees. The normal ones get pollinated and make a second crop, the gall-flowers receive the eggs and over-winter a brood for the next year. All I can say is WOW!

Filipendula ulmaria, MEADOWSWEET

The flowers have no honey only pollen.
The plant contains very high levels of salicylic acid, the seeds are taken by Robins who may be poisoned if these are eaten in excess.
The leaflet-blade galled by Dipteron gall-midge Dasyneura / Perrisia ulmariae causes up to 200 small reddish pustules on the upper surface, these become cone shaped and hairy.

FLATWORMS

First there was the New Zealand sort, now there are several. All are revolting, slimey, unpleasantly large very flat 'worms' that eat other useful worms and so destroy garden drainage and fertility. Mostly confined to the more acid damper regions these are a most serious problem. They can be trapped hiding under slabs and between stacks of saucers, tiles and so on. Do not handle them as they can cause skin reactions. Scissors are effective if cruel.

FLEA BEETLES

These minute critters destroy small seedlings and leave a multitude of tiny holes clean through many others. They are especially fond of Brassicas and related plants.
They may be discouraged by wet conditions and by dusting with lime or wood ashes. Flea beetles can be trapped by waving sticky fly paper close above them (honest they jump if disturbed, and then stick).
Flea beetles are repelled by the smell of tomato foliage, discarded side shoots have been used to keep them from seed beds.

Foeniculum vulgare, FENNEL

This just edible herb is often grown more for decoration than use.

Ancient giant fennel, now lost, was the container in which Prometheus carried fire to us humans (the pith burning slowly inside the dried stem).

Italian Finocchio form has an edible swollen base and swollen stems refreshing to chew, do not sow this early but after mid-summer or it will probably bolt, and only likes rich moist soil.

Fennel flowers are good hosts to hoverflies and predatory wasps and the smell may deter aphids from nearby plants.

Forsythia

Shoots get invaded by bacterium Corynebacterium fascians which causes fasciation, stems become broad, flattened and ribbed, splayed and curved, swollen Bud galls may form in clusters, this spreads to jasmine, plantains, Chrysanthemums, dogwood, Cotoneaster, Euphorbias, Hibiscus, holly and Inula.

Fragaria, STRAWBERRIES

It's said eating strawberries is good for our teeth, though not the 'modern' sugar and cream with them.

The Alpine varieties are all round companions bringing in pollinators and predators over their very long flowering season and providing an insulating dry tussock of dead leaves for critters to hide or hibernate.

Strawberries love mulches of pine needles, which also discourage slugs. Mulches of wheat or barley straw keep the fruits clean and so less get mould, but avoid oat straw as this may promote root rots.

In warmer climates before establishing a new bed sow soya beans then dig these in green to prevent root rots. Plantains nearby are bad as these are hosts to Myzus ascalonius aphids which bother both strawberries and shallots.

Not surprisingly THE main co-lives associated with this fruit are Birds. Not much else matters by comparison. Though oddly voles collect up fruits in little piles and eat off all the seeds!

Aphids of several strains especially the yellow Capitophorus fragaefoli are a problem transmitting virus diseases of which strawberries suffer many.

Leaves reddening and drying up especially in dry weather with a fine web underneath will be Red Spider mite Tetranychus urticae.

Leaves going yellow at the edges, crinkled puckered leaves and dying away could be one of several viruses, or Tarsonemid mite Tarsonemus pallidus, this lives in the centre of the plant, few runners develop, young leaves brown and the problem multiplies especially in warm humid conditions as their lifecycle takes only two weeks or so. The old boys found they could clean their most valuable plants of this mite by plunging them in water at 110 degrees Fahrenheit for twenty minutes then immediately cooling and planting them in a clean bed. Capsid bugs cause puckered holes in leaves and distorted fruits, as may various Strawberry beetles. Several different ground living beetles can be found attacking strawberries though only four damage the fruits directly. The Strawberry Seed beetle adult Harpalus rufipes spoils the fruits by eating the seeds, the larvae live on seeds of weeds and then pupate in rough vegetation.

A small black weevil adult, the Strawberry Blossom weevil Anthomonus rubi, often found on raspberries, damages the stem of the fruit causing it to abort, it may attack other soft fruits too leaving a tell tale puncture mark cutting through the stalk.

Another the Strawberry Rhynchites Caenorhinus germanicus, cuts through the leaf and fruit stalks as well causing them to wilt and die, the larvae live in the soil on the roots but allegedly do little harm.

Plants just doing poorly or suddenly wilting and dying should be dug up and examined as it will be vine weevil Otiorhyncus sulcatus, or the similar Strawberry Root weevil O. rugosotriatus, or the Red-legged weevil O. clavipes as found on currants and plums.

As well as weevils the roots are also eaten by leather jackets, wire worms and chafer grubs. This last, Phyllopertha horticola, lives for three years as a white larva with a brown head eating roots of many plants as well as strawberries before pupating into the beetle.

The above ground parts are galled by Leaf and Bud nematode eelworm Aphelencoides / Aphelenchus fragariae and A. ritzemi-bosi, these cause considerable distortions, weakening and stunting even causing death of the crown.

Similar deterioration may be another eelworm infestation. The Stem eelworm Ditylenchus dipsaci causes the leafstalks to thicken, leaves to become corrugated and flower buds to distort.

Another eelworm Xiphenema diversicaudatum lives on the roots and is important as it carries the Arabis mosaic virus which does far more harm. The same hot water treatment can treat eelworm infested plants as for Tarsonemid mites, see above.

Strawberries are said to be hosts to parasites of the Oriental fruit moth.

The Leaf Button / Strawberry moth Peronea conariana larvae, greenish with yellow head, hatches in late spring eating and webbing together blossom buds and leaves, often living in a web on the underside of leaves.

Strawberries also suffer Small / Garden Swift moth Hepialus lupulinus eating their roots.

Strawberries often suffer Grey mould Botrytis cinerea in damp conditions which starts as a small grey spot on the flowers or developing fruits and causes complete rot.

Leaf Spot Mycosphaerella fragariae causes small circular spots on leaves that start red, go grey then whitish with dark red edge and may wither the leaves.

Strawberry mildew Spaerotheca macularis produces dark patches on the upper surface and whitish grey patches on the lower leaf surfaces, it overwinters on leaves.

Leaf blotches Gnomonia spp. start as brown blotches with purplish borders surrounded by yellowing, on the leaf stalks may be seen the fungal spores called Black Spheroids.

If the plants weaken become smaller leaved with reddish tints and unproductive this may be Red Core / Lanarkshire disease Phytophthora fragariae, the sure sign is the roots are withered and blackened except for a red core.

Strawberry Crinkle virus causes loss of vigour and crinkled leaves, spread by creamy white Strawberry aphid Chaetosiphon fragaefolii which flit from plant to plant in early summer.

Strawberry Yellow Edge virus is another that reduces vigour, and causes a yellow edge to the leaves, also spread by aphid C. fragaefolii.

The Arabis mosaic virus mentioned above is spread by the eelworm Xiphenema diversicaudatum living on the roots and this virus causes the leaves to blotch, mottle and the veins to thicken.

A host of other viruses are unfortunately also possible.

Fraxinus excelsior, ASH

Seldom found above 1,000ft.

One of the briefest canopy periods of UK trees, coming into leaf late and falling early. Bark is mildly acidic ph 5.2-6.6.

The wood will burn well even when fresh cut, though better once dried.

The inflorescence is invaded by an acarine gall-mite Eriophyes fraxinivorus / Phytopus fraxini which swells, distorts and fuses the many floral parts into a brown lump up to half by three quarters inch, every flower truss on a tree may be galled, sometimes these remain on long after they've been vacated.

The leaflet is attacked by a Homopteran Psyllid Psyllopsis fraxini which rolls either or both leaflet margins down and across to the midrib, size and colour vary, yellow, red, purple to brown, inside the Roll gall the Psyllids are embedded in a mass of delicate fibres.

Often on younger rather than older trees the midrib and rachys get attacked by a Dipteron gall-midge Dasyneura / Perrisia fraxini which causes greeny russet pod shaped lumps up to two inches long on the underside, when these open on the topside the edges have minute saw like teeth, about half a dozen larvae drop out in autumn and pupate in the soil.

Another Dipteron, Ash-midge Clinodiplosis botularia, is often found together with the Dasyneura.

The wood of old trees may be tunnelled by Goat Moth Cossus ligniperda.

The trunks, stumps and large branches, dead and alive, support a semi-circular bracket fungus Polyporus / Polyporellus squamosus, brown scales with white edible flesh smelling of cucumber, this grows quickly and can reach many pounds in weight but harms trees causing the wood to decay with timber White rot, spreads onto beech, lime, poplar, willow and walnut.

Freesia

Difficult cut flower for amateur growers, honest, try them yourself!
Carries Bean Yellow mosaic; dark and yellow patches with bright yellow spots, this spreads to most Leguminous plants and also Alpinia, Chenopodium, Gladiolus, Babiana, Sparaxis and Tritonia.

FRENCH INTENSIVE gardening

French market gardeners took many huge crops a year using much labour and unbelievable amounts of manure, up to 300tons per acre per year. This led to their leases having clauses requiring the land to be lowered to the original ground level when they vacated! Many of their methods have been adopted such as raised beds. The mixture of crops, with up to five different ones growing together, were continually harvested and replanted with much labour. On the whole their system was too specialised and reliant on cheap labour to be widely used now.

FRUIT

This takes less labour than vegetables, and simpler to maintain, perennial and better for ecology, and often ornamental as well.

Fuchsia / Fuschia

Berries are edible, these make a delicious jelly, California Dreamer series can give thumb sized fruits.
Plants often devastated by Vine weevils and prone to Aphids, White flies and Red Spider mites.

Leaf-hoppers Erythroneura pallidifrons, pale yellow or white, eighth inch long, active insects may do some damage causing bleached areas on leaves, and spread to Geraniums, Calceolarias, Primulas, Salvias, and Verbenas.

Fumaria officinalis, FUMITORY

Unrelated to crop plants and germinating in winter this is recorded as having nitrous fumes from roots; so deserves investigation for a green manure.

FUNGI

These are converting material continuously, predating each other and everything else. Only a few are ever visible to us and then it is usually just the fruiting body. Truffles are a type that lives on oak and other tree roots and kitchen mushrooms are just ones that grow on old horse manure. Most give out a tiny amount of heat as like animals and plant roots they 'burn' oxygen, and some give off light; see Luminous plants.

Common fungi are the mildews and rusts which attack plants especially if the plant is under water stress or in stagnant air. Smuts, wilts, moulds and rots are likewise usually fungal attacks but may be in unison with bacteria. Plentiful air, light and water usually minimise damage. Allium, nettle, garlic and Equisetum sprays are among the best natural fungicides we have yet discovered.

Many pathogenic fungal spores germinate in a film of water and will not succeed in water that has been washed through unsterilised soil or compost, thus the potential value of spraying compost extracts on plants and adding these to your general watering.

FUSARIUM WILT

Many Fusarium fungi attack almost any plant, wilting, yellowing and withering leaves and shoots, usually working upwards from the base and killing smaller plants especially seedlings, these are often more prevalent in higher soil temperatures.

Fuschia see Fuchsia

As it was originally spelt but not pronounced.

Galanthus, SNOWDROP

Not natives though long here, sweet scented flowers though few stoop to find out.
Blooms have much nectar, open from about 10am to 4pm.
A mould covering leaves and bulbs is Grey mould Botrytis galanthina which will eventually destroy the bulbs.

Galium aparine, GOOSE-GRASS / CLEAVERS

This can germinate almost year round even during winter months.

Accumulates Calcium and Potassium.

Edible, not very palatable, the tea is considered a cure for cystitis.

Seeds have been roasted as a coffee substitute.

Loved by geese, honest they really do tuck into it, one of their favourite treats.

Alternate summer host for Myzus cerasi aphids which cause galled leaves on many of the cherry family.

The leaves are attacked by acarine gall-mites Eriophyes galii / Cecidophyes / Phytoptus rolling up into sickle shapes with a fuzz of hair inside, from pale green to brown and sometimes over an inch long containing numerous mites.

Host to Colorado beetle Doryphora decemlineata (US denizen not yet problem in UK).

Galium verum, LADY'S BEDSTRAW

This is mainly pollinated by beetles.

The shoots are attacked by a Dipteron gall-midge Geocryptta galii / Cecidomyia galii / molluginis which form rings of galls encircling the stems near the leaf bases with up to half a dozen spherical swellings of green going to reddish brown with short hairs.

Another gall-midge Dasyneura galiicola causes reddish terminal galls where the tips of shoots become swollen and distorted.

GEESE

These make great lawnmowers, and eat almost everything else including bark and stems, and steal windfall apples before you can get to them. They are very good at grubbing out buttercups and can be used to clear these from pasture.
Better than any guard-dog as more constantly alert, quicker to call alarm, perceived by intruders as dangerously aggressive, and goose eggs are far more useful....

Genista tinctoria, DYER'S GREENWEED

The flowers have no nectar only pollen.
Terminal leaves galled by Dipteron gall-midge Jaapiella genisticola / Perrissia / Asphondylia genistae, forming a half inch ball greenish yellow or brown and sometimes involving the flowers

Geraniums, NOT PELARGONIUMS!

Very good ground cover for shady moist spots.

Generally tough though green or greenish brown Aphids Macrosiphum solani can be a problem as also spread to Arums, tomatoes, carnations, Calceolarias and lettuce, especially under cover.

Leaf-hoppers Erythroneura pallidifrons, pale yellow or white, eighth inch long, active insects may do some damage causing bleached areas on leaves, also spread to Calceolarias, Fuchsias, Primulas, Salvias, and Verbenas.

Geranium robertianum, HERB ROBERT

Snails and slugs avoid extracts of this plant.

GERMINATION

More plants are lost at this stage than any other. Seeds need warmth, moisture and air to germinate. They only germinate when close to the soil surface and conditions are exactly right so sow as if each seed were your last. Many plants produce secretions that inhibit others from germinating so remove all weeds including hoed and pulled weeds from off seed-beds.

Geum rivale, WATER AVENS

This and G. pulchrina, often found to have froghoppers hidden in Cuckoo Spit.

Gladioli

Not awfully hardy these die away unless lifted and replanted annually.

Flagging plants and eaten corms is probably due to Swift moth grubs on the roots.

Over-wet conditions encourage Basal rot / Base decay Bacterium marginatum with rust like spots on leaves becoming black then leaves and stems rot off.

They share Grey Bulb rot Sclerotium tuliparum with tulips and narcissi.

Three diseases: Hard rot, Dry rot and Smut all come in and multiply on infected corms, do not plant any with any blemish such as spots or sunken patches. In Hard rot Septoria gladioli the leaves get yellow patches turning brown with hard dark spots on corms. In Dry rot Sclerotium gladioli the leaves yellow and brown in late spring, the stem decays and sunken spots of reddish brown are found in the corm. In Smut Tubercinia gladioli black raised spots appear on all parts and the corms decay.

Gladioli also suffer various penicillium and fusarium rots. May carry Bean Yellow mosaic; dark and yellow patches with bright yellow spots which spreads to many Legumes and also Alpinia, Chenopodium, Freesia, Babiana, Sparaxis and Tritonia.

And can carry Clover Yellow Vein virus; yellow mosaic, necrosis and wilting which spreads to most Legumes and also Antirrhinum, Atriplex, Chenopodium, Coriandrum, Cucurbita, Gomphrena, Nicotiana, Nicandra, Papaver, Petunia, Proboscidea, Rubus, Spinacia, Tetragonia and Viola.

Glechoma hederacea, GROUND IVY

This is sort of edible if you are desperate enough.
Accumulates Iron.
The leaf-blade is attacked by Dipteron gall-midge Dasyneura glechomae / Cecidomyia bursaria causing Lighthouse galls which may be in great number on the upper surface, each a sixth of an inch high, light green, pink, red or brown, round topped and hairy, these fall off in autumn leaving holes in the leaf, the insect pupates over-winter in the fallen case.
The Hymenopteran gall-wasp Liposthenus latreillei / Aylax glechomae / Diastrophus glechomae makes pea shaped pea sized galls on the leaves and slightly more oval galls on the stems and petioles, green turning to red and purple as these mature, slightly downy outisde hairy inside and becoming hard for over-winter till the insect emerges the next spring.

Gloxinia

Tender garden or house plants.

Attacked by Eelworm nematodes causing brown spots and blackened areas, which also attack ferns, Begonias, orchids and Salvias.

Glycine max, SOYA beans

These must have their mycorrhizal fungal partner or grow badly.

Too tender for most European gardeners, newer varieties may just crop here.

The green parts contain 0.25-0.3% Phosphorus and 1.3% Calcium. An acre in the USA yields above 15cwt of beans, about 13cwt dried giving 500-600lb of crude protein and containing 200-250lb oil and about 500lb carbohydrate.

The plants are hosts to Trichogramma wasps and have been used to deter cinchworms, chinchbugs, corn earworms, corn borers and Japanese beetles.

These can carry Clover Yellow Vein virus; yellow mosaic, necrosis and wilting which spreads to most other Legumes: and also Antirrhinum, Atriplex, Chenopodium, Coriandrum, Cucurbita, Gladiolus, Gomphrena, Nicotiana, Nicandra, Papaver, Petunia, Proboscidea, Rubus, Spinacia, Tetragonia and Viola.

They also carry Soybean mosaic virus; blistering, leaf cupping, necrosis, wilting and death, this also seriously affects other beans.

As bad is Bean Curly Dwarf mosaic; mosaic, stunting and rugosity, this also infects other Phaseolus species, pea, chickpea, lentil, broad bean, mung bean and Leguminous weeds.

Bean Southern mosaic; green mosaic with rugocity also infects beans, cowpeas, peas and other Legumes.

Thrips tabaci and Frankliniella occidentalis spread Tobacco Streak virus / Bean Red Node; red nodes, necrosis and red spots, also seed borne this also spreads to alfalfa, chickpea, fenugreek, Datura, sweet clover, Nicotiana, beans and many plants.

Whiteflies Bemesia spp. transmits Euphorbia mosaic; necrotic lesions and distortion, this also infects lentils and other Legumes.

Gomphrena decumbens

May be infected by Clover Yellow Vein virus; yellow mosaic, necrosis and wilting which spreads to most Legumes and also Antirrhinum, Atriplex, Chenopodium, Coriandrum, Cucurbita, Gladiolus, Nicotiana, Nicandra, Papaver, Petunia, Proboscidea, Rubus, Spinacia, Tetragonia and Viola.

Gossypium, COTTON

A tender crop plant grown for the hairy seed plumes.

In warmer climes cotton is protected from root rots if it follows a fallow of alfalfa but this also has allelopathic secretions detrimental to the cotton so needs time to be broken down.

Alfalfa has also been used as a sacrificial crop for Lygus bugs on the cotton.

GRASSES

Closely related plants to agricultural cereals, rice and maize. Tough grasses for play areas and utilitarian swards generally like lime, while the fine leaved 'bowling green' grasses like acid soil. This means different conditions and maintenance are necessary. The tough grasses make better swards for almost all purposes save bowling and putting greens which are specialised situations.

Clover helps grass immensely, so set the mower high to spare it and the flowering will then benefit bees and other insects.

Daisies indicate grass is being cut too close, and is probably short of lime, this will handicap worms so the sward may soon become badly drained and mosses will appear.

The best fertiliser to stimulate without overfeeding is well diluted urine, use this natural renewable resource and make a bonus water saving from less flushing.

In orchards grass will inhibit growth especially under pears but this effect is of use once the trees are established as excessive tree growth slows fruiting. The competition of grass is particularly bad for newly planted trees and shrubs especially if regularly cut, the soil should be mulched or weeded for a radius of at least the height of the plant.

Timothy grasses use their pollen to prevent nearby plants setting viable seed; just ten grains of their pollen on the stigma of other plants can prevent them setting viable seed!

Grasses may inhibit each other, their frost killed leaves inhibit re-growth and exudates of dead leaves inhibit germination of other species as well as the donor.

Many grasses are reluctant hosts to parasitic plants; Yellow Rattle Rhinanthus crista-galli, Lousewort Pedicularis and Eyebright Euphrasia officinalis.

All aerial parts of most grasses galled by nematode eelworm Tylenchus dipsaci, this causes considerable distortions, weakening and stunting.

Very rarely the Hessian fly, a minute yellowish grub, may cause poor growth as these sap the base of the leaves.

Many grasses are alternate hosts for such as Aphis granaria / avenae Corn aphid / Dolphin, of cereals, Frit Fly Oscinis frit and the devastating Ergot of rye Claviceps purpurea.

Cereals and grasses sustain serious damage to roots from Small / Garden Swift moth Hepialus lupulinus which also attacks parsnip, lettuce, potato, celery, strawberry and beans.

Damping off is a fungal attack with patches of grass dying back after yellowing or reddening and wilting, most prevalent in damp humid conditions, often where growth is poor due to low light or poor soil conditions.

In warmer weather especially in late summer Fusarium Patch or Snow mould can cause yellowish brownish burnt out holes, sometimes huge, dying going slimy and becoming covered in whitish or pinkish cotton.

If however there is a sticky redness, the grass looks bleached but does not waste away then it could be Corticium or Red Thread. A lens will reveal red spiky outgrowths from the tips.

Very rarely there may be little white mycelia showing on the burnt out spots which are more browny yellowish than bleached and this shows Dollar Spot.

Little black dots at the base of the stems indicates an Ophiobolus attack.

A general dirty yellowishness and a fine powdery coating will be a Mildew attack.

Fairy Ring champignon fungus Marasmius oreades, edible, buff tan cap with deeply cut and wide spaced whitish gills, smells of burnt almonds, this creates green rings, these are formed as the fungus moves outwards from its original spot leaving enriched soil behind for the grass.

Likewise Blewits Lepista saeva / Tricholoma saevum / bicolor / personatum grow in grasses in rings, they have buff tan caps with brown gills and an ink stained stem (stipe), they are edible, tasty and even remain edible once frosted, but must always be cooked.

The edible Horse mushroom Agaricus / Psalliota arvensis has a white cap, greyish gills and a slight scent of aniseed, if scratched the flesh turns yellow, also found in spruce forests (the inedible and similar Yellow stainer Agaricus / Psalliota xanthodermus / xanthoderma is yellow at the base of the stipe and smells of carbolic).

The best known of all edible mushrooms is the Field mushroom Agaricus / Psalliota campestris, white cap with pink gills, this is found in damp meadows especially round the edges in the lee of hedges.

Hygrophorus conicus / conica, inedible, has a reddish orange or yellow conical cap, yellowish gills, tastes bitter, turns black with age or when dried and often appears in fields and meadows after rain.

Likewise Stropharia coronilla appears after rains, it has a yellowish white to tan ochre cap with chocolate brown gills and spores and an unusually short stipe, it is inedible. St George's mushroom Calocybe / Tricholoma gambosa / gambosum / georgii appears in spring on the sunny edges of woods hiding in grassy clumps, it is edible and tasty, has a fleshy pale cap with narrow crowded gills, and white spores, it has a marked floury taste and smell.

GREEN MANURES

These are plants sown to produce fertility rather than for a direct crop. Tares, vetches, lupins and other Legumes are often used to fix Nitrogen, others like mustard produce masses of fine roots. Hungarian Grazing Rye, perennial ryegrass, Lolium perenne, produces lots of top growth.

Green manures can also be used for pest and or disease control where they awaken attacks and are then taken or incorporated before the problem has had time to reach maturity and reproduce. Manuring with mustard with the digging in coming almost as soon as it has developed the first true leaves awakens clubroot spores but is not then there to feed them so they expire.

The green manure may be incorporated by digging, sheet composting or composting elsewhere before returning. These are usually sown when the land is not needed and act as cover crops preventing soil erosion and leaching.

I prefer using less troublesome plants than the usual offerings which come from farming and are hard to incorporate or kill off.
I find Miner's Lettuce Claytonia perfoliata, Corn salad Valerianella and Limnanthes douglassii to be the most useful for winter, with spinaches, borage, buckwheat and Phacelia best in summer.

GROWTH regulators

The auxins and other hormones used by plants alter others growth as well as their own. Once used by chemists as precursors for weed killers and straw shorteners these also damage crops and co-lives even in minute doses from spray drift or later as residues.

Haplophyton cimicidum, MEXICAN COCKROACH PLANT

A tender shrubby US weed, poisonous, apparently an extract is made to kill cockroaches.

HEAVY FEEDERS

In crop rotation these are those plants that usually need to be given extra fertility such as compost or well-rotted manures. All Brassicas especially cauliflowers and broccolis, leaf and stalk vegetables like endive, leeks, celeriac & celery, sweet corn, potatoes, tomatoes, and cucurbits, all require their soil to be well fed to do well.

Hedera helix, IVY

Well known climbing evergreen, does not damage modern buildings though a slight threat to the old and decayed.
Without doubt one of the best providers for bees, flies and wasps late in the year, wasps can even be attracted away from ripening fruits to ivy flowers.
Ivy also gives plentiful shelter, fruit and nesting places to birds and many forms of life.
Be warned, birds, pigeons in particular, eating many berries may apparently develop poisonous flesh.
A spray of the leaves has been used against corn wireworms, whether of maize or wheat unknown.
Ivy especially on hot dry walls and any sneaking under cover may overwinter red spider mites, mealy bugs and other co-lives we probably don't wish to have more of.
Suffers from a yellowish Soft scale shared with hollies and myrtles, this species does not produce a hard shell.

Hedera helix var. cristata, PARSLEY / HOLLY IVY

The leaf blades are galled by acarine eriophyid mites, the already wavy edges get thickened, distorted, pouched, become hairy with pustules and finally have reddish tints.

HEDGE

Much better than a fence as hedges absorb energy from the wind warming the garden instead of causing eddies. It's also a habitat for inumerable creatures but does require more annual maintenance, and steals space in a small garden.

A hedge can be formal, cut to a precise shape regularly which limits the choice of plant, or informal which requires much more space and can be of many more different plants so is better for wildlife.

Hedysarum

Leguminous wild flower very similar to the crop Sainfoin, only occasionally grown in gardens now though quite attractive.

May be infected by Clover Yellow Vein virus; yellow mosaic, necrosis and wilting which spreads to most other Legumes and also Antirrhinum, Atriplex, Chenopodium, Coriandrum, Cucurbita, Gladiolus, Gomphrena, Nicotiana, Nicandra, Papaver, Petunia, Proboscidea, Rubus, Spinacia, Tetragonia and Viola.

Helenium amarum, BITTER SNEEZEWEED

American weed toxic to livestock so beware of possible risk from other species used as garden plants.

Helianthus annuas, SUNFLOWER

Edible seeds, much beloved by wild birds and hens, good for culinary purposes and oil these have been roasted for 'coffee'.

The flowers are very good for bees, Lacewings and predatory wasps.

The foliage is good for cows and sheep, and the stems are rich in potash.

Bundled together the dead stems make excellent wild life shelters hidden under evergreens or at the base of hedges.

Rust Puccinia helianthi causes brown powdery mounds on leaves and stems, the leaves dry and wither, the seeds may become infected.

Helianthus tuberosus, JERUSALEM ARTICHOKE

Edible if not palatable standby crop for when the potatoes fail, not much loved as they give you wind.

These make a screen very quickly so are useful for new gardens and their late sunflower like flowers are good for insects.

Can be attacked by fungus Sclerotinia sclerotiorum which causes white fluffy growths on stem and tubers with hard brownish black sclerotia forming on and in the stems and tubers, worst in wet acid soils.

If you need to get rid of these borrow some geese for a month.

Helleborus, HELLEBORES

The Christmas and Lent Roses are poisonous and were once used as pesticides.

Useful for insects as these are winter flowering when little else is.

These resent moving the more as they get older and larger!

Sometimes suffer Mildew Perenospora pulveracea with pale patches on top and a white powdery patch under the leaves eventually killing the plant.

Leaf spot Coniothyrum hellebori causes irregular black spots on top and lower leaf surfaces which yellow, wither and die then the plant too.

Hemerocallis, DAY-LILY

Will grow almost anywhere.
The flowers and buds of most species are edible, some almost tasty.
Leaves die down in autumn to form weed excluding mulch if not disturbed.

Heracleum sphondylium, HOGWEED

'Siberians' dry bundles of stems and scrape off a sugar.
Traditionally gathered to feed hogs, and rabbits.
Hairy parts can cause skin irritation in hot sun.
The flowers have been recorded as visited by 118 species of insect: 0 Lepidoptera, 13 species bee, 49 species Diptera flies and 56 other.
Alternate host for Leaf-hopper Eupteryx aurata shared with hemp agrimony, mint, stinging nettles and ragwort.

HERBS

Generally accepted as plants with culinary or household use.
Herbs often have a strong taste originally to discourage being eaten. They mostly have pervasive odours and can hide plants from pests while their flowers encourage beneficial insects. Hyssop, lemon balm, valerian, yarrow and chamomile are most generally helpful.

Herminium monorchis, MUSK ORCHID

The blooms have a strong odour especially at night which indicates a moth pollinator, and it is for fraud as only pollen and no nectar.

Hesperis matronalis, DAME'S VIOLET / SWEET ROCKET

Evening scented flowers, pollinated by moths but also visited in day by cabbage white butterflies and by bees Halictus leucopus, Andrena albicans, Volucella pellucins and Rhingia rostrata.

Hibiscus

Shoots invaded by bacterium Corynebacterium fascians which causes fasciation, stems become broad, flattened and ribbed, splayed and curved, this spreads to jasmine, plantains, Chrysanthemums, dogwood, Cotoneaster, Euphorbias, Forsythia, holly and Inula.

Hieracium, HAWKWEEDS

Dipteron gall-midge Cystiphora pilosellae commonly colonises the leaves forming small galls. All species and especially H. umbellatum and H. perpropinquum have their shoots galled by Hymenopteran gall-wasp Aulacidea hieracii / Aylax / sabaudi / graminis / Cynips, eggs are laid in a bud near the tip, the gall is oval or pyriform covered in silky grey hair, reddish at first then smooth and brown and about an inch long, inside are twenty larvae which over-winter in the gall.
Host to Chrysanthemum Rust Puccinia hieraci.

Hieracium pilosella, MOUSE-EAR HAWKWEED

The blooms open at 8am and close at 3pm.
Dipteron gall-midge Cystiphora pilosellae makes galls in the leaf mid-rib.

Hippophae rhamnoides, SEA BUCKTHORN

The leaves host the aphid Capitophorus eleagni which alternates between this and carrots.

Holcus lanatus, MEADOW SOFT GRASS / YORKSHIRE FOG

This grass is generally disliked by cows, sheep and horses both fresh and as hay.
Host to Brassica Clubroot disease and Stem eelworm Tylenchus devastatrix.

HONEY

Made by bees from nectar from flowers. No flowers no honey no bees, so plant as many flowering plants as you can. Nectar is now shown to contain not just contain sugars but dozens of amino acids to feed pollinators, and antibiotic compounds to protect the plant against any diseases carried by them.

HONEY FUNGUS see ARMILLARIA

Hordeum distichon / vulgare, BARLEY

Cereal grown mostly for animal feed and for beer after malting.

Ashes contain 4% potash, 17% soda, 3.4% lime, 10% magnesia, 2% Iron oxide, negligible Manganese oxide, 41% phosphoric acid, 0.3% sulphuric acid, 22% silica and a little chlorine.

The inflorescence stalk is attacked by the Dipteron chloropid Chlorops taeniopus Gout fly or Ribbon-footed corn-fly which lays eggs on the leaves or stalks, the larvae get into the shoots which thicken and form cigar shaped galls, the flower fails and the fly after hatching moves to an alternate host, often couch grass.

In a trial germination was reduced by soil organism Gliocladium roseum, this was counteracted by Azotobacter chroococcum but ONLY when this was grown in a nitrate free medium. In other words seeds not only do not need soluble fertilisers but using them will hinder success.

Hosta, MEGASEAS

Known for their susceptibility to slugs.
Vine weevils cause slow death.
Some species have scented flowers.
The bird-dropping-like slug of the Lily beetle Lilloceris lilli, a bright reddy orange rather smart looking beastie, destroys the leaves also eats lilies, lily of the valley, hollyhocks, Solomon's seal, potatoes and tobacco.

HOVER-FLIES

Incredibly useful co-lives. These lay their eggs on aphid infested plants, the green or reddish green larvae consume six hundred aphids apiece in a fortnight before pupating into hovering flies often somewhat resembling small bees or wasps. As with Lacewings the adults need nectar and pollen, many varieties prefer yellow flowers. The recommended plants for attracting them are buckwheat, coriander, dill, fennel, goldenrod, lavender, mint, Phacelia, Sedums and veronicas. In the wilder places broom, yarrow, vetch, creeping thistle and knapweed are main attractants.

Humulus lupulus, HOP

Vigorous perennial dioecious climbers with large number of cultivars existing and more now lost.
Female plant 'flowers' are the hops (despite the dusty resin being termed pollen which it is manifestly not). The male plants are discouraged on continent as seeds in the hops for brewing hinder the bottom fermenting yeasts used in foreign lagers but not the top fermenting yeasts used in good old British beer.
The reason for adding hops was not for their bitter flavour but for their preserving qualities so a cheaply made lower alcoholic brew would keep saleable for longer.
The young shoots are edible but bitter, so change the water thrice.

Weakened by wireworms which may be lured onto trap plantins of potatoes.
Host to Stem eelworm Tylenchus devastatrix.
Hops suffer hosts of aphids, controlled best by Stethoras ladybirds which also eat whiteflies.

Hyacinthus orientalis, HYACINTH

These are often robbed of their sap by insects making holes through the fleshy base of flowers.

Hyoscyamus niger, HENBANE

Oddly scented, oddly flowered, uncommon, highly poisonous weed that accumulates phosphates up to 45% of it's mineral content.
Host to Colorado beetle Doryphora decemlineata in the US.

Hypericum

Medicinal uses.
Flowers have no nectar but visited by insects for pollen.

Hypochaeris radicata, CAT'S EAR

The shoots and stems are attacked inside by Hymenopteran gall-wasp Phanacis hypochaeridis / Aylax showing as wrinkled succulent greenish swellings usually about half to three quarters of an inch but occasionally up to six inches long, the larvae pupate within to emerge the next spring.

Hyssopus officinalis, HYSSOP

Perennial, barely edible, just hardy herb with little household utility, but a superb bee plant that makes lovely honey.

Ilex, HOLLY

This grows in heavy shade, and has poisonous berries. Bark can be retted to a sticky glue used as 'bird-lime'. Apparently good for extracting heavy metals from environment.

Thorny leaves good for discouraging mice and moles from holes.

Beyond a certain height foliage loses the spines as the plant 'knows' no giraffes are likely in cold climates.

Holly is prone to leaf browning and dropping off if waterlogged.

Prey to a Leaf miner leaving obvious tunnels and there is little effective control other than squidging or accurate needling.

Bothered by yellowish Soft scale shared with myrtles and ivies, this species does not produce a hard shell.

Leaves often mined by Dipteron agromyzid Phytomyza ilicis, this makes blotches that are greenish yellowish white, amoeba shaped in the middle of the leaf and unlike most leaf miners here a gall is formed as the two surfaces swell and bulge to form a cavity, as these age purplish or brown flecks and stains form.

Shoots invaded by bacterium Corynebacterium fascians which causes fasciation, stems become broad, flattened and ribbed, splayed and curved this spreads to jasmine, plantains, Chrysanthemums, dogwood, Cotoneaster, Euphorbias, Forsythia, Hibiscus and Inula.

INTERCROPPING

Growing different crop plants together instead of in separate areas. Much of companion planting is about effective intercropping; with each participant and their needs considered. At it's most complicated the whole garden becomes integrated with flowers, herbs, fruit and vegetable areas no longer separately discernible, an armchair gardening folly, difficult to manage in reality.

Imperata cylindrical, COGON-GRASS

Soils under cogon-grass have reduced fungus populations of many Aspergillus species with increases in A. flavus and reduced growth of Melilotus parviflora.

Inula conyza, PLOUGHMAN'S SPIKENARD

The stems support agromyzid stem-borer Melanagromyza aeneoventris.
The shoots get invaded by bacterium Corynebacterium fascians which causes fasciation, stems become broad, flattened and ribbed, splayed and curved, this spreads to jasmine, plantains, dandelions, Chrysanthemums, dogwood, Cotoneaster, Euphorbias, Forsythia, Hibiscus and holly.

IRON

Important nutrient accumulated by plants and essential for animal health.

Iris

Huge number of very different species and thus different requirements, so do read the label.

If large pieces of leaf disappear in midsummer, you will find rather tiny caterpillars of the Sawfly Rhadinoceroea micans.

Simple poor growth is proabably an eelworm infestation.

Flagging leaves and eaten out rhizomes indicate Swift moth caterpillars.

Winter flowering Iris suffer Angle Shades moth Phogophora meticulosa green or olive brown caterpillars feeding on leaves, flowerbuds and blooms.

Leaf spot Heterosporium gracile causes yellow brown spots and stripes on the leaves from late summer.

Roots showing softness or rotting have Rhizome rot Pseudomonas iridis, confirmed by an evil smell.

Iris foetidissima, GLADDON IRIS

Poisonous, the rubbed leaves have odour of stale roast beef sandwiches.

Iris pseudacorus, YELLOW IRIS / FLAG

This marginal plant secretes nectar and is visited by Humble bees and Rhingia species.

Jasminum, JASMINE

Shoots get invaded by bacterium Corynebacterium fascians which causes fasciation, stems become broad, flattened and ribbed, splayed and curved, this spreads to plantains, dandelions, Chrysanthemums, dogwood, Cotoneaster, Euphorbias, Forsythia, Hibiscus, holly and Inula.

Juglans, WALNUTS

These become very big trees and take a long time to fruit, the male and female flowers often not coming out at same time and are wind pollinated.
Be warned handling walnut leaves and especially the shucks of the fruits as these soften, will stain your skin and clothes indelibly black.
Varro remarked on the sterility of land near walnuts.
Often trees carry huge quantities of yellow lichens unseen on the upper side of branches.
Some nuts are dead inside but this is as often from the year being too dry as from any disease.
Squirrels do their usual.

Blister Mite are leaf blisters caused when leaf-blade is galled by acarine gall-mite Eriophyes tristriatus typicus / Phytoptus / Erineum juglandinum / Phyllerium juglandis, making a shiny bulge on top surface but infestation is underneath where mites live in hollow filled with downy hairs.

Surprisingly rather rarely you may find a rather familiar looking maggot in your walnut as these are attacked by the same Codling Moth as haunts apples.

Blotches on the leaves made of spotty bits forming a whole and not just one plain blotch is likely Bacterial Blight Xanthomonas juglandis which will also cause twigs to die back from black streaks on the shoots, and spots on leaves and fruits, the fruits become rotted, shell-less and soggy inside.

Leaf Blotch or Leaf Spot fungus Marssonina juglandis / Gnomonia leptostyla causes yellowish brown patches greyish on the underside of the leaves going brown with spots also appearing on the shuck or fruit covering.

The trunks, stumps and large branches, dead and alive, support a semi-circular bracket fungus Polyporus / Polyporellus squamosus, brown scales with white edible flesh smelling of cucumber, this grows quickly, can reach many pounds in weight but harms trees causing the wood to decay with timber White rot, spreads to beech, horse chestnut, lime, poplar and willow.

Juncus articulatus, JOINTED RUSH

The inflorescence of this and of J. effusus, SOFT RUSH, is attacked by Homopteran Psyllid, a jumping plant louse Livia juncorum which forms a rosette Tassel gall with about seventy red or brown tufts or tassels (when hung upside down) up to three or more inches long, often several will be found low down in the rushes, this louse is in turn often predated by Dipteron Lestodiplosis liviae.

Juniperus communis, COMMON JUNIPER

The small green scaly berries have been used as flavouring and medicine.
Apex of shoots galled by Dipteron gall midge Oligotrophus juniperinus which form a cluster of needles somewhat resembling an artichoke and this is known as the Juniper berry or Whooping gall as it was once used to treat whooping cough!

Junipers suffer stem galls caused by various species of rust fungi Gymmnosporangium which cause swellings, the fungi spores then migrate to other trees where they also cause galls. G. juniperi moves to apple and mountain ash where it causes orange yellow below red on top galls on foliage. G. sabinae moves to pear where it causes the thickened Pear-leaf Cluster-cups on the foliage and sometimes on stems and fruits, causing leaf loss and poor wood ripening. G. clavariaeforme / Rostelia lacerata moves to hawthorn where it forms orange to brownish cluster-cups on stems and leaves which then suffer early death.

Kniphofia

A relatively recent introduction from South Africa these prefer dry winters and wet summers.
Their flowers are full of nectar in quantity and this has already been discovered and is now regularly enjoyed by Blue Tits. I have shaken a dozen flower spikes over a dish and collected a wineglass full for breakfast.

Laburnum anagyroides

Poisonous, decorative Leguminous tree with yellow racemes.

Leaf miners cause whole leaves to brown in blotches and die.

LACEWINGS / FLY-GOLDINGS

Chrysopidae family, light green insects with four lace-like wings, very good aphid controls, each adult lays five hundred eggs, each hanging on a thread-like stalk and each larvae eats about four hundred aphids in a couple of weeks, the adults need nectar and pollen sources. Lacewings are most useful as they're one of the few predators who consume woolly aphids.

Lactuca sativa, LETTUCE

Edible though developing 'opiates' in the milky sap when near flowering and these cause intense bitterness so plants must be grown carefully to avoid stress and bolting and to be succulent.
If it's hot sow lettuce in shade as it will not germinate above 65 degrees F.
Lettuce has been shown to take up natural antibiotics from the soil.
Lettuce suffer from a host of different aphids, at least a half dozen on the leaves early in the season particularly Macrosiphum solani, greenish, also often found on underside of leaves.

Then later come the Lettuce Root aphids Pemphigus bursarius which stunt growth, though growing chervil nearby may help protect them. This root aphid over-winters as eggs on poplar trees especially Populus nigra later moving on to the leaf stalks there forming galls which split in midsummer when the aphids move back onto lettuce. (Anthocorid bugs destroy these galls and reduce the pest numbers and these apparently 'live' on chervil.) Old time gardeners used a solution made from elderberry leaves boiled in soft soap to drench the roots and claimed this killed the root aphids.

The Root Knot eelworm Heterodera marioni can cause lettuce roots to develop galls the size of dots or as big as plums, this may spread to tomatoes, cucumbers and beans.

Symphalids Scutigerella immaculata may eat the roots at ground level causing corky patches and letting in rots.

Lettuce also suffer damage to roots from Small / Garden Swift moth Hepialus lupulinus and both roots and leaves attacked by fat, black striped larvae of Great Yellow Underwing moth Noctua / Tryphaena pronuba.

Downy mildew Bremia lactucae turns leaves yellowish brown and stunts the plants.

Grey Mould Botrytis cinerea often starts in wounds, turns the leaves and then whole plant grey and rotten.

Ring spot Marssonina panattoniana is prevalent in cold wet conditions; brown patches on underside of leaf ribs appear first then brown spots on outer leaves which fall out after turning whitish to leave white margined holes, then rot moves into centre and often kills plant, spread on debris.

Lettuce Mosaic virus is transmitted by aphids and on the seed, the leaves mottle while the veins go transparent and growth is stunted, also invades more than twenty genera in ten families.

Lettuce Infectious Yellow virus, spread by whiteflies, also invades cucurbits.

Turnip mosaic virus, spread by aphids, also invades most Cruciferous plants.

Bidens Mottle virus, spread by aphids, also invades lettuce and endive and does serious damage in Florida.

Beet Western Yellows virus, spread by aphids, also invades many other plants as does Lettuce Necrotic Yellows virus, also spread by aphids.

Lettuce Big Vein virus, spread by soil borne fungus Olpidium Brassicae on surface of zoospores.

Can also be infected by virus Broad Bean Wilt; yellow mosaic and distortion this also infects spinach, pea, broad bean and other Legumes.

Lettuce Mottle virus, spread by aphid Hyperomzus lactucae.

Commonest is probably Cucumber mosaic virus, spread by more than 60 aphid species, invades more than 800 plant species.

LADYBIRDS

Many different varieties each adapted to eat some but not other aphid species, both by the adults and their less well known larvae; which resemble minute black crocodiles and eat even more aphids. So no aphids no ladybirds therefore somewhere some plant has to be infested. Thus encourage aphids on sweet cherries, redcurrants, honeysuckles, vetches and stinging nettles and other plants to feed ladybird larvae for better control elsewhere.

Provide ladybird adults with winter hideaways of rolled up corrugated cardboard and bundles of sweet corn stems and leaves hidden in hedge bases.

Latest list of plants benefitting ladybirds rates goldenrod, fennel, mint, lavender, sedums and veronicas as amongst best, I would certainly add red dead nettle.

Ladybirds are also particularly attracted to the smells of creeping thistle and couch grass -some comfort there then if you have these weeds you probably have less aphids, also they're attracted to chopped Berberis leaves and mayweed flower-heads, and most find aphids fattened on vetches preferable but not the vetch aphid itself Megoura vicia which also occurs on peas and beans. This aphid though eaten by some ladybirds is toxic to others. Commonest are the two and seven spotted varities. Newer larger invasive species may eat our natives and replace them, probably to our crops detriment, a larger, cannabalistic, Harlequin variant is currently increasing in numbers.

Two spot ladybirds do best when fed nettle aphids, pea aphid, and peach-potato aphids and do badly on black bean and elder aphids.

The seven spot ladybird lays it's eggs on plants near ground level, the two spot prefers plants higher off the ground.

Ladybirds, mostly two spot, some seven and fourteen spot, on stinging nettle patches help control aphids on nearby broad bean crops.

Between 41 and 51 degrees Fahrenheit aphids breed faster than ladybirds can control them but above 52 degrees F, 11 degrees Centigrade, ladybirds can eat aphids faster than they can be replaced so long warm sunny weather means less aphid problems whereas there are more during long cool springs and autumns.

Ladybirds prefer to sit on glossy rather than waxy leaved Brussel's sprouts and in spring choose warm basking places such as on rubber tyres, black plastic, rusty metal and similar- so all that junk may have some use...

Lamium album, WHITE DEAD NETTLE

Although considered a weed this is a nectar producer over a long season, indeed I still suck the flowers soon after dawn as I did as a kid (leave it later and the bees will already have had it all).

The flowers are especially adapted for humble bees particularly Anthidium manicatum.

Presence nearby may help deter potato bugs (sic).

In summer attacked by Homopteran aphid Capitophorus / Rhopalosiphum / Aphis / Myzus ribis which also causes leaf blistering galls on redcurrants.

Lamium amplexicaule, HENBIT DEAD-NETTLE

Similar to red dead nettle the leaves of which are stalked where as those of henbit are not stalked. Interestingly this has two sets of flowers, the normal we observe and also hidden, cleistogamous, flowers in autumn without petals or stamens that set seed unnoticed.

Lamium maculatum, SPOTTED DEAD-NETTLE

This has a deeper tube to nectary which is by-passed by Bombus terrestris biting holes, B. rayellus then utilises these bitten holes.

Lamium purpureum, RED DEAD NETTLE

In spring this is an important flower for many insects.

In summer hosts Homopteran aphid Capitophorus / Rhopalosiphum / Aphis / Myzus ribis which moves to cause leaf blistering galls on redcurrants.

Larix europaea / decidua, LARCH

Seldom found above 1,200ft line.
Larches are galled by Cnaphalodes spp. heteroecious on Spruces.
Several Boletus fungi grown on larches especially the edible and tasty Boletus / Suillus / Ixocomus grevillei / elegans with an orangey yellow very slimy cap, a resinous scent and light green flesh.
Another Boletus the very edible Boletus / Boletinus cavipes with a lemon yellow, orange, even reddish brown, cap and whitish flesh, is most often found on larches on clay soils.
Clitocybe clavipes, edible, is found most often in mossy litter under larch but also in pine and oak woods, it has a browny black to olive green cap and smells of bitter almonds.
Hygrophorus / Limacium lucorum, edible, lemon yellow cap and stem and slightly slimy appears in late autumn and nearly always under larches.

Lathraea, TOOTHWORT

A semi-parasitic plant found on roots of trees especially hazels.

Lathyrus odoratus, SWEET PEA

Poisonous and not an edible pea!
The flowers must be picked daily as any seed forming
stops further flowering.
May suffer from Earwigs and Aphids and Symphalids
attacking roots under glass.
Hates dry conditions but in very wet conditions leaves
may yellow and plant wilts with Stem rot Fusarium spp.
and or Botrytis at ground level.
Yellow mottling or brown streaking on the stems and
discoloured foliage with poor flowering suggests virus
once called Streak.
May be infected by Clover Yellow Vein virus; yellow
mosaic, necrosis and wilting which spreads to most other
Legumes: and also Antirrhinum, Atriplex, Chenopodium,
Coriandrum, Cucurbita, Gladiolus, Gomphrena, Nicotiana,
Nicandra, Papaver, Petunia, Proboscidea, Rubus, Spinacia,
Tetragonia and Viola.

Laurus nobilis, BAY

This makes a big tree if not cut back by wind and frost.
Confused in literature with the poisonous Prunus
laurocerasus, Laurel, this is the one for culinary use. The
leaves are used as flavouring, I prefer, unlike most writers,
old leaves to fresh.

Lavatera, TREE MALLOWS

Useful late flowerers with much pollen.
These may get Hollyhock rust Puccinia malvacearum,
which infests many hosts but does not alternate between
them at different stages, however be warned that it will
spread to common mallows, hollyhocks, Abutilons and
Sidalcea, in all of them it infests the leaves and petioles
forming yellow to brown pustules on the undersides often
causing swelling and distortion.

Lavendula officinalis, LAVENDER

Edible in moderation as a flavouring; try lavender
shortbread and / or lavender rice pudding. (I knew a
family who regularly rubbed lavender on their lamb roasts
until I enlightened them and planted a rosemary.)
Long used to keep pests out of clothes the smell also
keeps some away from nearby plants in the garden. Thus
often planted under roses to keep the aphids off and hide
the bare legs.
Prone to Cuckoo spit.

LEATHER-JACKET / DADDY-LONG-LEGS / CRANE-FLY / BOTS

Tipula oleracea are pointed violently wriggling brown leathery cases, following nasty looking grey grubs with no legs, which later become a fearsome looking but actually harmless giant 'mosquito'.

The grubs do horrendous damage to lawns but also to other plants, and unlike most pests these continue to eat throughout winter too. These like damp and dark and can be brought to the surface for the birds or chickens by laying carpet, cardboard or opaque plastic sheet over well soaked ground then rolling it back first thing in the morning.

These grubs can also be baited onto chips of potato, carrot or similar, and by germinating grain, bran and even bread hidden under pieces of bark, wet newspaper or cardboard.

Steinernema feltiae nematodes available commercially kill Leather Jackets if they are watered on when the soil is wet and warmer than 10°C (50°F).

LEGUMES

The largest family of plants that fix Nitrogen from the air
(several others can, though these are mostly tropical).
They achieve this with nodules on their roots which
contain bacteria and fungi who do the fixation in
exchange for nutrients from the plant. Trees such as
Laburnum, Judas tree and Caragana, shrubs such as
Brooms and Tree Lupins are Leguminous as well as the
clovers, peas, beans and lupins we usually think of. All of
them benefit other plants by supplying Nitrogen as their
root hairs and associated microorganisms decompose.
Beans are Legumes and should be grown more, they
enrich the soil and if not eaten fresh can be easily dried
for storage.
Most Legumes especially clovers are an alternate host for
Clover Yellow Vein virus, spread by aphids, which attacks
many plants including cucurbits and especially squash.
They host Muskmelon Vein Necrosis virus spread by
aphids.
Legumes can also be infected by Watermelon Curly
Mottle virus spread by whiteflies.

Lens culinaris, LENTIL

Leguminous crop grown in warmer climes.
Whiteflies Bemesia tabaci transmit Euphorbia mosaic;
necrotic lesions and distortion, also spreads to soybean
and other Legumes.

May also carry Clover Yellow Vein virus; yellow mosaic, necrosis and wilting which spreads to most other Legumes and also Antirrhinum, Atriplex, Chenopodium, Coriandrum, Cucurbita, Gladiolus, Gomphrena, Nicotiana, Nicandra, Papaver, Petunia, Proboscidea, Rubus, Spinacia, Tetragonia and Viola.

Also infected by Bean Curly Dwarf mosaic; mosaic, stunting and rugosity, this also infects other Phaseolus species, soybean, pea, chickpea, broad bean, mung bean and Leguminous weeds.

Levisticum officinale, LOVAGE

A large (head height plus) edible herb of moist places which adds 'body' to vegetable stocks so substitutes for salt.

LICHENS

These are fungi combined with algae, see ALGAE.

LIGHT

Most important. If you shade plants with others, walls or dirty glass do not be surprised when they fail to prosper. Most care is needed for plants under cover, in winter when light is short and for seedlings in early spring.

LIGHT FEEDERS

In crop rotation these are the plants that do not usually require extra fertility. Most root vegetables and the Legumes do fairly well in soil with residual fertility from previously fed crops and the decomposing roots they have left behind.

Ligustrum, PRIVET

These hungry semi-evergreen shrubs impoverish the soil all round inhibiting most plants near them and have poisonous fruits and sickly sweet flowers.
The leaves get tunnelled by Leaf Miners Gracilaria spp, causing blisters and curling.

Lilium

A huge range of bulbous plants, all need well drained, leaf mould rich soils, some need acid conditions, some prefer full sun, others partial shade, some need shallow planting and some deep, ie. check their labels!
Primary bothersome co-life currently is the bird-dropping-like slug of the Lily beetle Lilloceris lilli, a bright reddy orange rather smart looking beastie, destroys the leaves, also eats Lily of the valley, hollyhocks, Hostas, Solomons seal, even potato and allegedly tobacco.
Aphids do little apparent harm but spread virus diseases.

The Madonna lilies and their hybrids are especially prone to Leaf spot Botrytis cinerea which starts as reddy brown leaf spots then dries up the stems and distorts surviving flowers.

Lilies contract Mosaic virus, as well as mottling this can cause blooms to remain unopened so any plant with mottled variegated or distorted leaves is best destroyed immediately.

Limnanthes douglassii, POACHED EGG PLANT

This useful low growing annual has dense ferny foliage and makes good groundcover and winter green manure. It self seeds profusely.

Excellent hoverfly attractant liked by all bees.

Linaria vulgaris, YELLOW TOADFLAX

The nectar is only accessible to long lipped bees whilst other insects are excluded.

The roots are attacked by Coleopteran weevils Gymnetron linariae / collinum which larvae live in small spherical galls, G. hispidum causes elongated galls on the stems.

The shoots are galled by Hymenopteran gall-wasp Aulacidea hieracii / Aylax / sabaudi / graminis / Cynips which over-winter in the gall.

Linum usitatissimum, FLAX

As a field crop (for seed for oil) or as green manure it's very beautiful in flower, and very attractive to a host of insects and a good bee plant.
It leaves a tough fibrous haulm which makes excellent compost, if slowly.
Ashes contain 26% potash, 1.5% soda, 26% lime, 0.2% magnesia, 4% iron oxide, negligible manganese oxide, 40% phosphoric acid, 1% sulphuric acid, 1% silica and 1% chlorine.

Listera ovata, TWAYBLADE

This scarce native is exclusively pollinated by Ichneumon wasps.

Lolium perenne, PERENNIAL RYEGRASS / HUNGARIAN GRAZING RYE

Superb deep rooter, good cover crop and much recommended green manure, productive but hard to kill off.
Sheep prefer it young and dislike it once mature.

Lolium temulentum, DARNEL

Although a grass this has poisonous seeds, these were apparently roasted to give off an early form of riot control gas.

Lonicera, HONEYSUCKLES

Mostly the well known evening perfumed climbers though also several shrubby species, and the tiny leaved L. nitida evergreen hedge.
Suffer massive aphid attacks, which 'turn into' ladybirds.
May be colonised by reddish brown oval Peach scale which spreads to Cotoneaster, Escallonia and flowering currants.

Lonicera periclymenum

Varieties with shorter nectaries are more accessible to bees.
Homopteran aphids Siphocoryne xylostylei / Aphis / Rhopalosiphum feed on the base of the corollas and causes them to become stunted, deformed, swollen and hairy often turning into a globular mass.
The inflorescence is also attacked by a micro-Lepidoptera Many-plume moth Orneodes hexadactyla causing the flowers to gall.
Mildew is a common problem aggravated by dry roots.

Lotus corniculatus, BIRD'S FOOT TREFOILS.

Leguminous. Flower and sometimes leaf-bud galled by Dipteron gall-midge Contarinia / Diplosis / Cecidomyia loti, flower distorted fails to open and becomes downy, yellow, pink or reddish brown. If the leaf is galled it forms a miniature bunch of bananas greenish yellow or brown.

Lotus major, GREATER BIRD'S FOOT TREFOIL

Leguminous and plant contains 6% ash itself containing 23% potash, 21% lime, 5% magnesia and 11% phosphoric acid.

LUMINOUS PLANTS

The mycelium or root system of fungi can glow such as Rhizomorpha subterranean found in old rotting wood. In others it's the actual mushroom. Garish fungi, such as the Olive tree agaric Agaricus olearius, glow dayglow yellow, then also glow in the dark when alive but not once dried. Likewise the mycelium in rotting wood seems to glow only as long as it remains moist.

Coal mines at Cardiff had Polyporus annosus growing there which could be seen glowing from a great distance. Another mine in nineteenth century Germany had a luminous gallery for visitors lit by masses of fungal mycelium on the walls.

Pleurotus and mushrooms with white spores and an eccentric or obsolete stem are most luminous especially the Agarics. Those on oaks are reckoned to be particularly bright.

(Do not expect to see this unless it is a warm, humid and totally dark situation!)

Lupinus, LUPINS

Leguminous with their roots galled by bacteria Rhizobium beyerinckii Leguminous partner, thus these common garden flowers add to soil fertility, and also improve soil texture and Calcium levels.

Dried plant contains 4% ash.

Most lupins are poisonous.

Lupin foliage traps dew for the insects making them especially beneficial, they also suffer vast populations of huge aphids so large they almost seem worth bar-b-q-ing.

Weevils Sitona lineata, grey ones out at night, eat crescent shaped pieces from the leaves.

Sudden death may be Root rot Thielaviopsis basicola where the roots turn black with white fungus marks, worst on lime rich soils.

May be infected by Clover Yellow Vein virus; yellow mosaic, necrosis and wilting which spreads to most other Legumes and also Antirrhinum, Atriplex, Chenopodium, Coriandrum, Cucurbita, Gladiolus, Gomphrena, Nicotiana, Nicandra, Papaver, Petunia, Proboscidea, Rubus, Spinacia, Tetragonia and Viola.

Also can carry Peanut Mottle virus; necrosis and wilting, this seriously affects beans.

Lycium barbarum, GOJI / DUKE OF ARGYLL'S TEA PLANT

A scrappy, straggly, thorn bearing lax climber with a tiny flower and a small edible berry which I find not very palatable however reputedly this is highly beneficial as health giving medicine.

Lycopersicon esculentum, TOMATOES

Interestingly tomatoes have been shown to take up antibiotics from the soil.

Tomatoes can be protected from Botrytis by coating them with certain yeasts, these may occur naturally when honeydew from aphid infestations drips onto them, an interesting concept in crop protection.

In the greenhouse White fly, Thrips, Leaf-hoppers, Red Spider mite and Mealy bug are their usual troublesome.

Spring tails cause the plants to wilt and can be found on the roots as tiny whitish purplish critters which hop about but are easily eliminated with soft soap.

Symphalids Scutigerella immaculata may eat the roots at ground level causing corky patches and letting in rots. Both these last are commonest in plants raised under glass.

The roots are attacked by nematodes / eelworms Heterodera spp. especially H. marioni known to attack over 800 different plants, these cause gall swellings on roots, the males leave to search for females, these remain in the old galls, swell and turn into a cyst of up to five hundred eggs, these develop into juveniles within the cyst and later leave, up to a year or more later, the roots may get woody galls the size of dots or as big as plums.

Most Potato eelworms especially Heterodera schachtii also attack tomatoes, plants will wilt during day and small white cysts will be found on roots.

The Tomato moth Polia oleracea caterpillar, greenish to reddy brown or yellow, up to two inches long, eats the leaves underside first then whole lot, it eats at night and if disturbed drops, onto waiting sheets of newspaper if you're clever.

Bits of the leaf repel flea beetles from other crops. Tomato leaf spray has been used against asparagus beetles and asparagus roots kill Trichodorus, a nematode that attacks tomatoes.

Including Tagetes in crop rotations reduces these nematode populations by 85%.

Bacterial canker Corynebacterium michiganense may affect the leaves which brown on one side only of the leaf stalk which has yellow brown streaking inside, the fruit may have spotting and streaking from the stalk end. The bacteria can survive several years on strings, canes and debris and beware 'suspicious source' seed as this may be infected.

Botrytis Stem rot causes grey sunken areas on stem usually in badly made pruning wounds.

Seedlings suffer Damping Off caused by many different fungi, Phytophthora cryptoga, P. parasitica, Corticum solani and others, clean compost, clean water, dryish bright conditions and good ventilation help prevent the wilting and dying.

Once seedlings get larger they then may suffer Foot Rot from similar fungi, however plants may grow away from these if not killed and where the stem can reroot above the lesion.

Root rot Colletotrichum atramentarium attacks later stages of plant including mature, most often mid to late summer, roots turn brown not healthy white, symptoms are wilting of older leaves during day but recovering at night.

Tomato canker / Stem-rot fungus Didymella lycopersici is a root disease, fruit may be infected, dark brown lesions occur on stem base at or below soil level, these can be seen to have tiny black spores, pinkish tendrils extend and may infect other tissues especially through wounds, leaves may get grey lesions in damp conditions. In bad cases large plants suddenly wilt, you may find a black ulcer or canker rotting the stem base, it's carried through winter on debris, strings and supports.

Wilt or Sleepy Disease is similar caused by Verticillium albo-atrum, affected plants can be saved by earthing up at base, syringing foliage but keeping soil dryish, and keeping plants warmer (above 77° F), just because it is temperature dependent so Verticillium is not often seen in summer.

Fusarium wilt is opposite, occurs most often in hot periods.

Leaf Mould / Rust, Cladosporium fulvum, causes yellowish blotches on top of leaves with purplish underneath, leaves become brown and brittle, this is prevalent under cover and in warm humid conditions especially where plants are over-crowded, spreads by spores so remove all debris and litter after crop finished, it weakens plants and reduces crops but fruits otherwise unaffected.

Beware that tomatoes may harbor Wart disease which attacks the roots, see potatoes.

Tomatoes, particularly if outdoors, share Potato Late Blight Phytophthora infestans with potatoes with similar dire results.

Tomatoes are also susceptible to Early Blight Alternaria solani which looks much the same at first with black or brownish spots on the leaves and stems. However these are a bit more angular in shape and on the stems the spots are sunken and not streaked. On the fruits Late blight causes random rotten spots, Early Blight causes the fruit to rot mostly at the flower end this becoming covered with a black mat of mycelium. Tagetes erecta grown with the tomatoes protects them from the Alternaria but not the Phytophthora.

Tomatoes are invaded by over 40 viruses worldwide. Raspberries share Tomato Black Ring virus.

Tobacco Mosaic virus causes serious losses, leaves mottle dark green and young growth is distorted, then as fruiting starts brown streaks appear on stems which become brittle. Often infection starts with a smoker who carries it in on their hands or their tobacco, commercial growers stopped most attacks when they banned smokers from their greenhouses, also transmitted on pruning equipment.

Tomato mosaic virus, spread by aphids, on tools, in soil and on seed, may reduce yields by a quarter, also invades tobacco and Datura.

Cucumber mosaic virus is also found invading tomatoes and peppers and aubergines.

Tomato Ringspot virus, spread by nematodes, also invades Cucurbits and hundreds of other plants both woody and herbaceous.

Tomato Spotted Wilt virus, spread by thrips, also invades cucurbits.

Beet Curly Top virus is spread by leaf-hoppers and also invades Cucurbits and many other plants.
In warmer climates the sweet potato whitefly Bemisia tabaci spreads Tomato Yellow Leaf Curl virus, Tomato Leaf Curl virus, Tobacco Leaf Curl virus, Chino del tomate virus, Tomato Yellow Dwarf virus and Tomato Golden mosaic virus.
Tobacco Etch virus and Vein Banding mosaic virus spread by aphids also invade tomatoes.

Lycoris radiata

Japanese bulbous weed, planted to prevent rodent damage to paddy field banks and footpaths as these will not make holes near the bulbs.
Ground up the bulbs are included in plaster for barns also to prevent rodent damage.

Lysimachia vulgaris, YELLOW LOOSESTRIFE

Are only blooms known visited by a rare bee Macropsis labiate, must be for pollen as no nectar.
Two forms, one showy and in open spaces seldom self fertile, other form less showy and found in shade habitually self fertile.
Hosts virus Tomato Black Ring also spreads to raspberries.

Lythrum salicaria, PURPLE LOOSESTRIFE

Exclusively pollinated by Cilissa melanura bees.

MAGNETISM

Many claim this affects growth, this seems highly likely, however one should consider whether all effects will always be beneficial.

Magnolia

One of the oldest of flowering plants, shown to generate warmth helping the spring pollinators who visit, also warmth makes scents more volatile and thus reaches patrolling insects telling them of comfort station nearby.

Malus, APPLE

Grown everywhere so very many associated co-lives, and therefore many parasites and predators of those as well.

Be careful to store only perfect fruit and to keep these away from strong herbs, potatoes and carrots. Separate late from early ripeners and use dried nettles to help preserve and ripen them.

Said that in ripe fruit the round seeds will be most like parent and flat seeds more like a crab.

Cooking varieties have greater need of wood ashes, which they all enjoy.

June Drop is not a disease or a pest attack but looks disastrous; around midsummer depending on the tree's assessment of it's cropping ability it drops a large number of fruitlets leaving fewer to swell and ripen.

Bitter Pit is another not very common problem sometimes found with old trees on worked out soils, especially on acid soils. Basically a shortage of water causes lots of small brown spots to appear throughout the flesh especially just under the skin. Mulches improving soil moisture and enhancing the microlife population reduce this physiological condition; it's not a pest or disease as it does not spread.

Watery Core or Glassiness of the fruit is another physiological disorder where the core seems to be waterlogged. It's worst in young, over fertilised trees in high temperatures with extremes of water stress, I find Charles Ross particularly prone.

Apples are said to benefit from nasturtiums underneath to drive away the Woolly Aphis, Penstemons to keep their Sawflies away, chives and garlic to discourage fungal diseases and alfalfa / Lucerne to bring nutrients up from deep down.

Apples give off ethylene gas as they ripen, this may inhibit plant growth and cause premature maturation in flowers and fruits.

Of the co-lives wasps and birds are often troublesome. Wasps usually rely on birds to start the holes for them and our friends the Blue tits and Blackbirds are common culprits pecking holes in ripening fruits. Birds peck fruit such as apples and pears selectively thus Lord Lambourne and Cox's Orange Pippin are much more heavily damaged than Laxton's Fortune and Worcester Pearmain. And leave windfalls, ideally cut open, to fob them off.

Very corky scarred or distorted leaves and fruits may be showing earlier damage from Apple Capsid Plesiocoris rugicollis, adult quarter inch long and green, attacks making small punctures in the leaves and shoots (brown or black marks), then moves onto the fruits where their punctures cause corky patches that expand with the fruit making them unsightly and prone to other problems. They hatch in spring from eggs buried under the bark, moult five times getting bigger and eventually grow wings and mate.

Apple Suckers Psylla mali look much like aphids though under a lens are red eyed, yellow green with green wings, they cause similar problems to aphids with distorted leaves and failed flower buds, damage is lessened as only one batch a year, from overwintering eggs.

In hot dry conditions Fruit Tree Red Spider mites, Panonychnus uni can cause their usual trouble browning leaves and bringing on autumn colouring early in summer, usually predated by the Capsid bug Anthocoris nemorum.

Bryobia mites Bryobia rubrioculus are dependent on apple and pear trees with no alternate hosts. These suck sap, breed rapidly and they and their damage much resemble red spider mite except they're not hairy and have longer front legs.

Chafer beetle adults of Melolantha melolantha and Phyllopertha horticola eat the leaves and small fruitlets, while their larvae eat the roots.

Bark beetles Anisandrus dispar, bore into the wood all the way to the middle, usually on already weakened specimens which it further degrades, interestingly the grub is thought to get most of it's sustenance not from the chewed up wood but from fungi growing on the tunnel walls.

Several weevils attack parts of apple trees though seldom badly, in particular Leaf weevil Phyllobious oblongus and P. piri adults may graze and thus harm seedling trees though their larvae mostly eat the roots of grasses.

The Apple Fruit Rhynchites weevil R. aquatus is brownish red, attacks the fruits a fortnight after petal fall, damage is quite distinctive as if a biro pen has been pushed hundreds of times into the flesh.

The Apple Twig Cutter weevil Rhynchites caeruleus, has a dark blue adult, rather beautiful and well named for the larvae does just that to the ends of twigs which fall off in summer, the adults emerge and over-winter to eat leaves and bark before laying their eggs from late spring.

The yellowish Apple Blossom weevil, Anthonomus pomorum, causes flower buds to brown and stay shut, the 'cap' can be lifted off to show the grub within and prove it's not frost damage.

The white Apple Bud weevil, Anthonomas cinctus, often attacks pears worse in both causing dead buds and shoot tip damage.

Leaf-hoppers Erythroneura alneti and Typhocyba froggatti are greenish jumpers that suck the sap as adults and also as nymphs causing leaves to wither or colour early.

Aphids are often evident and in at least eight varieties. The Green apple aphid Aphis pomi, the Oak apple aphid Rhodslosiphum invertum and the Rosy apple aphid Sappapthis mali are commonest, these usually do modest harm, though heavy infestations cause leaf curling and distortion, plus their honeydew causes sooty moulds. Branches, roots and stems are attacked by Homopteran aphid Eriosoma lanigerum / mali / Schizoneura / Aphis lanigera the dreaded American Woolly aphid or American blight. Swellings and cankers form with woolly fluffy covering protecting these aphids spread aerially on wind buoyed up by the fluff. Woolly Aphis is remarkably common in old untended overgrown orchards and seldom seen in open well pruned ones. A North American wasp Aphelinus mali has been introduced to Europe and may now help to control Woolly Aphis which has not proved palatable to most local fauna. Growing trailing nasturtiums in profusion under the trees is reputed to drive Woolly Aphis away but takes several years. Our best natural controls are Lacewings whose larvae eat them and the Red Velvet mite Allothrombium fuliginosum which apparently particularly relishes woolly aphids.

Scale insects are often found on old trees and in overgrown orchards and particularly on wall specimens. Mussel Scale, Mytilococcus / Lepidosaphes ulmi, an elongated scale that lies flat on the bark, the eggs overwinter under their dead parents old scales, usually on twigs but may move onto fruit.

San José Scale, Quadraspidiotus perniciosus, may completely coat trees, each female produces 400 young with three generations a year, even small infestations cause die back and fruit damage.

Oystershell Scale, Quadraspidiotus ostreaeformis, has the obvious shaped shell, the larvae overwinter before settling down to make a scale in spring, seldom found in such numbers as the others but may then cause similar damage.

Earwigs Forficula auricularia, cause ulcerous holes in fruit messed with excreta, worst in trees surrounded by grass. Holes with 'maggots' in the apples are probably either Apple Sawfly or Codling Moth. The sawfly, Hoplocampa testudinea, a dirty whitish caterpillar with a brown head, makes big rotten holes in the middle with a tunnel usually from the top. This is the worst pest as it may leave one and damage another or even several apples and sometimes making a ribbon scar across a fruit as it travels, damaged fruit usually fall early, the larvae overwintering in the soil. The sawfly caterpillars attack from when the fruit first swells till early summer about the time of the June Drop and then through summer and early autumn it's the Codling's turn.

The Codling Cydia pomonella, a pinkish caterpillar with a brown head, makes an even bigger mess in the middle, often enters from the side of the fruit, but does at least ruin but the one fruit apiece.

For the rather numerous other caterpillar co-lives bothering apples see Volume 2 Really Help Butterflies.

Fireblight Erwinia amylovaca is a serious bacterial infection that spreads into the wood from the initial attack usually on the flowers which look as if burnt, and eventually kills trees (though almost all susceptible varieties have already expired). Known in the USA for two centuries it arrived in the UK in 1957 and has since wiped out many of our choicest Rosaceae.

Juniper stem galls are caused by rust fungi Gymmnosporangium juniperi which moves to apple where it causes orange yellow below and red on top galls on foliage.

Powdery mildew Podosphaera leucotricha very commonly attacks young leaves and shoots leaving them narrowed, distorted, curled even withered and covered with powder and worst cases stunts buds. Similar to aphid attacks in appearance but usually earlier in the season, mildew attacks can often be disregarded unless flower buds are damaged as these then give fewer poorer fruits if any. The dead but infective shoots appear grey in winter. Some varieties, ie Cox and Bramley, are notoriously badly affected.

Apple Canker Nectria galligena is a serious fungal disease, often much worse in dank stagnant overgrown conditions than in drier open sunny orchards. The spores enter through wounds, even leaf scars, causes sunken spots which rot the bark and ulcerate it exposing the wood and swelling up all round until it rings the twig, limb or even trunk and the tree dies, Cox's Orange Pippin and James Grieve are particularly troubled but Newton Wonder, Worcester Pearmain and Bramley's Seedling are much more resistant.

Scabby patches, often greenish to start with but turning dark on the fruits are usually Apple Scab Venturia inaequalis. Cox and Worcester Pearmain suffer badly whereas Charles Ross and Beauty of Bath are rarely touched. Scab is associated with canker as it often lets the latter in to do more damage on the twigs and limbs. If Scab attacks the fruits early it distorts them and cracks appear, attacking late they develop normally with only skin damage. At first the infected spots are dark, then they sink and become corky and black, sometimes perfectly round in shape. They may proliferate when apples are in store.

Very similar though not so serious is Sooty Blotch Glaeodes pomigena, dark patches looking as if the fruits have been touched with soot, often worst in damp years and shade and developing further in over-humid storage. When the flower truss turns brown and the fruiting spur dies back it is Blossom Wilt Sclerotinia laxa, Cox and James Grieve and Lord Derby are very prone, Bramley is seldom touched.

Brown Rot Sclerotina fructigena and S. mali are fruit problems that like scab may also attack other parts. This Brown Rot is not necessarily the other brown rot of decay but rough raised rings of spots running around the fruit on the skin of a yellow cream hue that slowly mummify the fruit. Any wounds, or rough treatment causing bruising, may either get a simple rot that's brown and/or Brown Rot with the latter going on to either dry out the fruit, or, in store it may turn it black with a white fluff that allegedly infects the surrounding fruits. This is not easy to control except by ensuring minimum entrance points by careful handling, good pest control and ensuring storing fruits are picked with the pedicel (little stalk) intact. Brown Rot rarely affects Bramley's Seedling and likewise other varieties that resist canker well also resist brown rot, and the related disease Blossom Wilt. Brown Rot also affects plums similarly so keep these as far away as possible. With plums often the fruits get a brown rot with whitish bubbling but with apples it tends to stop at the flower and stem stage.

Crown gall Pseudomonas tumefaciens bacteria cause cauliflower galls on the roots which hinder growth by interfering with the passage of nutrients.

An annual fungus Inonotus hispidus does much damage to old trees living on the trunk forming a large (up to 10lb) bracket of russet, whitish underneath with big pores, juicy and meaty though inedible, and dripping moisture in damp conditions, this has been used to make a yellow dye, also found on pears.

Many Viruses invade apples, often unnoticed such as Chlorotic Leaf Spot virus, Stem Pitting virus, and Scaly Bark virus. Rubbery Wood virus, a self explanatory description seen in some old specimens of a few varieties including James Grieve but particularly Lord Lambourne. Bad cases become weeping, it would be attractive in a way but the yields drop. Rubbery Wood also invades Sunset, Miller's Seedling, Worcester Pearmain, Golden Delicious.

Flat Limb is another self explanatory virus.

Mosaic virus causes a mosaic of light patterns in the leaves reducing the vigour and crop, many varieties get affected especially Bramley's, Worcester Pearmain and Lord Lambourne.

A virus is thought to cause Chats where the fruits stay small, smaller than crabs, ripen and fall early and of little use, Chat Fruit virus is often found in Lord Lambourne.

Star Crack is often confused with capsid damage and it's spread by the apple capsid Plesiocoris rugicollis but is a virus infection with no control, the tiny corky patches are star shaped and as the apple expands become indented. Star Crack virus shows up most in Cox's Orange Pippin, Bramley's Seedling, Laxton's Fortune, Charles Ross, the Cox may even get the shoots killed by resultant cankers.

Malva sylvestris, COMMON MALLOW

Blooms visited by many insects

Often infested by Hollyhock rust, Puccinia malvacearum, which is unusual as it infests many hosts but does not alternate between them at different stages, however be warned that it will spread to hollyhocks, tree mallows, Abutilons and Sidalcea, in all of them it infests the leaves and petioles forming yellow to brown pustules on the undersides often causing swelling and distortion.

Matricaria chamomilla, WILD CHAMOMILE

This is well confused in sources as GERMAN and with SCENTED MAYWEED, M. recutita and PINEAPPLE MAYWEED, M. matricarioides, and SCENTLESS MAYWEED, Tripleurospermum inodorum / M. inodora.
Accumulates Potassium, Calcium and Sulphur and has traditional medicinal as well as companion effects.
Blooms have strong smell said distasteful to bees, however visited by Prosopis signata and Sphecodes gibbus, and by hoverflies and wasps, yet mostly fertilised by flies.

Matthiola, STOCKS

Yellowish green caterpillars of the sawfly Pteronidea spiraeae are found on the underside of leaves devouring them.

Don't forget these are distantly related to Brassicas and 'suspicious' plants can carry in unwanted co-lives such as Clubroot.

Medicago sativa, ALFALFA / LUCERNE

A Leguminous perennial that roots remarkably deeply, accumulates Iron, Magnesium, Phosphorus (0.5%), Potassium (1.5%), Calcium (3%) as well as fixing Nitrogen. It may yield up to eighteen tons per acre green drying to about three containing nearly half a ton of mineral ash. Needs new soil inoculating with companion bacteria before it will grow well, this is sold with the seed commercially.

Used as a sacrificial crop for corn wireworms, and for Lygus bugs on cotton but allelopathic secretions from it are detrimental to the cotton.

Alfalfa residues inhibit Trichoderma virides an important soil microorganism.

Can suffer fungal Violet root rot / Copper-web Helicobasidium purpureum which also attacks asparagus, beet, carrot, parsnip, potatoes and even clover, and is harboured by several weeds.

Alfalafa mosaic causing necrosis and wilting also invades beans and many other plants.

Clover Yellow Vein virus; yellow mosaic, necrosis and wilting which spreads to most other Legumes and also Antirrhinum, Atriplex, Chenopodium, Coriandrum, Cucurbita, Gladiolus, Gomphrena, Nicotiana, Nicandra, Papaver, Petunia, Proboscidea, Rubus, Spinacia, Tetragonia,
 and Viola.
Thrips tabaci and Frankliniella occidentalis spread Tobacco Streak virus / Bean Red Node; red nodes, necrosis and red spots, also seed borne this also spreads to chickpea, fenugreek, Datura, sweet clover, soybean, Nicotiana, most beans and many plants.

Melilotus arvensis, FIELD MELILOT

Leguminous, may carry Clover Yellow Vein virus; yellow mosaic, necrosis and wilting which spreads to most other Legumes and also Antirrhinum, Atriplex, Chenopodium, Coriandrum, Cucurbita, Gladiolus, Gomphrena, Nicotiana, Nicandra, Papaver, Petunia, Proboscidea, Rubus, Spinacia, Tetragonia and Viola.

Melissa officinalis, LEMON BALM

Most famous of all bee plants this lemon scented herb benefits almost everything and should be in every garden. Rubbed on your or pets' skins will please bees and deter other insects.

Mentha, MINTS

These love rich moist soil, allegedly detest wood ash (I'm sure I've seen mint growing on sites of old bonfires), and are more than somewhat invasive. Thus the common recommendation to plant spearmint and table mints in containers part buried in the soil to minimise their expansionist tendency.

Their odour can be used to repel rodents, clothes moths, fleas and flea beetles and spearmint discourages aphids by discouraging their 'owners' the ants.

Sprays of mint tea repel ants and Colorado beetle.

Mints are wonderful autumn bee plants and also aid hoverflies and predatory wasps.

Mint Rust Puccinia menthae causes swollen shoots with yellow pustules turning brown, you can cleanse roots of the black spores for forcing or transplanting by heating them in water for 10 minutes at 112°F.

Powdery mildew Oidium sp. may attack the whole plant especially in dry poor conditions.

Mentha piperita, PEPPERMINT

Oil is much used for scent and flavour, production is improved by stinging nettles, with chamomile it is reduced but that of the chamomile increased.

Like most of the family will help keep Brassicas free of cabbage white butterfly caterpillars.

Loved by bees and other beneficial insects.

Exudates from peppermint can reduce infestations of clubroot fungus of Brassicas.

Mentha pulegium, PENNYROYAL

Used as a personal, household and garden insect repellent since time immemorial.

Mentha rotundifolia, BOWLES MINT / APPLE MINT

Leaves contain chemical smelling of pineapple and similar to Amyl acetate capable of altering other plants growth in same way as ethylene.
Alternate host for leaf-hopper Eupteryx aurata shared with hogweed, hemp agrimony, stinging nettles and ragwort.

MICE

Pests with little good to be said for them excepting they are not rats.

Mice droppings are rice size, rats' are like raisins. Strong herbs such as mint or camphor plant, Euphorbias, wormwood and corn chamomile repel them as may the everlasting pea, Lathyrus latifolius, Narcissi, Scilla and Muscari families of spring bulbs.

Grain may be protected with leaves of dwarf elder, Sambucus ebulis, which have a strange foetid vanilla scent and purgative properties.

In trials mice showed most distaste for cinnamon, pepper, pine needles and extract of rhubarb root.

MICROCLIMATE

Some places are more favourable than others not only on the grand scale but also in a similar way in any garden. A warm south facing corner is subject to conditions utterly unlike the edge of a shaded ditch. The individual climate in each place can be as different as across a country and different plants will enjoy each. The skill is in matching them up, and / or manipulating the microclimate to the crop. Growing different companions is one of many ways of altering the immediate microclimate increasing or decreasing moisture, shade, wind etc.

MILDEWS

Divide into two types, powdery and downy. The powdery forms do less damage in general than the downy, grey matted mildews. Both attack plants under stress 'eating' from the outside, the commonest causes are plants too dry at the roots and stagnant air. Good growing conditions suitable to the plant, careful pruning and training to allow access of air and light will do much to alleviate mildews. The Alliums nearby will offer some protection but this needs time to work, removing diseased material will speed up the effect. Garlic and Equisetum teas, seaweed and nettle sprays make plants tougher and more resistant as may mustard seed flour and milk.

MILLIPEDES, not Centipedes

Blanjulus guttulatus and Polydesmus complanatus. When disturbed these curl up, are slow moving, have two pairs of legs per segment and are generally harmful to plants. (Centipedes run away, move quickly and have one pair of legs per flattened segment, generally are useful to plants as centipedes predate many 'pests'.)

Millipedes eat living and dead material, burrow into corms, roots, tubers, fruits and eat seeds, seedlings, stems and often enlarge holes made by other critters, these holes then allow in fungal and bacterial diseases. They breed in spring, the eggs laid in a buried sealed nest hatch in ten days.

MILK

Animals that eat strong flavoured plants, especially the Alliums, have tainted off flavour milk for several days. Milk has been sprayed, whole and skimmed, against many pests and diseases. It blocks their pores and they asphyxiate. It's even been used as a fertiliser.

MINERALS & MINERAL ACCUMULATORS

Plants are made up of air, light and water, only a few per cent of any plant consists of minerals but these are vital. Plants need them to function and recycle them from older leaves when short, this causes visual symptoms and can aid recognition of a deficiency. Similar symptoms may be caused by virus or other diseases or simply by the senescence from old age or season.

Many plants, often weeds, concentrate minerals in themselves that are particularly short in their soil making them available to other plants when composted. Weeding is not a chore but collecting minerals for better compost! The minerals in the soil are mostly insoluble as rock dusts and are made available to plants in the first case by the action of micro-organisms which can be encouraged. Use seaweed extracts, Biodynamic and herbal sprays, water and mulching and a greater diversity of plants.

Mineral accumulators are plants especially rich in elements. Some common plants have relatively high levels of certain elements compared to their surrounding competitors and are thus especially worth gathering for compost. Others accumulate elements you may not wish to make more available such as Cadmium, Lead and Nickel. This same ability that makes these accumulators also makes these tough competitors stealing away all their companions nutrients.

Particularly noted accumulator of:
Boron: Euphorbias.
Cadmium: Japanese knotweed.
Calcium: Alfalfa / Lucerne, buckwheat, cabbage family, coltsfoot, comfrey, corn chamomile, corn marigold, creeping thistle, daisy, dandelion, Equisetum, fat hen, foxglove, goose-grass, great plantain, horseradish, Locust / Robinia, lupins, melons, oak bark, purslane, scarlet pimpernel, sheep's sorrel, shepherd's purse, silverweed, soya beans, stinging nettles, thistles, yarrow.
Cobalt: Bulbous buttercup, comfrey, Equisetum, ribwort plantain, rosebay willow herb, tufted vetch.

Copper: Bulbous buttercup, chickweed, coltsfoot, creeping thistle, dandelion, great plantain, ribwort plantain, sow-thistles, spear thistles, stinging nettles, tufted vetch, yarrow.

Iron: Alfalfa / Lucerne, broad beans, bulbous buttercup, chickweed, chicory, coltsfoot, comfrey, creeping thistle, dandelion, Equisetum, fat hen, foxglove, great plantain, ground ivy, groundsel, oats, silverweed, stinging nettles.

Lead: Minuartia verna.

Magnesium: Alfalfa / Lucerne, borage, coltsfoot, daisies, Equisetum, ribwort plantain, salad burnet, sheep's sorrel, silverweed, yarrow.

Manganese: Bulbous buttercup, chickweed, comfrey.

Nickel: Alyssum bertolonii.

Nitrogen: Most young growth has higher % Nitrogen than older more fibrous material, though in some such as borage may be converse. All Leguminous plants fix Nitrogen so their roots and root remains are especially useful. The following have relatively high haulm levels of Nitrogen when green: borage, broad-leaved dock, chickweed, fat hen, groundsel, knotgrass, purslane, sow-thistles, stinging nettles.

Phosphorus: Alfalfa / Lucerne, broad beans, thorn-apple, valerian, vetches, yarrow.

Potassium: Alfalfa / Lucerne, Artemesias, broad-leaved dock, bulbous buttercup, cabbages, chickweed, chicory, coltsfoot, comfrey, corn chamomile, couch grass, fat hen, goose-grass, great plantain, horse radish, purslane, stinging nettles, Tagetes, tansy, thistles, vetches, yarrow.

Selenium: Astragalus.

Silica: couch grass, dandelion, great plantain, Equisetum, knotgrass, sheep's sorrel, stinging nettles.
Sulphur: Alliums, Brassicas, coltsfoot, fat hen, horseradish, purslane.
Zinc: Japanese knotweed, field pennycress (Thlaspi).

Minuartia verna, SPRING SANDWORT

Unusually accumulates lead and other metals in leaves.

MITES

Many of these minute insects are plagues on plants especially the Red Spider mite, however a few such as the Red Velvet mite Allothrombium fuliginosum are predators and this particularly relishes woolly aphids.

MOLES

Well known of seldom seen underground mammal with very tough hard wearing fur, thus moleskin trousers.

Many plants are said to repel moles, find one that really works and you will have fame and fortune. Euphorbias and most other spurge family plants, castor oil and Incarvilleas, and countless other suggestions, all have been claimed to deter moles but none have ever proved consistently if at all efficacious. Likewise poke sharp, twiggy, thorny things in their tunnels, flood them, gas them with car exhaust, put foul, disgusting things down there. You will only discourage them for a while or drive them to the neighbours temporarily! Why not accept them and appreciate the fine soil they leave? This soil is excellent for adding to most potting composts.

Several rare beetles are almost only ever found living in mole' nests; Aleochara spadicea, Heterothops nigra, Quedius vexans, Q. longicornis, Hister marginatus, Onthophilusglobosus, Medon castaneus, Oxypoda spectabilis, O. longipes, Oxytelus sculpturatus, Choleva angustata, Choleva nigrita.

MOLLUSCS see SLUGS and SNAILS

Morus nigra, MULBERRY

Slow growing large trees with delicious fruit loved by birds and us.
Often one of last to come into leaf in spring, and stays in leaf late in autumn.
Can be pollarded, coppiced and hard pruned for fodder.

M. alba is the better species for sustaining real silkworms.

MOSSES

Once dried these are excellent packaging and frost protection, sphagnum moss is antiseptic and was used medicinally, and mosses are good at extracting heavy metals from their environment.

MOSQUITOS, gnats, flies as well as true mosquito

These are discouraged by the smell of strong herbs and some trees such as walnut and elder. The highly poisonous castor oil plant discourages them. Unfortunately they like smell of people more and especially if these are not garlic eaters, the critters home in on our exhaled carbon dioxide. Most pungent scents rubbed on the skin will help but none will give complete freedom, pennyroyal, Eucalyptus and the mints are useful (especially avoid rue which will blister the skin in hot weather).

MULCH

Almost anything applied to the soil surface to suppress weeds and or retain moisture is mulch. Peat was once widely used despite ecological damage to peatbogs. Make any mulch go further with underlayers of wet newspapers.

Organic mulches rot down releasing nutrients so are usually best, grass clippings used in thin layers and then often topped up are not expensive and effective.

Oak leaf mulch repels many pests, as do cocoa shell and raw wool. Conifer needle mulches are brilliant with strawberries repelling many things and allegedly improving the flavour (I tried this and it made no perceptible difference, perhaps a deeper and for longer mulch is needed).

MUSHROOMS, CULTIVATED

Usually grown on fermented horse manure the common edible mushroom Agaricus / Psalliota campestris needs constant temperatures and humidity. A cellar or cave is ideal, I found down in the bilges of a houseboat I once had worked really well.

Cracking of the caps is because of too dry conditions. Rose Comb is a symptomatic result of some pollution or damage causing the cap to distort to a hen comb shape. The mushrooms are often ruined by Sciarid and Phorid flies whose larvae tunnel through the stems and caps.

Springtails / Brown fleas, Fungus Gnats and several mites also prove troublesome.

Several fungi attack the desired fungi/mushrooms;

White Mould / Bubbles disease is Mycogone perniciosa which coats the mushrooms with a white mould and they become stunted and distorted.

Brown Blotch is a stain on the cap from Pseudomonas tolaasii.

The mycelium in the bed is competed with by White Plaster mould Monilia / Oospora fimicola which looks as if plaster has been scattered on the surface.

Brown Plaster mould Papulaspora byssina / Myriococcum praecox first makes white matted or fluffy patches and these brown and go powdery.

Mushroom-bed Sclerotium fungus Xylaria vaporaria forms white threads and black sclerotia (have smell of cucumber) which can be pulled up if the protruding end (often pink) can be spotted.

Mushroom-bed Brackets are the toadstool fungus Clitocybe dealbata with white stems, caps and gills.

Common soil microbes Verticillium spp. Fusarium spp. and Cephalosporum spp. can invade the mushroom mycelium.

MYCORRHIZAL organisms

Fungii and bacteria living on the roots of plants are usually beneficial, sometimes essential this interplay of plant, bacteria and fungus is more widespread and of greater importance than we have so far understood. Rhizobium bacteria on Legumes are the commonest and its estimated they fix 100 million tons of Nitrogen per year from the air for the eventual benefit of plants and us all. These are available commercially and probably useful in worked out soils but a shovel full of muck is probably equally beneficial and cheaper.

Myrrhis odorata, SWEET CICELY

Edible plant in all parts, strongly aniseed scented, in need of improvement, very happy in damp places.
Flowers much visited by insects, the seedpods are large, good chews and once used in furniture polishing.

Myrtus

Many species and most a bit tender, usually evergreens with scented flowers (smell of garlic sausage). Edible berries are produced on almost all species.
May be attacked by a yellowish Soft scale shared with hollies and ivies, this does not produce a hard shell.

Narcissus, DAFFODILS

Poisonous.

If mixed in a vase with flowers of lily of the valley they (sic), at least one or other, will wilt. (*odd as apart from N. poeticus most bloom before lily of valley*).

Daffodils believed to discourage mice as may other narcissi, grape hyacinths and scilla. In the USA this family have been used against cabbage worms, Colorado beetles and squash bugs.

Often Narcissus fly Meroden equestris / Eumerus spp. causes leaves to yellow first, then fail as their grubs eat out the centre.

Sometimes bulbs decay away from Grey Bulb rot Sclerotium tuliparum which will also spread to tulips and gladioli amongst others.

Yellow Stripe Ramularia narcissi causes yellowish green streaks on the leaves, sometimes on the flowers, the leaves may then distort and the bulbs go blind.

Nasturtium officinale, WATERCRESS

Edible but classic advice is beware of possible contamination if eating uncooked.

I find this needs clean calcium laden running water to be immersed in to be most succulent. Alternatively grow this in containers of constantly moist compost. Growing this in still or stagnant water gives poor growth and competition from algae.

This can become infected by a mosaic virus, probably from cucumber, with characteristic mottling in yellow.

NEMATODE EELWORMS

These are mostly microscopic. Small 'worms' may be just that or the larger saprophytic worms that are mostly harmless. Although we use some specialised parasitic nematodes to control pests most are considered pests and these are generally too small to see though they may cause damage that can be seen (such as the strings of spheroidal cysts on potato roots). The first sign is plants sicken and do badly with no obvious reason.

An eelworm infestation will be especially likely where the same plants have been grown for many years in the same soil. Thus nematodes are serious pests to crops such as potatoes and tomatoes, and popular flowers such as Begonias, Chrysanthemums, Coleus, Delphiniums, Gloxinias, Iris, tulips, Narcissis, orchids and Salvias.

Onion and leek leaves swell, distort and their bulbs crack and rot.

Other bulbs show softening, and leaf and stem shortening.

With Phlox, sweet William, ferns and Chrysanthemum the Leaf & Stem eelworms swim up the wet surfaces and penetrate the leaves and stems causing browning, splitting, stunting or whippiness.

Root Knot eelworms cause galls from tiny spots to huge lumps on the roots and ruin crops such as beans, cucumbers, lettuces and tomatoes with little remedy though they are worst in light warm soils.

On potatoes eelworms form visible cysts on the roots. These can be reduced by prior plantings of Solanum sisymbrifolium. It seems all of the Tagetes marigold family give off secretions that kill nematodes and can be planted to clean the ground. Crotalaria, castor oil plants, Calendula officinalis, sage, asparagus, Petunias and some Dahlias discourage them. The bulbs and roots of some such as strawberries, tulip, Chrysanthemums and Phlox can be cleaned up by heating their roots in a water bath at 110°F for 20 minutes or so.

High levels of organic matter in the soil especially additions of garden compost help control them by increasing numbers and varieties of predatory fungi.

Applications of dried powdered leaves of Caltharanthus roseus, the Madagascar periwinkle, dramatically reduce soil infestations of Root Knot nematodes.

Weeds are often sources of re-infection; Annual meadow grass, chickweed, fat hen, groundsel, knotgrass and shepherd's purse harbour nematodes that attack most root vegetables, Brassicas, lettuce and onions, fruits such as strawberries and blackcurrants and many ornamentals.

Nepeta cataria, not mussinnii, CATNIP

Most cats love this so it should be planted where you want them to lurk. A patch near the strawberries can really keep down bird damage. Or if you are bothered by cats snoozing on your warm patio then put a bed of catnip in another sunny spot and they will soon gravitate there. The scent repels ants, aphids, fleas, flea beetles and in the USA Colorado beetles, darkling beetles, Japanese beetles, squash bugs and weevils. So would probably make a useful personal insect repellent if you have no problem with that hint of cat pee.

Nicandra physaloides, SHOOFLY plant / PERUVIAN CHERRY

Poisonous somewhat dangerously resembling Physalis. This is claimed to repel whiteflies but is such a vigorous large plant it soon becomes too big for most greenhouses.

May be infected by Clover Yellow Vein virus; yellow mosaic, necrosis and wilting which spreads to most Legumes and also Antirrhinum, Atriplex, Chenopodium, Coriandrum, Cucurbita, Gladiolus, Gomphrena, Nicotiana, Papaver, Petunia, Proboscidea, Rubus, Spinacia, Tetragonia and Viola.

Nicotiana affinis, SWEET TOBACCO

Deep flower tubes with strong scents are attractive to night flying moths.
The bird-dropping-like slug of the Lily beetle Lilloceris lilli, a bright reddy orange rather smart looking beastie, may eat the leaves having spread from lilies, lily of the valley, hollyhocks, Solomon's seal, Hostas and potatoes.

Nicotiana sylvestris, WOODLAND TOBACCO

Deep flower tubes with strong scents attract night flying moths.
The plant has sticky leaves that trap small insects such as whiteflies.
Alternative host for Tomato mosaic virus, spread by aphids, on tools, in soil and on seed, may reduce yields by a quarter, also invades Datura and other Solanaceae.

Nicotiana tabacum / robusta, TOBACCO

Highly effective people killer the smoke and extracts of nicotine most effectively kill insects and spider mites. Now considered too dangerous to use it was an early insecticide, natural and very effective against rather too many forms of life. It was dangerous sprayed without protection, and worse when burnt to fumigate a whole greenhouse, store or whatever.

Tobacco is a powerful nerve poison, one cigarettes worth can kill.

The common widespread use injured careless people so was banned. (Then a foul but lethal spray became illicitly made from cigarette |butts and soapy water but this cannot be recommended.)

Tobacco is related to potatoes and tomatoes so they have similar problems and preferences.

Crops badly damaged by Tobacco mosaic virus which spreads amongst tomatoes, peppers and many other plants.

Tobacco Ringspot virus, spread by nematodes, also invades cucurbits and many other plants both woody and herbaceous.

Tobacco Leaf Curl virus and Tobacco Etch virus spread by aphids also invades tomatoes.

May be infected by Clover Yellow Vein virus; yellow mosaic, necrosis and wilting which spreads to most Legumes and also Antirrhinum, Atriplex, Chenopodium, Coriandrum, Cucurbita, Gladiolus, Gomphrena, Nicandra, Papaver, Petunia, Proboscidea, Rubus, Spinacia, Tetragonia and Viola.

Leaf-hoppers Orosius argentatus spread Tobacco Yellow Dwarf / Bean Summer Death; yellowing and wilting. Thrips tabaci and Frankliniella occidentalis spread Tobacco Streak virus / Bean Red Node; red nodes, necrosis and red spots, also seed borne this also spreads to alfalfa, chickpea, fenugreek, Datura, sweet clover, soybean, beans and many other plants.

NITROGEN

One of the nutrients most required for plant growth and the most easily lost from the soil. Naturally replaced by growing Legumes as green manures and companions and by encouraging other micro-organisms that fix it from the air. If you apply soluble chemically based Nitrogen you first inhibit and destroy the very organisms that are supplying the equivalent of a ton of fertiliser per acre per year for free, and then encourage the proliferation of sorts that break down fertility back to Nitrogen again.

Nuphar lutea, YELLOW WATER-LILY / BRANDY-BOTTLE

Fruity scent of flowers, although no nectar, attracts Meligethes beetles as pollinators.

Nymphaea alba, WHITE WATER-LILY

Sweet fruity perfume from flowers which open at 7am
and close at 4 pm, others claim open midday. These close,
and partly submerge in evening.
One of the plants known to warm their flower heads,
these aid the Cetoniaea beetle pollinators.
A brown beetle Gaterucella nymphaeae and its brown
backed yellow-bellied larvae can strip water lily leaves and
flowers.
Leaves are also eaten from underneath by Caddis flies
who are caterpillars living in their own mandible crafted
tubular homes of litter.
A greenish brown caterpillar of the Brown China Marks
moth eats the leaves from above.
Leaves full of holes edged by decay were attacked by Hole
rot Ramularia nymphaea.

Ocimum basilicum, BASIL

One of the tastiest herbs in the garden and a shame it
needs so much warmth to do well as flavour is lost when
frozen or dried.
It has been sprayed as an emulsion against (for the smell I
suspect as doubtful it has pesticidal properties) asparagus
beetle and used as a trap plant for aphids.

Oenothera, EVENING PRIMROSE

Very good pollen provider and is attractive to night flying moths.
In emergencies this has edible but bitter roots.
Prone to the same eelworms as Phlox.

OIL

Most aromatic herbs are giving off oils to trap moisture. Dictamnus gives off so much it, allegedly, can be lit momentarily on hot days. These oils may be concentrated and then used as scents and pest repellents. Other oils from seeds and plants can be used as pesticides directly by coating pests so they cannot move, breathe or breed.

Onobrychis vicifolia, SAINFOIN / ESPARSETTE

A Leguminous plant once used as field crop and green manure.
The dried plant yields 6.25% ash containing 0.53% phosphoric acid and 1.3% lime.
Flowers said to make poor wax but delicious honey.

Ononis arvensis / repens, REST-HARROW

Exclusively fertilised by bees, though carrying no nectar.

Onopordum acanthium, COTTON THISTLE

Another plant known to warm up their flower heads to aid pollinators.
Host to Celery Fly Acidia heraclei.
The stems sustain stem boring caterpillar Myelois cribrella.

ORCHIDS

Houseplant forms can be attacked by Eelworm nematodes causing brown spots and blackened areas, which also attack ferns, Begonias, Coleus, Gloxinias and Salvias.

Origanum vulgare & species,
MARJORAM / OREGANO

All this family are beneficial with strong aromatic oil that makes them favourites in the kitchen. Best flavoured Orgeanos are sadly tender.
The golden form of Marjoram only turns yellow when the sun is warm and bright enough and makes a cheerful and beneficial ground cover.
The oil gives some control over Botrytis Grey mould.

Orobanches, BROOM-RAPES

Parasitic plants especially of brooms and clovers. O. minor mainly bothers clovers, O. rapum genistae gorse and broom, and O. ramose attacks hemp and maize.

Oxalis acetosella, WOOD SORREL

Some of this family were eaten in the past but as the name indicates these can have high levels of oxalic acid and so are risky, and they're barely palatable anyway. Interestingly these have two sets of flowers, the normal ones we observe and then hidden, cleistogamous, flowers in autumn without petals or stamens that set seed unnoticed.

Paeonia, PAEONY

These need really rich moist soil to do well and larger plants can be reluctant to bloom again for a while once moved.

Ants are often seen on the flower buds but do little harm unless they're also farming aphids.

Wilting shoots with leaves turning brown and the roots rotting but the plant somehow surviving is a sure case of the Rust Botrytis paeoniae shared in common with Lily of the Valley.

Dahlias should also be avoided because their Crown gall is thought the same Bacterium tumefaciens as the Root gall causing root deformities in paeonies.

Papaver, POPPY

Seed is edible used on breads and confectionaries.

One species is the source of opium and so may be illegal to grow in some countries. The others are all too easy to grow some becoming self seeding weeds.

Garden poppies are loved by bees for their big crop of pollen for they have no honey.

Fruit capsules are galled, though this not easily noticed as often no external sign, by Hymenopterous gall-wasp Aylax / Diplolepis papaveris and A. minor.

May be infected by Clover Yellow Vein virus; yellow mosaic, necrosis and wilting which spreads to most Legumes and also Antirrhinum, Atriplex, Chenopodium, Coriandrum, Cucurbita, Gladiolus, Gomphrena, Nicotiana, Nicandra, Petunia, Proboscidea, Rubus, Spinacia, Tetragonia and Viola.

Parietaria officinalis, PELLITORY

This nettle relation is easy to mistake for a dock family weed such as bistort.
Alternate host for many garden co-lives: leaf-hopper Eupteryx urticae Cidnorhinus quadrimaculatus, Flower beetle Brachypterus urticae, Leaf miner Agromyza anthracina, Nettle ground bug Heterogaster urticae, Common nettle capsid Liocoris tripustulatus, Large nettle aphid Microlophium carnosum Psyllid Trioza urticae.

Passiflora, PASSIONFLOWERS

These are mostly tender, and need warm rather than just frost free conditions as they're prone to root rots when cold and damp. Very thirsty in growth.
Although remarkably easy to grow these are sometimes not self fertile and need cross pollinating with another to set good crops.
Plagued by Mealy bug these are not often bothered by other pests though the usual suspects may hole their leaves.

Prone to virus diseases especially Passionfruit Woodiness virus; mosaic, blisters and distortion with woody pericarp to fruits, this may spread to your beans!

Pastinaca sativa, PARSNIP

Very slow germination, fresh seed is needed every year. The seeds have high levels of allelopathic compounds that inhibit germination of seeds of many plants and also contain antibiotics which protect them against botrytis, liquid extracts have proved protective to French beans. Foliage is attacked by Celery and Parsnip Fly Tephritis / Trypeta onopordinis.

The flowerhead of the wild species may be attacked by Dipteron gall-midge Kiefferia / Schizomyia / Asphondylia / Cecidomyia pimpinellae which causes the walls to thicken and the ovary to swell considerably, greenish yellow to purple or brown, but as parsnips are seldom flowered this does not often get seen in gardens.

The flowers attract hoverflies and predatory wasps and make a sacrificial crop against Carrot Blossom moths and also liked by Carrot Root fly Psila rosae, see carrots.

Main problem for parsnips is Canker, also called Rust, usually a mixture of diseases rotting tissues after some wound or crack allows entry especially of Bacterium carotavorum.

Leaf Spots of Ramularia pastinacae, small brown spots, rarely serious unless over-crowded.

Sclerotinia Rot can be serious, see carrots, Daucus.

Parsnips may get Downy mildew which damages leaves with pale spots whitish underneath, Powdery mildew is more common, caused by Erysiphe polygoni which has various strains for specific plants, use fresh seed and improve hygiene.

Pelargonium, not 'GERANIUMS'

Bacterial Leaf spot Bacterium pelargonii starts as watersoaked dots, irregular shaped usually and brown, the leaves yellow then go brown and finally red.
Another Leaf spot Cercospora Brunckii makes round brick coloured spots on leaves, these are slightly raised and in bad cases fused together.
Grey mould Botrytis cinerea is problem over-winter if cold and damp, often starts on petals.
Wet roots cause Black leg Pythium spp.where plants turn black from the base up.
If leaves turn sickly yellow, or pale spots appear on stem then it's the more contagious Stem Rot Fusarium pelargonii.

Penstemon

These, pretty though not very hardy, flowers grown under apples apparently repel their sawfly.

PEPPER DUST

Both black pepper and also chilli pepper are ways to discourage those larger nose guided pests from areas. This only works while dry conditions, and can cause some distress so not nice!

Petroselinum hortense, PARSLEY

Apparently toxic to parrots.
Curled leafed variety was developed to prevent accidental poisoning by Fools Parsley, Aethusa cynapium, a wild plant closely resembling the ordinary parsley.
Health giving herb for us in moderation that loves moist soil, difficult to establish or move. Let it self seed where it will.
If short of Magnesium the leaves become pale, marbled with a purplish hue.
As a camouflage plant it has often been used to mask carrots and onions from their root flies though it suffers from Carrot Root fly itself, see carrots, Daucus.
Sow parsley in meadows to attract hares as they love it.
It has been sprayed as a tea against asparagus beetles.
Like dill supposedly loved by bees especially Prosopis species, but I find it attracts more hoverflies.
Grown under roses the smell will help repel their Aphis.
Parsley seeds contain antibiotics which protect them against botrytis, liquid extracts have proved protective to French beans.

Suffers Leaf Spot Septoria petroselini causing small brown spots going white with black dots, commonly seed borne. Rust Puccinia aethusae occurs with rusty pustules under the leaves in summer and more, darker ones in autumn.

Petunia

These may protect beans from beetles.
Also believed to repel leaf-hoppers, aphids and rose chafers.
Some of the very popular P. surfinia varieties have a virus disease that causes them to weaken and do badly.
May be infected by Clover Yellow Vein virus; yellow mosaic, necrosis and wilting which spreads to most Legumes and also Antirrhinum, Atriplex, Chenopodium, Coriandrum, Cucurbita, Gladiolus, Gomphrena, Nicotiana, Nicandra, Papaver, Proboscidea, Rubus, Spinacia, Tetragonia and Viola.

Phacelia tanacetifolia

Pretty plant used as ground cover, green manure and as an attractant to many beneficial insects especially hoverflies.

Phaseolus coccineus, RUNNER BEANS

South American perennials and tender though their (poisonous) roots can be over-wintered as with Dahlias for an earlier crop.

These need pollinators or no crop though very latest varieties are becoming self fertile.

The flowers are often bitten into by buff-tailed and small earth humble bees whose tongues are too short to reach the nectar by legitimate means, this results in reduced pollination of the seeds and so flowers produce pods with fewer seeds than the standard or may just abort.

Will grow well with, and up sweet corn, which they protect from corn armyworms (US co-life).

Red spider mite can be a problem in hot dry years. Anthracnose and rarely Halo blight may attack as for French beans, see below.

Phaseolus vulgaris, DWARF / FRENCH / HARICOT / WAX-POD / SNAP / STRING / GREEN BEANS

These beans came from South America but have spread worldwide.

Mostly dwarf there are running / climbing forms of these which give more per sq. ft.

Prone to Red Spider mite in hot years and under cover.

The Bean Seed fly Delia cilicrura lays eggs in the soil close to the plants the whitish larvae tunnel into the stems and seeds, the adult is often attracted by decaying material, also attacks runner beans.

The Bean beetle Bruchus rufimanus, the Pea beetle B. pisorum and the Broad Bean beetle Acanthoscelides obtectus all cause holes and transparent patches in the seeds, the adults lay eggs on the pods and the larvae eat into the seeds, the pupae may not be noticed in saved seed and then sown with the next crop.

The Root knot eelworm can cause their roots to get galls the size of dots to as big as plums.

Parsley and parsnip seeds contain antibiotic chemicals that protect them against Botrytis, liquid extracts have proved protective to French beans. Dutch researchers have found that French beans could also be protected from Botrytis by coating them with certain yeasts. These may occur naturally when honeydew from aphid infestations on other plants drips onto them, an interesting concept in crop protection.

At Ryton Gardens they have shown that interplanting Brassicas with French beans significantly reduces pest levels on both.

Anthracnose often miscalled canker, rust or blight, Colletotrichum lindemuthianum, causes specks, spots and lesions, dark brown sunken cankers and die back on all parts, worse in wet years and under glass, spots on pods start reddish brown and enlarge, become slimy then infect the seeds, which should not be resown.

Halo Blight, Bacterium medicaginis / Pseudomonas phaseolicola is spread by rain, the semi-transparent spots on leaves surrounded by pale yellow halo, if joining together the leaves become brown and wither, even the stems may succumb and the plants wilt, also damage to seeds, this is seed carried so do not sow seeds with blisters, also attacks runner and other beans.

Root rots, Fusarium solani and others, cause plants and or crop to simply fail.

Leaf Spots Asochyta pisi, A. pinodella and Mycosphaerella pinodes cause brown spots with darker margins especially in damp weather on leaves and pods, may stunt growth, seeds become discoloured and infected and should not be resown, overwinters on debris.

Beans are infected by a huge number of viruses worldwide spread by different vectors.

Aphids spread:

Alfalafa mosaic, mottling with yellow dots, spread by fourteen species and wide range of alternate hosts.

Bean Common mosaic, green mosaic with stunting, also seed spread.

Bean Leaf Roll; mosaic and distortion, also invades other Legumes and is a problem with peas.

Bean Yellow mosaic; dark and yellow patches with bright yellow spots which also infects many other Leguminous plants and also Alpinia, Chenopodium, Gladiolus, Freesia, Babiana, Sparaxis and Tritonia. Broad Bean Wilt; yellow mosaic and distortion (also infects spinach, lettuce, pea, broad bean and other Legumes). Blackeye Cowpea mosaic; chlorosis, necrosis and wilting, also seed spread, infects most beans.

Clover Yellow Vein; yellow mosaic, necrosis and wilting which infects most other Legumes and also Antirrhinum, Atriplex, Chenopodium, Coriandrum, Cucurbita, Gladiolus, Gomphrena, Nicotiana, Nicandra, Papaver, Petunia, Proboscidea, Rubus, Spinacia, Tetragonia and Viola.
Cowpea Aphid-borne mosaic: mosaic, necrosis and wilting.
Cucumber mosaic; green mosaic and blisters (infects 800 plant species and in 19 is seed borne as well as aphid spread).
Passionfruit Woodiness; mosaic, blisters and distortion.
Pea mosaic; yellow mosaic.
Peanut Mottle; necrosis and wilting.
Soybean mosaic; green mosaic with stunting, blistering, leaf cupping, necrosis, wilting and death.
Watermelon mosaic spread by more than 20 aphid species, usual mosaic symptoms plus pods mottle and distort, also infects many cucurbits and Legumes.
Whiteflies spread:
Melon Leaf Curl virus spread also invades Cucurbits.
Bemesia tabaci spreads Bean Golden mosaic; golden mosaic and stunting, also infects wild Legumes.
Same whitefly spreads Bean Dwarf mosaic; yellow mosaic and stunting, found on weeds Sida spinosa and S. rhombifolia. Euphorbia mosaic; necrotic lesions and distortion, also infects lentil, soybean and other Legumes.
Rhynchosia mosaic; yellowing and stunting.
Beetles spread:

Bean Curly Dwarf mosaic; mosaic, stunting and rugosity, also infects other Phaseolus species, soybean, pea, chickpea, lentil, broad bean, mung bean and Leguminous weeds.

Bean Mild mosaic; green mosaic.

Bean Pod Mottle; mosaic and rugosity.

Bean Rugose mosaic; mosaic with severe rugosity.

Bean Southern mosaic; green mosaic with rugocity also infects soybeans, cowpeas, peas and other Legumes.

Blackgram Mottle; mottling and distortion.

Cowpea Chlorotic Mottle / Bean Yellow Stipple; yellow spots and slight stunting, also affects other Legumes.

Leaf-hoppers spread:

Beet Curly Top; curling, yellowing and stunting, mostly a problem in arid regions where it infects a wide range of plants.

One, Orosius argentatus, is especially feared in tobacco farming areas as it spreads Tobacco Yellow Dwarf / Bean Summer Death; yellowing and wilting.

Nematodes especially of genus Xiphinema spread:

Tobacco Ringspot; mosaic, necrosis with stunting, can spread to large range of woody and herbaceous plants, -as can Tomato Ringspot; another mosaic, necrosis and stunting.

Thrips tabaci and Frankliniella occidentalis spread Tobacco Streak virus / Bean Red Node; red nodes, necrosis and red spots, also seed borne this also affects alfalfa, chickpea, fenugreek, Datura, sweet clover, soybean, Nicotiana, other beans and many plants.

Fungi, chytrid Olpidium Brassicae, spread Tobacco Necrosis / Stipple Streak to beans; necrosis with stunting, also affects wide range of shrubby and herbaceous plants. Unknown vectors spread Tobacco mosaic virus to beans; necrotic local lesions, yellowish green blotches, leaves crinkle, turn down and deform.

PHEROMONES

Smells that are usually too faint for us to notice but carry messages to other forms of life. Many are employed by insects trying to find mates, we now use some of these to make sticky traps more effective. Some pheromones are mimmicked by plants in the same way to attract specific insects for pollination, and less subtle attractants may be used such as the smell of rotting meat as well as sweet honey like perfumes. Other pheromones may give instructions such as when the smell of a bee stinging incites others to do the same instantly. Sage-brush which has high levels of methyl jasmonate shortly after it is attacked by pests has been found to then initiate production of high levels of their own protective chemicals in tomato plants nearby.

Phleum pratense, TIMOTHY/ CAT'S-TAIL GRASS

Eaten with relish by cows, horses and sheep.

Phlox

Very prone to nematode problems, unusually live in the stem and the leaves not the roots so take care if propagating, another or same is common with Oenothera Evening primrose so these should be kept apart.
Cuckoo spit may be troublesome in hot dry years.

Phragmites australis / communis REED

The inflorescence stalk is attacked by Dipteron chloropid Lipara lucens / Lasioptera arundinis which cuases a greenish yellow torpedo shaped gall up to two or three inches long containing a single larvae, in autumn these turn brown and are enveloped by leaves, the new fly emerges and lays soon after so fresh galls form year round, the larva may be parasitised by Pteromalus spp. Chalcid wasps and by Polemon liparae braconids, often the vacated gall becomes a nest for other critters especially of Prosopis pectoralis a small black solitary bee which in turn may be parasitised by two ichneumon wasps, Gasteruption spp. and Chrysis cyanea the ruby-tailed wasp.

Phyteuma tenerum, ROUND-HEADED RAMPION

The flowers are attacked by Coleopteran weevil Miarus campanulae / campanulata which causes the ovary to swell into a gall, often lopsided, containing one or two larvae.

Phytophora infestans, BLIGHT

Fungal blight of potatoes, also affects tomatoes, worst in warm wet summers and from over-wintered volunteer tubers. Spacing, effective earthing up and removal of haulm once an infection starts will produce a crop most years, growing early varieties gives lower yield but crop before blight starts.

Many different trees, raspberries, sunflowers and cucurbits may make potatoes more prone to this disease. Growing cannabis sativa may deter blight but will encourage interest in your horticultural endeavours from the local constabulary.

Allium, nettle and Equisetum and seaweed sprays may offer some protection.

Picea excelsa / abies, NORWAY SPRUCE

Seldom found above 2000ft. line.

Leaf bases galled to form a pseudocone by Homoterous aphid Adelges abietis / A. allarumabietis / Chermes / Sacchiplantesf, this odd gall may be found on Christmas trees and may also gall Sitka spruce, P. sitchensis which is also galled similarly by Gilletteela cooleyi aphids which migrate to Douglas fir.

Spruce may also be galled by Cnaphalodes spp. heteroecious with larch.

The stumps often grow Staghorn fungi Calocera viscosa which are club shaped, springy and slimy.

Gelatinous tongue shaped bracket fungi Pseudohydnum gelatinosum / Tremellodon gelatinosus of white through blue to brown with soft dense teeth on the underside grow on the stumps, and also on those of pines.

The edible and tasty Boletus / Leccinum / Krombholzia piceum with a rusty brownish orange cap is found under spruces.

Another Boletus the edible and tasty Boletus / Xerocomus / Ixocomus badius with a chestnut chocolate brown cap, whitish flesh, often found on roots, stumps and fallen cones.

The litter grows the very tasty edible Boletus edulis / bulbosus with a light grey to brown cap, sweet white flesh, most often found on acid soils.

Very similar to, and often found with, the last mentioned is Tylopilus / Boletus felleus which has acrid pinkish flesh and is inedible.

Another fungus found in the litter are Fairy Clubs Clavariadelphus / Clavaria ligula much resembling small yellowish clubs, inedible and very bitter.

Two Russula species are common in spruce forests, R. foetens with a yellowy brown cap resembles Boletus edulis when young but is bitter and inedible, once older the mushrooms stink of burnt oil. R. achroleuca has a smoother yellower cap and an even more bitter acrid taste. R. paludosa with a rose or strawberry coloured to orangey yellow cap is considered edible, it prefers damp pine or spruce forests, peat bogs and the company of bilberries.

Lactarius deliciosus is found in grassy mossy litter under spruce, it has an orangey red cap with green stains, if cut it has a carrot coloured sap which turns green as it dries, it is edible, tasty and traditionally pickled in vinegar for its spicy flavour.

Spruce and birch woods are 'home' to Fly Agaric, the classic fairy tale magic mushroom, red with white flecks, Amanita muscaria and the similarly poisonous A. regalis with a liver coloured cap.

Often found in spruce and pine woods is another Amanita, spissa, this has a greyish cap with grey warts, it smells of raw potatoes and is not poisonous but too risky to consider as it so resembles the more poisonous species.

Clitocybe odora, edible, is found in needle litter, it has a coppery blueish green cap and smells of fennel or aniseed when fresh. C. inversa, edible, also likes deep rotting needle litter, it has an orangey yellow to red cap, often found in clusters or even circles.

Tricholoma argyraceum has a brown grey cap with yellowish gills, it is found in late autumn, often on the edge of forests and has a floury smell.

The well known edible Horse mushroom Agaricus / Psalliota arvensis has a white cap, greyish gills and a slight scent of aniseed, if scratched the flesh turns yellow, also found in meadows and fields (the inedible and similar Yellow stainer Agaricus / Psalliota xanthodermus / xanthoderma is yellow at the base of the stipe and smells of carbolic).

Pluteus atromarginatus, edible, grows on stumps and rotting wood, it has a light to dark grey or brownish cap and streaked stipe, the gills start white then go pink with red spores and have black margin, also found on pines.

Cortinarius / Myxacium caeruleipes is edible but unpalatable, has a brownish olive cap, yellow to brown spores and the light purple stipe has the remains of a gelatinous veil left on it as little fibrils, it smells of raw potatoes.

Picris hieracioides, HAWKWEED OX TONGUE

Blooms visited by at least twenty seven, another reference 29 different insect species: 3 butterflies and moths, 16 species bee, 9 species Diptera flies and 1 other.

PIERIS BRASSICAE, CABBAGE WHITES

Large, White and Green Veined butterflies, most serious pests of Brassica family. Do NOT destroy small yellow silky cocoons as these contain the Ichneumon Fly Microgaster glomeratus who will lay about sixty eggs in a Large White caterpillar parasitising it. Another Ichneumon Fly Pteromalus Brassicae lays up to two hundred and fifty eggs on the newly formed chrysalis parasitizing it. Wasps also predate these caterpillars, particularly of the Small White.

Pimpinella anisum, ANISE

A pungent seeded annual herb, used in cooking and in ointments against insects, their bites and stings.
A host to predatory wasps it deters aphids and reduces cabbage worm attacks.

Pimpinella saxifraga, BURNET-SAXIFRAGE

The blooms attract 23 insect species: 0 Lepidoptera, 3 species bee, 8 species Diptera flies and 12 other.
The flowerhead may be attacked by Dipteron gall-midge Kiefferia / Schizomyia / Asphondylia / Cecidomyia pimpinellae which causes the walls to thicken and the ovary to swell considerably, greenish yellow to purple or brown

Pinguicula, BUTTERWORTS

Leaves are covered with sticky hairs to catch small insects.

Pinus, PINES

Bark is very acidic ph 3.4-3.8. Not much grows under pine trees!
They inhibit composting and most plants but mulches of their needles discourage slugs and snails.
Gelatinous tongue shaped bracket fungi Pseudohydnum gelatinosum / Tremellodon gelatinosus of white through blue to brown with soft dense teeth on the underside grow on the stumps and also on spruces.

Boletus fungi especially the edible and tasty Boletus / Leccinum / Krombholzia vulpinum with a rusty brownish orange cap found underneath pines. Another Boletus the edible and tasty Boletus / Xerocomus / Ixocomus badius with a chestnut chocolate brown cap, whitish flesh, often found on roots, stumps and fallen wood. Yet another Boletus the edible and tasty Boletus / Suillus / Ixocomus variegatus with a yellowish brown cap, whitish flesh is often found in large numbers where soil is acid and sandy. Pine forests also grow edible Gomphidius mushrooms, G. rutlus / viscidus with yellow, orange or brown caps and flesh which turn pinkish as these dry.

In dry weather in pine forests mushrooms are seldom found though Russula lepida is an exception, with a vermillion pink cap with a bloom and a distinct taste (it is inedible) of menthol and resin. R. emetica is similar in appearance but preferring moister conditions, this has a strong fruity smell, although poisonous raw some have claimed it is harmless once cooked. R. paludosa with a rose or strawberry coloured to orangey yellow cap is considered edible, it prefers damp pine or spruce forests, peat bogs and the company of bilberries.

Lactarius pinicola is often found under pines, it has an orangey red cap with circular markings, it is edible, however the similar L. torminosus is slightly poisonous, easier to identify is another edible species L. volemus which bleeds lots of 'milk' when young, this smells of pickled herrings!

Often found in spruce and pine woods is Amanita spissa, this has a greyish cap with grey warts, it smells of raw potatoes and is not poisonous but too risky to consider as it so resembles the more poisonous species.

Clitocybe clavipes, edible, is found most often in mossy litter under larch but also in pine and oak woods, it has a browny black to olive green cap and smells of bitter almonds. C. inversa, edible, also likes deep rotting needle litter, it has an orangey yellow to red cap, often found in clusters or even circles.

Tricholomopsis / Tricholoma rutilans, edible, grows on the stumps, it has a yellowish cap covered in reddish scales with a yellow and red stipe. Tricholoma saponaceum, inedible, comes with caps in shades of every colour, all fading to red as the caps mature, these also smell of soap. Black pines on calcareous soil are associated with the edible Tricholoma terreum with a greyish or grey brown cap which has the scent and flavour of raw potatoes and one of the last mushrooms found each year. Other late species are the similar looking and edible T. portentosum and T. flavovirens though the last has browner more yellowish cap, both have a floury smell and are found most on sandy soils.

Hygrophorus / Limacium hypothejus / hypothejum / vitellum, edible, brownish cap and yellow gills and stipe, is nearly always found under pines.

Pluteus atromarginatus, edible, grows on stumps and rotting wood, it has a light to dark grey or brownish cap and streaked stipe, the gills start white then go pink with red spores and have a black margin, also found on spruces.

Cortinarius / Myxacium mucosus / mucosum is edible but unpalatable, has a brownish olive cap, yellow to brown spores and the stipe has the remains of a gelatinous veil left on it as little fibrils, it smells of raw potatoes.

The Common Earth-ball Scleroderma citrinum / aurantium, inedible, is very aromatic with a spicy smell, the fruit is round and white when young going brownish with a scaly appearance as the dark green spores are released, it is found in many woods but especially those on sandy soils.

Pinus lauricio-nigricans, AUSTRIAN PINE

Rust fungus Basidiomycete Coleosporium secionis spends part of its life on Scots and Austrian pines alternating with groundsel and cultivated cinerarias.

Pinus sylvestris, SCOT'S PINE

Shown to have mycorrhizal associations with 119 fungal partners to enable them to thrive in poor soils.

In alkaline soils their roots contain less resin than in acid soils and are more easily damaged by pathogenic fungi. Twigs are galled by acarine gall-mite Eriophyes pini which cause stems to swell into fatter lumps.

Pisum sativum, PEAS

Have a high requirement for Manganese and may get
Marsh Spot if deficient shown by seeds having dark rusty
patch on cotyledons, worse in over-limed and unbalanced
soils, seaweed sprays alleviate this.
Root exudates from peas increase availability of N, P, K
and Ca.
The large green Pea aphid Acyrthosiphon / Macrosiphum
pisum / pisi feeds on leaves and stems, can wither the
growing tips in summer, and spreads Mosaic virus.
The Bean beetle Bruchus rufimanus / granaria, the Pea
beetle B. pisorum and the Broad Bean beetle
Acanthoscelides obtectus all cause holes and transparent
patches in the seeds, the adults lay eggs on the pods and
the larvae eat into the seeds, the pupae may not be
noticed in saved seed and then sown with the next crop.
The Pea and Bean weevil Sitrona lineata and spp. eat
notches from the shoots and young leaves, as they are
brownish the small adults are difficult to see especially as
they often eat from the underside of leaves, the adults
overwinter in the soil and lay eggs on the roots of most
Leguminous plants but these cause little damage.
The Pea Midge Contarina pisi has small white jumping
larvae which usually eat flowers, terminal buds and also
the pods.

Pea and Bean thrips Kakothrips robustus / pisirorus causes silvering of the leaves and pods, the adults are black and tiny, the larvae yellowish, in large numbers these may stunt growth. Thrips do other damage to peas; often they start attacks at ground level on the stem stunting seedlings, destroying growing points, distorting growth and turning pods brown.

Very similar symptoms are caused by Pea eelworm nematodes Heterodera schachtii and Anguillulina dipsaci. All aerial parts galled by nematode eelworm Tylenchus devastatrix, this causes considerable distortions, weakening and stunting.

The Pea Moth Laspeyresia nigricana gives those most annoying small greenish white grubs in the peas, very early and very late crops often miss this as the moth is flying in midsummer.

If you are growing peas for the first time on 'virgin' soil then use commercially supplied Legume inocculant or compost containing pea residues to ensure the right fungi and bacteria are available.

Pea Wilts, Fusarium oxysporum, F. pisi, F. redolens, and F. solani strains, are seen as wilting, often at flowering time with the leaves greying and yellowing, tthen the leaves roll from the edges, if the stem is slit there is an orangey red discolouration inside, this is serious and needs burning with the roots and no peas growing there for five years! Soils containing Fusarium equiseti and other strains produce highly phytotoxic substances causing scorching of foliage and reduced growth of pea stems. Roots may also rot when attacked by F. solani, and also by Aphanomyces euteiches, and Black-Root rot Thielaviopsis basicola, all of which are worse in poor soil conditions especially excessive wet.

Powdery mildew, Erysiphe polygoni, powdery white deposits, also attacks swedes and turnips, but in different strains to peas, most serious late in season and especially in dry summers, this has been controlled by powdered ginger and sweet flag extracts (which also stimulated vigour).

Downy Mildew, Perenopspora viciae, greyish furry growth, seldom a problem save in very wet years.

Pod and Leaf Spots, Ascochyta pisi, A. pinodella and Mycosphaerella pinodes, spread by infected seeds and on debris, worse in wet seasons, improve hygiene and do not save seed.

Grey Mould, Botrytis cinerea, common grey furry mould worse in wet seasons and over-crowded plants, improve hygiene.

Peas suffer many viruses:

Pea mosaic; yellow mosaic virus, also attacks beans, sweet peas, pale green yellowing and mottling of leaves, white spots between veins and deformation, and 'breaking' of flowers, spread by aphid Acyrthosiphon pisi.

Bean Leaf Roll virus can also attack peas where it is more serious than for beans.

Broad Bean Wilt virus; yellow mosaic and distortion spreads to lettuce, spinach, broad bean and other Legumes.

Clover Yellow Vein virus; yellow mosaic, necrosis and wilting which spreads to most other Legumes and also Antirrhinum, Atriplex, Chenopodium, Coriandrum, Cucurbita, Gladiolus, Gomphrena, Nicotiana, Nicandra, Papaver, Petunia, Proboscidea, Rubus, Spinacia, Tetragonia and Viola.

And can be infected by Bean Curly Dwarf mosaic; mosaic, stunting and rugosity, also spreads to other Phaseolus species, soybean, chickpea, lentil, broad bean, mung bean and Leguminous weeds.

Bean Southern mosaic; green mosaic with rugocity also spreads to soybeans, cowpeas and other Legumes

Plantago, PLANTAINS

Hosts for many plant pests over-winter especially Myzus ascalonius aphids which attack strawberries and shallots and the common Stem Eelworm Tylenchus devastatrix.

Shoots get invaded by bacterium Corynebacterium fascians which causes fasciation, stems become broad, flattened and ribbed, splayed and curved this spreads to jasmine, dandelions, Chrysanthemums, dogwood, Cotoneaster, Euphorbias, Forsythia, Hibiscus, Holly and Inula.

Plantago lanceolata, RIBWORT PLANTAIN

Accumulates Cobalt, Copper and Magnesium.
The inflorescence sustains Tortrix paleana / icterana forming a loose gall only noticeable by swelling of flower spike, inside up to half a dozen larvae live until they emerge in midsummer leaving their pupal skins stuck between undeveloped flowers.
The leaf-blade is attacked by nematodes Anguillulina dipsaci which cause swellings between the veins and loss of chlorophyl, the nematodes escape when leaves decay, this nematode attacks and galls nearly three hundred different plants.
The plants are attacked by Coleopteran weevils Gymnetron pascuorum whose larvae cause galls to develop.

Plantago major, GREAT PLANTAIN

Wind pollinated.

Accumulates Calcium, Copper, Iron, Potassium and Silica.

Poa annua, ANNUAL MEADOW GRASS

Annual weed and source of nematodes that attack many crop and ornamental plants especially Stem Eelworm Tylenchus devastatrix.

Poa nemoralis, WOOD MEADOW GRASS

The stem is attacked by Dipteron gall-midge Poamyia poae / Hormomyia causing it to split and many dozens of adventitious roots form in two neat rows, envelop and interlace to form an oval shape about a third of an inch long, light green or brown, often the stem bends at this point, larva lives and pupates inside.

Poa pratensis, BLUE-GRASS / SMOOTH-STALKED MEADOW-GRASS

Eaten by cows and horses, not so readily by sheep.

Poa trivialis, ROUGHISH / ROUGH-STALKED MEADOW GRASS

Cows, horses and sheep eat this readily.

POLLEN

Apart from obvious utility this is used by plants, especially maize, timothy grass and hawkweeds, to inhibit the growth or germination of other plants and possibly to alter the behaviour of animals. The pollen of some, such as that of bracken, is carcinogenic, and that of Lilium longifolium can kill cats. Pollen plants are as essential for many insects including bees as are nectar producers.

POLLINATION

Many crops are totally dependent on pollination but cannot sustain their pollinators year round thus to ensure pollinators then other plants need be grown to carry these between crops by providing other necessities for their life cycles.

Polygonatum odoratum, SOLOMON'S SEAL

Suffers from greyish Sawfly slug worms Phymatocera aterrima which strip the stems bare almost overnight, plants in shade may escape serious attack, most are devastated but some recover.
The bird-dropping-like slug of the Lily beetle Lilloceris lilli, a bright reddy orange rather smart looking beastie, also destroys the leaves, this usually eats lilies, lily of the valley, hollyhocks, Hostas, potatoes and tobacco.

Polygonum amphibium, AMPHIBIOUS BISTORT

The leaf-blade is attacked by Dipteron gall-midge Wachtiella / Cecidomyia / Dasyneura persicariae which rolls the leaves and swells them to many times their original thickness and turns them spongy and greenish yellow, orange, pink, and purple or red near the petiole.

Polygonum arvensis, KNOTGRASS

Accumulates Nitrogen and Silica.
Host for pests over winter and source of nematodes that attack many crop and ornamental plants.

Blooms have little honey and are seldom visited by insects.

Polygonum fagopyrum, BEECH-WHEAT

I believe this is old names for Fagopyrum esculentum, BUCKWHEAT, especially as bees said to make good wax but poor honey on it.

Polygonum persicaria, REDSHANK / PERSICARIA / SPOTTED PERSICARY

Analysis of dry matter, as % - N 3.12, P 1.16, K 3.12, Ca 4.93 Na 2.53, Crude ash 10.58.
Leaf-blade attacked by Dipteron gall-midge Wachtiella / Cecidomyia / Dasyneura persicariae which rolls the leaves and swells them to many times their original thickness and turns them spongy and greenish yellow, orange, pink, and purple or red near the petiole.

Populus, POPLAR

Seldom grows above 1,600ft line.
Big trees, not good companions near buildings or drains, make excellent shelter belts further away.
Foliage was pruned for fodder for stock.
Resinous exudations used by bees for propolis.

Not good near lettuces as winter host for Lettuce Root aphid.

Most poplars leaf-mid-ribs get attacked by Homopteran aphid Pemphigus filaginis, this forms a swelling nearly an inch long and half as wide, on the upper surface of a major vein or midrib, underneath is a matching groove, starts greenish yellow turning reddish later, in summer the aphids move to various members of the Compositae. The leaf-blade, flowers and even the fruits get galled by an ascomycete fungus Ascomyces aureus / Exoascus / populi / Taphrina / populina which makes the beautiful (when seen en masse) Gold leaf, a pouch swelling usually on the upper but sometimes on the lower surface lined with the gold mycelium, the galls often coalesce and vary in size from half to one and a half inches, the mycelium is often a food soiurce for Psyllids.

Wood especially deadwood consumed by Goat Moth Cossus ligniperda.

The trunks, stumps and large branches, dead and alive, support a semi-circular bracket fungus Polyporus / Polyporellus squamosus, brown scales with white edible flesh smelling of cucumber, this grows quickly can reach many pounds in weight but harms trees causing the wood to decay with timber White rot, also grows on beech, horse chestnut, lime, willow and walnut.

Although the edible Oyster mushroom Pleurotus ostreatus can be found on almost any decaying deciduous tree stumps it is most often found on poplar and commercially it's grown on poplar wood, with a grey or blueish grey cap, once cooked it has a pleasant fish like taste, and is one of the few mushrooms that may be found in winter.

Pholiota destruens, inedible, slimy beige to brown caps with numerous whitish scales, brownish gills with ragged edges, bitter with strong mushroom smell, is often found on stumps, dead and live wood, and also on willows.

Populus alba, ABELE / WHITE POPLAR

Young stems attacked by Lepidopteran moth Gypsonoma aceriana / Hedya / Spilonota which usually makes one gall per stem, about an inch or just under long, the caterpillar eats at the pith and pushes its droppings out a hole and some stick on the stem, after the causer has left the stem may continue in growth in the same direction without branching but the gall often cracks the stem longitudinally and the cavity may enlarge and be used by other critters or become infected by disease.

Populus aurora candicans

Attractive to some, variegated, tree very prone to surface running roots and shooting suckers up everywhere to the point of being a weed a seriously bad choice within running distance of any building or drain.

Populus x canadensis var. serotina, BLACK ITALIAN POPLAR

Often used in wet situations as more tolerant than most trees.
This has leaf glands at the union of blade and petiole attacked by acarine gall-mite Eriophyes diversipunctatus which causes them to swell, sometimes up to half an inch across and turning red.

Populus nigra var. italica, LOMBARDY POPLAR

The lower leaf petioles are attacked by Homopteran aphid Pemphigus bursarius / Aphioides / Byrsocrypta which forms a Purse gall, a lop sided urn shaped pouch about two thirds of an inch long with a beak shaped end often split and exuding a white fur or powder, in late summer the galls become reddish brown, coated with honeydew and cast skins, the, all female, aphids move to Compositae such as lettuce and sow-thistle where they infest the roots without causing galls, reproduce parthenogenetically, then return to the poplars where they produce male and females who leave over-wintering eggs on the bark, seldom more than a couple form on any petiole, these aphids are an important food source for many critters particularly Diptera such as the chamaemyid Leucopis bursaria.

The leaf petiole is also galled by Homopteran aphid Pemphigus spirothecae / affinis, this forms a Spiral gall, a distorted ribbon shaped spiral of several turns touching but not fused, about a third of an inch long, dark green to red and chocolate, the mother aphid gives rise to thirty or so offfspring in summer which then reproduce in turn a month later, these leave the gall and lay eggs on the bark, these hatch into males and females, the latter lay over-wintering eggs, the cavity is then often colonised by saprophytic moulds Penicillium glaucum and Cladosporium herbarum. .

Populus tremula, ASPEN

The leaf petiole is attacked by Dipteron gall-midge Syndiplosis petioli, a gall forms somewhat resembling the pouch gall made by aphid Pemphigus bursarius but pear not urn shaped and the escape hole is round and flush whereas the aphids leave a gaping hole lined with white fur. Rarely more than one or two found per petiole.

The leaf-blade is attacked by Dipteron gall-midge Harmandia globuli / tremulae, the gall is a smooth thimble shape and in colour and shape resembles the egg of the puss-moth Cerura vinula, it is about an eighth of an inch across each way and usually only in small numbers up to a dozen per leaf, found on the top surface attached to a main vein with a concavity underneath, starts yellow and goes to red then purple through summer.

Several Boletus fungi grow on Aspens especially the edible and tasty Boletus / Leccinum / Krombholzia aurantiacus / aurantiacum / aurantiaca with a red orange cap, greyish pink flesh, also found on birch.

Portulaca, PURSLANE

Accumulates Calcium, Nitrogen, Phosphorous, Potassium and Sulphur.

Richest plant source of omega 3 oils essential for animal nutrition, very good hen food.

POTASSIUM

Potash, after Nitrogen the nutrient soonest lost from soil. Essential for disease resistance and fruiting so wood ashes should be eagerly sought and used. Gooseberries and cooking apples show shortage soonest. Leeks and celeriac need plenty, tobacco accumulates it, as do tansy and sunflowers. Rock potash, seaweed products, poultry manure and urine are rich sources.

Potentilla, CINQUEFOIL

These are vigorous weeds with many cousins, many resemble wild strawberries, and mistaken for a wild variety are sometimes 'rescued', given a nice spot and run rampant without ever, of course, fruiting.

Potentilla anserina, SILVERWEED

Accumulates Calcium, Iron and Magnesium.

Potentilla erecta, TORMENTIL

Aerial branches galled by Hymenopteran gall-wasp Xestophanes brevitarsis / tormentilae which cause swelling and distortion eventually turning brown.

Potentilla reptans, CREEPING CINQUEFOIL

Rhizome and petiole galled by Hymenopteran gall-wasp Xestophanes potentillae / Cyips / Aylax / abbreviatus / splendens which form swellings like beads on a string, green becoming pink then brown.

Poterium sanguisorba, SALAD BURNET

Wind pollinated, edible, accumulates Magnesium.

Primula, POLYANTHUS / AURICULA etc.

Although primula and cowslip flowers have ben used for flavouring wine some can cause irritation to mammals, P. obconica is notorious for causing dermatitis.
Disappearance, sudden, or slow death is probably Vine weevils.
Serious debility though is Root aphids PentAphis auriculae, these are pale greeny white and mealy, their covering the roots causes foliage to yellow and wilt.
Leaf-hoppers Erythroneura pallidifrons, pale yellow or white, eighth inch long, active insects may do some damage causing bleached areas on leaves, also found on Calceolarias, Fuchsias, Salvias, and Verbenas.

Proboscidea louisianica, UNICORN / DEVIL'S CLAW

Claimed medical uses.
US weed which may be infected by Clover Yellow Vein virus; yellow mosaic, necrosis and wilting which then infects most Legumes and also Antirrhinum, Atriplex, Chenopodium, Coriandrum, Cucurbita, Gladiolus, Gomphrena, Nicotiana, Nicandra, Papaver, Petunia, Rubus, Spinacia, Tetragonia and Viola.

Prunus, STONE FRUITS & others

Large genus with many common associated co-lives, these have been entered with those species most likely to have them, but bear in mind that there is a continuous drift to and from others in this genus.
Although most Stone fruits love lime, too much may cause pale green leaves with a yellowish tinge from a shortage of available Iron.
Many have glands at base of leafstalk providing 'nectar' to ants and other 'friends'.
Beware any variety bred as a pretty double flowered form as these often have no nectar or pollen and help few insects.
All are safest pruned in summer to avoid the fungal Silver-leaf disease.

Prunus amygdalus, ALMOND

Never plant sweet almonds near to peaches, nectarines or bitter almonds or their nuts may not be sweet but bittter. See P. persica peach below as these two are very similar, in particular their foliage is attacked by Peach leaf curl fungus ascomycete Taphrina / Exoascus / deformans, causing flattening and elongation of leaves, these forming baggy pouches usually bright red, then falling early.

Prunus armeniaca, APRICOT

These fruit on spurs more like apples so though they may crop as bushes they're easily fan trained on warm walls and thus often suffer many more co-lives including 'greenhouse' ones.

Commonly find Aphids, Mussel scale, Webspinning sawflies (sic), Capsids, and especially when on walls Red Spider mites.

Apricots tend to get symptomatic Die-back that simply needs pruning out.

Shot holes start as brown spots become holes and later form scabs and spots on shoots and fruits which ooze gum.

Mosaic virus transmitted by aphids mottles the leaves yellow and they may become brittle (to be sure it's not Iron deficiency, if the virus the symptoms will remain unaffected by seaweed sprays).

Prunus avium, GEAN / MAZZARD / WILD CHERRY

One of the main ancestors of SWEET CHERRIES
These make big trees, and the surface running roots make them no friends to lawns, paths or drives!
Cherries sometimes suffer from interveinal yellowing due to a shortage of available manganese.
A total lack of fruit may be a lack of pollination as Cherries are most tricky however almost any sweet variety can be pollinated by a Morello if in flower at the same time.
Flowers often ruined by wet weather causes them to rot and let in several diseases. The fruits also split easily when rain follows a dry spell while swelling.
From the point of view of securing the crop the only co-life worth considering is the birds.
Cherries suffer Capsids and Mussel scale (see under Malus) and the same Sawflies that bother pears and plums also attack cherries, see pears.
If our climate warms more the Cherry Fruit fly Rhagoletis cerasi may become more common in the UK though seldom seen here at current time, it lay it's white maggots in the fruits which go soft and brown around the stalk and rotten inside, the maggots drop to pupate in the ground overwinter.

Terminal leaves are attacked by Homopteran aphid Cherry Black-fly Myzus cerasi, eggs overwinter in bark and aphids start on new leaves and apical buds causing distorted, reddened, folded and crumpled leaves, even halting the growth entirely, in summer these aphids move onto Galium spp. bedstraws and Veronica speedwells then return to lay eggs in autumn. Cherries may crop despite suffering these devastating attacks, and the aphid attack often 'turns into' ladybirds, which go on to patrol the rest of the garden.

The Cherry Fruit moth Argyresthia curvella / nitidella caterpillars, clear green with brown head, enter the flowerbuds and eat those and the fruitlets, fall to ground pupate and energe within two months to lay eggs in bark crevices and bud scales, the larvae emerge in two batches, some immediately when they eat till they overwinter in silk cocoons hidden in the bark, and another set that wait to hatch later in spring.

Cherry Bark Tortrix Enarmonia formosana is a pink caterpillar tunneling under the bark, may also attack apple, pear and plum trees especially those in decline. Gummosis seen as gloop oozing from cracks in the bark with yellowing leaves and dieback may be Bacterial Canker, Pseudomonas mors-prunorum & P. prunicola often made worse by water logging especially on acid or heavy land, infection occurs in autumn through wounds and kills twigs, stems even branches, the first sign may be yellowing withering leaves often upwards curling.

Cherry Leaf Spot / Cherry Blight / Shot-hole disease Blumeriella jaapi / Cylindrosporium padi / Coccomyces hiemalis is a fungal disease common in US and Europe mostly on Sour cherries, overwinters on fallen leaves, infection can cause early leaf fall even before the cherries ripen.

Shot Hole Disease (not Shot-hole disease above) Clasterosporium carpophilum casues small round holes in the leaves and sunken red rimmed spots on the fruit which then shrivels, it overwinters in lesions on stems and may cause premature leaf fall.

The fruits and flowers are attacked by Brown Rot Sclerotinia fructigena & S. laxa, may attack leaves then cause Blossom Wilt, next, on flowers and rots fruit, see Malus.

Cherries are often badly attacked by Blossom Wilt Sclerotinia laxa with flowers and leaves dying with no obvious cause even buds remaining unopened and all looking as if scorched.

Cherries suffer Gloeosporium Rot Gloeosporium fructigenum and other species where the fruits turn brown and shrivelled on the tree or in store, it is a fungal infection living on small cankers on the shoots which shower spores onto the fruits.

Rarely the leaves suffer Cherry Leaf Scorch Gnomonia erythrostoma turning yellow then brown and hang on all winter to re-infect the next crop in spring, the fruits may get small hard black spots in the flesh, wild trees often harbour this disease.

Cherry Leaf Curl Taphrina cerasi is similar fungal attack to peach leaf curl and causes discolooured leaves, early leaf fall and a Witches Broom effect in cherries with stems proliferating where a leading bud was stunted.

Silverleaf disease Stereum purpureum is not such a big problem for cherries as for plums, poor growth, die back and poor cropping are indications but the confirming sign is that silvery look to the leaves in summer when an air gap forms under the membrane, fruitng bodies later form on affected branches.

Cherries are often invaded by viruses unnoticed.

Leaf Roll virus can kill mature trees which often 'seem to have died of drought'.

Tatter Leaf virus appears in early years, it's spread on pollen, symptoms disappear but cropping may be reduced up to 50% for life.

Little Cherry virus appears in many varieties especially Waterloo, often in Kanzan.

Rasp-Leaf virus is a lethal combination of two less virulent viruses, the result of soil borne infection carried by nematode eelworms; Prune Dwarf, itself pollen spread, combined with either Raspberry Ringspot or Arabis Mosaic. Either these also appears in raspberries and strawberries and the Arabis Mosaic in blackcurrants. And Prune Dwarf also causes Sour Cherry Yellows, six weeks after flowering leaves yellow and shed, often after warm days and cool nights.

Prunus cerasifera, MYROBALAN PLUM

Reliable insipid fruit, the bushes make good informal hedges and sacrificial crops to other fruits.

Prunus cerasus, SOUR CHERRY

More slender and twiggy than Sweet cherries these may also be pruned more easily and less riskily, self fertile. One of the few succulent fruits that may not eaten by wasps if others are available.
Cherry Leaf Spot / Cherry Blight / Shot-hole disease Blumeriella jaapi / Cylindrosporium padi / Coccomyces hiemalis is a fungal disease common in US and Europe mostly on Sour cherries, overwinters on fallen leaves, infection can cause early leaf fall even before the cherries ripen.
Morello Sour cherries in particular often badly attacked by Blossom Wilt Sclerotinia laxa with flowers and leaves dying with no obvious cause, even killing unopened flower buds, all looking much like they have been scorched. This often follows wet weather.
Cherries suffer Gloeosporium Rot Gloeosporium fructigenum and other spp. where the fruits turn brown and shrivelled on the tree or in store, it is a fungal infection living on small cankers on the shoots which shower spores onto the fruits.

Silverleaf disease Stereum purpureum is seldom such a big problem for cherries as for plums; poor growth, die back and poor cropping are indications but the confirming sign is a silvery look to the leaves in summer when an air gap forms under the membrane, fruiting bodies later form on affected branches.

Prunus domestica, PLUM / DAMSON / GAGE

These need some lime in their soil.
In years that escape the frosts all the plum family tend to crop so heavily they break branches and or exhaust the tree so thin early with shears if necessary before the fruits swell, or prop the branches if that's too late.
Fruit Gumming is caused by stressful conditions such as hot and dry, with the fruits oozing a clear chewy gum in droplets and leaving gummy lumps when cooked.
Keep away from Anemones as share a common fungal disease.
US reports garlic protects them from their Curculio beetles.
Birds and Wasps are always troublesome to the sweeter fruits and leave us the sour and unripe.

The common, annoying, co-life is maggots in the fruits. Whitish greeny yellowish with a brown or orange head is the Plum Sawfly Hoplocampa minuta and H. flava which lay in the flowers and the larvae, creamy white with yellow brown head, eat inside the fruitlets, destroying up to five apiece, then fall and pupate in the soil underneath. Prefers Czar and Victoria, spurns Ponds Seedling and Monarch.

A similar and more common problem is the Plum Fruit moth Laspeyresia funebrana whose pinkish larvae are found inside the first ripening fruits, the larvae fall to pupate and start a second generation who overwinter in cocoons in the ground.

AnurAphis padi aphids can curl the leaves. Mealy aphids, especially Brachycaudus helichrysi / Hyalopterus arundinis completely coat the underside of leaves which also curl, with crop reduction and withered shoots, these then move to their alternate host of China asters Callistephus which may be stunted seriously.

Brown scale Euleconium corni lay 2000 eggs each, these hatch in autumn hide in the bark, move to leaves and shoots in spring where they settle to form scales, they not only suck sap but their honeydew and sooty mould hinders lower leaves.

The Red Legged Weevil Otiorhynchus clavipes found on currants and raspberries sometimes moves onto plums where it eats flowers, fruitlets, leaves even the bark of tender stems.

Capsid bug Lygus pabulinus causes the foliage to be spotted and pitted and seldom bothers fruits much.

Leaf-blade attacked by acarine gall-mite Eriophyes / Phytoptus similis causing odd little protuberances on the leaves, when up to sixty galls, yellow, orange or purplish, mostly on upperside, oval but coalescing, this also attacks Bullaces.

Whole branches and limbs dying or with tunnelled bark and wood, often with an odd smell, may have Shot-hole Borer Anisandrus dispar beetles, tiny black beetles whose larvae bore almost any fruit tree though mostly preferring Stone fruits, and in particular plums already carrying Bacterial canker, these have two broods a year.

Cherry Bark Tortrix Enarmonia formosana is a pink caterpillar tunneling under the bark, mainly on cherries but also attacks apple, pear and plum trees especially those in decline.

Bacterial Canker causes stunted shoots yellowing and withering leaves with shot hole like spots and cankers ulcerating limbs, the ubiquitous Victoria is often badly attacked, as is Csar. This fungus also attacks the leaves causing Shot-hole and Leaf Spot especially in wet years. If there is die back with small but no large canker to be seen and with tiny hairs or jelly like pimples it may be Branch Die-back Diaporthe perniciosa / Dermatea prunastri.

Brown Rot / Blossom Wilt Sclerotinia / Monilia Laxa and Monilia fructigena cause the same interrelated nest of symptoms as on apples with Withered Tips, Twig Blight and cankers, and rotten, dropped and mummified fruits. Brown Rot Sclerotina fructigena, S. laxa, and S. mali can attack most parts like scab. It is known as Blossom Wilt when the flower truss turns brown and the fruiting spur dies back. This Brown Rot is not necessarily the other brown rot of decay but the fruits get a brown rot with whitish bubbling.

Sooty Blotch Glaeodes pomigena similar to that in apples causes round brown patches on the fruit skins and worst in wet years.

Silverleaf disease Stereum purpureum is a big problem for plums, you seldom see an old plum tree; poor growth, die back and poor cropping are indications but the confirming sign is a silvery look to the leaves in summer when an air gap forms under the membrane, fruitng bodies later form on affected branches. Trichoderma virides, a fungus parasitic on others can be injected into the trees to prevent such attacks but is not available to amateurs in the UK. An important point is to avoid pruning any of these or other Stone fruits, or their ornamental forms, any time other than in summer in dry conditions to prevent the fungus gaining access via the wounds. Any winter damage should be pruned back immediately and I cauterise the wounds with a blowtorch before sealing with a suitable compound, such as beeswax melted and applied with a brush.

Plum fruits are attacked by Plum Leaf Curl fungus ascomycete Taphrina pruni / Ascomyces / Exoascus / institiae, causing it to shrivel and go brown, the leaves are curled and blistered, the fungus overwinters on the bark. This is also believed to cause Bladder bullace / Pocket plum / Starved plum / Mock plum, causing flattening and elongation of fruit, kernel fails and flesh inedible, pale green, greyish or dusty orange and up to two and a half inches in size. Similar fungal attacks may be found on most others in prunus family.

As with most plants mottled leaves indicate a Mosaic virus spread by aphids with no cure.

Plum Pox is another similar virus causing mottling and blueish or reddish depressed rings and spots on the fruits which then also lack sugar.

Prune Dwarf appears in Italian Prune, Switzen, causing leaf distortion and stunting but in most cultivars shows as poor leaf colour with cropping 70-80% reduced.

Bark Split virus, self descriptive, often invades Cambridge Gage more than others.

Prunus laurocerasus, CHERRY LAUREL

Poisonous, makes a big evergreen tree if not cut back by wind and frost.

The leaves preserve grains and seeds from weevils and burning leaves dangerous to us as well as insects.

Leaves, especially wilted, stems and seeds contain much cyanide based compounds however it's just possible the fruit flesh may be made edible with processing or improvement and could be worth investigating.

Prunus padus, BIRD CHERRY / HAGBERRY

An ornamental with bitter black probably poisonous fruits, said to be good for attracting caterpillars on to it away from other fruit trees.

Prunus persica, PEACH / NECTARINE

Usually self fertile, surprisingly easy to grow from seed, may fruit in four or five years and often come nearly 'true'.

Do well in big tubs housed outdoors till late winter, brought under cover for flowering and fruiting, then going out again for autumn and into winter. This handicaps most of their co-lives and reduces the pruning. Permanent housing under cover is strongly not recommended as they will not get a winter chill and fail to thrive, to say little of their co-lives proliferating!

Remember these are fruits that overcropping seriously spoils. If you want sweet luscious globes then thin early, thin often and never leave two fruitlets closer than a hand width apart. Be especially vigilant at splitting doubles as these never swell cleanly.

Outdoors trees often suffer total losses of bloom from frost, and beware as the fruitlets remain sensitive for weeks after setting.

Although these need lime too much may cause Chlorosis with pale green leaves with a yellowish tinge due to a lack of available Iron.

A shortage of lime can cause soft or Split Stones, which as name suggests split and open the flesh at the flower end helping infestation by moulds and earwigs.

In dry years it's wasps, and in wet years it's rot's spoil the crop, surprisingly birds are seldom a problem.

With Nectarines it's the weather, even here in East Anglia these seldom ripen outdoors without at least a warm wall. Except for exceptional summers better move these under cover from late winter till just after harvest.

Ants can be their usual annoying selves and will farm scale.

Aphids cause the leaves to curl, and several different species abound: Leaves often have the somewhat polyphagous Peach Potato Aphis Myzus persicae, amber, yellow, red even black, which alternates with many plants especially thistles.

The Mealy Peach aphid Hyalopterus amygdali, a mealy greeny amber, migrates to live on reeds.

The Peach aphid Appelia / AnurAphis schwartzi, greenish yellow to brownish pink, and the Black Peach aphid Brachycaudus persicaecola are less common and unusually these remain on the peaches overwinter. Webspinning sawfly Neurotoma nemoralis larvae, green with black heads, make tents to feed on the leaves inside. Capsids may do some damage, and on walls of course expect Red Spider mites and Mussel Scale (see under Malus).

Earwigs are a secondary problem, if the flower end of the stone splits they get in and eat out the kernel while the flesh remains fine. Take note- if you do not spot that small split in the flower end then you can enjoy the bizarre experience of biting into the sweet flesh to suddenly find your mouth wriggling with earwigs; a little macabre and most disconcerting!

Shot Holes Clasterosporium carpophilium start as brown spots become holes and later also forming scabs and spots which appear on shoots and fruits and which may ooze gum.

Peach Powdery mildew Spaerotheca pannosa var. persicae may cause greyish white powdery patches on the leaves and shoots and reduces yields, it overwinters on buds and may severely stunt growth.

Peaches are very prone to Peach Leaf Curl, the foliage is attacked by fungus ascomycete Taphrina / Exoascus / deformans, causing flattening and elongation of leaves, forming baggy pouches usually bright red and falling early. This gets in as the buds open and swell so worst in wetter areas and thus can be prevented almost entirely by keeping the shoots dry. Permanent housing under cover eliminates this problem, then raising far too many others. Small bushes and wall trained forms can be protected overhead with a plastic sheet from mid-winter till the buds have opened. Once trees reach full size many shrug off attacks of curl anyway. This fungus visits others in family especially almond.

Mosaic virus mottles the leaves yellow, to be sure it's not chlorosis this will remain unaffected by seaweed sprays.

Prunus spinosa, BLACKTHORN / SLOE

Superb hedge plant, tough and resistant to stock and if well made to most animals down to the size of a small dog.

Fruit though technically edible is acid sour.

Pseudotsuga douglasii, DOUGLAS FIR

Gilletteela cooleyi aphids migrate to Douglas fir from Picea sitchensis Sitka spruce which was galled to form pseudocones.

Germination and natural regeneration suppressed directly and indirectly by (unspecified) soil actinomycete bacteria.

Psidium, GUAVA

This fruit should be grown in greenhouses but more for the perfume as for eating.
A shrubby thirsty tree this is very prone to Mealy Bug but otherwise easy.
The evergreen form, Cherry or Strawberry Guava, is even more decorative with less well scented but more palatable fruit, and is less plagued by Mealy Bugs.

PSYLLIDS

These are much like aphids though often more mobile. These and the similar Leaf-hoppers, are tiny yellowish active insects which attack leaves leaving bleached areas and dropping honeydew and are both treated much the same as Thrips. They are especially damaging under cover and spread to Calceolarias, Fuschias, Pelargoniums, Primulas, Salvias and Verbenas

Pteris / Pteridiumaquilinum, BRACKEN / BRAKE

A very invasive weed that gives off carcinogenic spores.

Although poisonous apparently some animals will consume this, it is said the best way to rid a plot of bracken is to put pigs on it for a year or so.

Allegedly Trifolium subterraneum, Subterranean Clover, is sown through bracken, stock like this so trample and weaken the bracken while trying to get at it. Pigs become even more effective!

Bracken is rich in Potassium, locks up other valuable nutrients and an acre may contain over forty tons of the rhizome.

Bracken contains compounds that are insecticidal, especially to aphids and to Diamond Back moths Plutella maculipennis.

The 'leaf' pinnae can develop rolled galls of Dasyneura / Perrisia / Cecidomyia filicina / pteridis, these are difficult to see and easily confused with the more hairy but similar galls caused by Eriophyes pteridis mites.

Pulmonaria officinalis, LUNGWORT

Provides excellent low cool groundcover and blooms early in year the flowers very rich in nectar.

Pyracantha, FIRETHORN

Great masses of flowers for insects, masses of berries for birds, and nasty thorns that prick you savagely making wounds that often get infected.

These have apparently recently become prey to an (unspecified) Leaf miner.
They can get Nut scale, similar to Peach scale except base of each is widened just above junction with stem, this spreads to elms, hazels, hawthorns and pears.

PYRETHRUM

Ancient insecticide made from Chrysanthemum cinerariaefolium.
Quick to break down it's believed harmless to mammals, it stuns insects but sometimes fails to kill so a mixture with derris or other stronger insecticide was often marketed instead of the pure substance.

Pyrus communis, PEAR

A good pear is harder to grow than a good peach, these need warmth, shelter and continuous moisture.
Harsh winds will blacken foliage as if burnt.
Lots of small fruits dropping may be just June Drop natural self-thinning as with apples.
Pear rust, see below, is carried over on Juniper making these bad companions.
Pears have noticeably less frequent visits of many of the same co-lives of apples; Leopard moth, Vapourer, Tortrix even Codling moths and Twig Cutters all may be found but not often, even aphids seldom bother pears.
However pears have some co-lives more their own.

The Sinuate Pear Tree borer Agrilus sinuatus beetle larvae, ivory white and legless, eats mostly sapwood causing premature leaf fall and may kill branches, the larvae eat for two years then pupate in situ before the adult leaves to mate and lay eggs.

White tents formed in the leaves in summer with many caterpillars, orangey yellow with pale brown stripes and black heads, that exude a red fluid if disturbed are the Social Pear Sawfly Neurotoma flaviveniris, these also visit plums and cherries.

If the leaves are looking patchy, blotchy or skeletonised then look for slug like yellow green or blackish Slug Worms / Pear Slug sawfly Caliroa cerasi larvae on the tops of the leaves.

Another sawfly Hoplocampa testudinea, a dirty whitish caterpillar with a brown head, makes big rotten holes in the middle of the fruit with a tunnel usually from the top.

Capsid bug Lygus pabulinus makes brownish black spots on the leaves and the fruits develop lumps of corky pitted tissue. Some apparently capsid damage is actually Stony Pit or Dimpled Pear, see below.

May get Nut scale which is similar to Peach scale except the base of each is widened just above junction with stem, this spreads to elms, hazels, hawthorns and pyracantha.

Leaf-blades get Pear Leaf Blister mite / moth (sic) attacks caused by acarine gall-mite Eriophyes pyri / piri / Phytoptus arianus / arionae / Typhlodromus pyri / small swellings on mostly upper side of leaf, yellowish green to red and purple, turn brown black and crack at maturity, may also cause irregular reddish brown pustules on fruit. This conflated with Pear Leaf Blister moths Cemiostoma scitella which are very small, the adults overwinter in bark cracks and lay eggs in young leaves which are mined by the green larvae, these fall with leaves in autumn to pupate and overwinter.

Pear Leaf midge Dasyneura pyri causes the leaves to fold upwards at the edges as the eggs are laid in the folds of young leaves, several generations a year can lead to a build up with some reduction in plant growth.

Fruit may be destroyed by Dipteron gall-midge Lestodiplosis pyri / Cecidomyia / nigra / pyricol causing Black pear which seems conflated and same as Pear Gall Midge Contarinia pyrivora, eggs are laid in flowers then yellowish white larvae eat inside of fruitlets, when these blacken and fall to the ground the midges leave (to over-winter in soil), and can cause serious fruit loss.

Bryobia mite Bryobia cristatus suck sap breed rapidly and they and their damage much resemble red spider mites except they're not hairy and have longer front legs, they're on the tree in late spring and early summer and alternate living on grasses and other herbaceous plants the rest of the year.

Summer Fruit Tortrix moths Cacoecia reticulana overwintering larvae eat leaves then pupate to emerge and lay eggs in eary summer, the hatching larvae web a leaf together, usually to a fruit, and feed inside on leaf and fruit, these mature pupate and lay so that the next generation hatch in early autumn to feed before overwintering.

Cherry Bark Tortrix Enarmonia formosana is a pink caterpillar tunneling under the bark, mainly on cherries but also attacks apple, pear and plum trees especially those in decline.

Pear rust at another stage is also Juniper Stem Gall rust, the fungi Gymmnosporangium sabinae moves to pears where it causes the thickened pear-leaf cluster-cups on the foliage and sometimes on stems and fruits, causing serious leaf loss and poor wood ripening.

A simple weather problem is blackening and browning of the leaves from cold dry winds with or without frost, but if flowers, shoots and leaves wither back going dark brown it might be Fireblight Erwinia amylovaca. This seriously infectious bacteria was known in the USA for two centuries then arrived in the UK in 1957 and has since decimated our Rosaceae so almost all susceptible varieties such as the glorious Laxton's Superb have already long expired.

Pear Scab Venturia pirina is a fungal attack, small spots cause early leaf fall and corky spots on fruit, has similar appearance to apple scab though a different species. It may cause whole twigs to wither, if bad this lets in Pear Canker as well. Pear Canker much resembles Apple canker as the same fungus Nectria galligena attacks both. The pear suffers ulceration and swollen distorted growth in the same way, and as with apples, some varieties are more prone such as William's, Conference and Doyenne du Comice.

An annual fungus Inonotus hispidus does much damage to old trees living on the trunk forming a large (up to 10lb) bracket of russet, whitish underneath with big pores, juicy and meaty looking though inedible, and dripping moisture in damp conditions, this has been used to make a yellow dye, also spreads to apples.

Stony Pit or Dimpled Pears is a virus, the fruits are smaller with dimples or pits, hard and gritty at the bottom where they are usually darker green. If only the odd fruit affected then it may well be Capsid or even weather damage. Stony Pit rarely appears in Williams' but does so severely in Beurre Hardy, Beurre d'Amanlis and Doyenne du Comice.

Pears also get invaded by Vein Yellows virus.

Blister Canker virus often invades Williams', Doyenne du Comice, and Laxton's Superb.

QUASSIA

Extracts from the bark of this tropical tree was used as an early selective insecticide as it killed aphids but not ladybirds.

Quercus, OAKS

Seldom grows above 1,500ft line.
These reputedly sustain more forms of life than any other plant in the temperate zone. These co-lives are so numerous many will have to wait for a separate appendix. Those listed below are under the species most likely to display them though the 300 plus co-lives will drift from one to another of our now very intermixed species and hybrids.
Oaks accumulate Calcium in their bark though it remains acidic ph 3.8-5.7.
The leaves contain much tannin and when used as mulch discourage slugs and snails but may inhibit some plants.
The weevil Rhyncharaenus quercus mines the leaves of all oaks and forms a gall as the surfaces bulge.
Dead branches support Tremella mesenterica, an inedible fungus with a brain like appearance, bright yellow while moist.
Large brown bracket fungi of Peziza arvernensis are found amongst fallen leaf litter, distinguished by fine warts on the spores.

Oak litter can grow the highly poisonous Boletus satanus with a light grey to brown cap, pale blue flesh, most often found on calcerous soils.

The litter also grows the very tasty edible Boletus aestivalis / edulis ssp / reticulatus with a light brown cap, sweet white flesh, most often found on calcerous soils and also under beech.

Oak litter favours the Panther Cap Amanita pantherina, this is highly poisonous though giving much the same initial effects as alcohol, and is easily confused with the Blusher A. rubescens which is edible but risky unless you really know your mushrooms!

Even worse is the Death Cap A. phalloides, usually greenish but sometimes white, with white gills, the flesh is sweet and pleasing to the taste so very easily eaten in error with dire results, also found under hornbeam.

Clitocybe clavipes, edible, is found most often in mossy litter under larch but also in pine and oak woods, it has a browny black to olive green cap and smells of bitter almonds.

Collybia dryophila, edible, buff tan cap with crowded whitish gills, very widely distributed not only under oaks but almost anywhere including above the tree line and especially in peat bogs.

Pluteus cervinus, edible, grows on stumps and rotting wood, it has a light to dark grey or brownish cap and streaked stipe, the gills start white then go pink with red spores, also found on birch, hornbeam and beech.

More common in the warmer parts of the continent than in the UK is the highly poisonous Entoloma / Rhodophyllus sinuatum / lividum / sinuatus, this has pale greyish cap, pink to orangish gills and pink spores, it likes calcareous soil and is also found under hornbeams and beeches. Pleurotus or Agaric mushrooms with white spores and an eccentric or obsolete stem are sometimes very luminous on oaks.

Quercus petraea, SESSILE OAK

This and Q. robur have their stems galled by Homopteran coccids Asteriolecanium variolosum / quercicola / Coccus / Asterodiaspis / Planchonia / fimbriata which form pit-galls or krebgalls, where a wall of bark like tissue is built up around where the (female) is sucking sap, these may be one or two or many in groups.
The leaf-blade is galled by Dipteron gall-midges Macrodiplosis spp, M. dryobia and M. volvens, both forming pockets by folding the edges, towards the under side in the former and the upper in the latter, the colour fades from green to brown or chocolate. Sometimes another gall-midge Clinodiplosis liebeli is found in with the Macrodiplosis midge larvae.
Both oaks also support over thirty cynipid gall-wasps, these usually form two different galls, one formed by the usual fertilised eggs and another alternate sort formed by the unfertilised parthenogenetic eggs, each taking it in turn to give rise to the next generation alternately female and male and female.

Biorhiza pallida / aptera / terminalis / Andricus / Cynips quercus-terminalis / aptera, causes the terminal or axillary bud to form the well known Apple gall / King Charles' apple / Oak apple which is almost spherical, spongy and often reddy pink and inch or so in diameter finally turning black, at the same time another generation is forming similar root galls about half that size and brownish.

Many parasites live on the larvae in aerial galls and even a few on root ones. Andricus kollari / Cynips / lignicola / quercus-petioli / tinctoria / circulans attacks the terminal or axillary buds forming a Bullet gall / Devonshire gall / Marble gall / Oak nut (and sometimes incorrectly called Oak apple), this starts as a green spherical ball about an inch or so across and turning brown with age, it is not native and was introduced in the nineteenth century from the Middle East for ink and the dyeing industry, unfortunately although it has 'gone native', it develops insufficient tannin to be useful. Over the years it was feared to reduce the acorn crop and so starve the nations pigs, however several predators and parasites have learned to hunt this wasp and even lesser spotted woodpeckers have found them a handy meal.

The buds and catkins are galled by Andricus fecundator / fecundatrix / pilosus / Aphilothrix / Cynips, the Artichoke gall / Hop gall / Hop strobile / Larch-cone gall is more common on bushes than trees, is over an inch long and dark green or russet with a solid core surrounded by deformed bud scales thus resembling an artichoke, the larvae invariably emerges as a female which lays unfertilised eggs in the male flower buds which will become catkins (usually choosing Q. robur as it comes into flower a fortnight earlier than Q. petraea), the resulting Hairy catkin galls are small pointed pale green or russet and covered in whitish hairs, from these male and females emerge to mate and lay eggs in the buds which become more Artichoke galls.

Another gall-wasp Andricus curvator often moves in with them utilising their efforts and many parasites and predators live on both these cynips. A. curvator / collaris / perfoliatus / Cynips axillaris / tegmentorum / fasciata / Aphilothrix can lay in leaf buds that have not been already galled but seem to prefer the ready-made, they then change these from Artichoke galls into Collared-bud galls which can be spotted as a tiny brown cigar sticking between the swollen bud scales. The females, unfertilised, then lay their eggs on the leaves giving rise to Curved-leaf galls pale green or brown swellings about half an inch long most often found on shoots springing from the main trunk.

The twigs are galled by Andricus testaceipes / sieboldi / Cynips / corticalis, particularly common on hedgerow trees down near the root zone, these form fluted Red barnacle galls arising out of the twigs with a pointed end which push up the tissues like a cap, these galls are about a quarter of an inch high, soft and red turning browner and harder with age, the females emerge to lay unfertilised eggs in the leaves which form Leaf-vein galls on the petiole or midrib of oval green swellings about the same size from which the male and females emerge to then repeat the barnacle stage.

Andricus inflator / globuli / Cynips galls the shoot tips causing a Twig gall swelling, green or brown and about two thirds of an inch long, the males and females emerge and the latter then lay in the terminal or lateral buds which swell to form Globular galls about a sixth of an inch long, spherical or oval and green, brown or blueish, these mature in autumn and the woody core drops out to protect the larvae until it emerges to start twig galls again.

Andricus nudus / malpighii / Aphilothrix lays fertilised eggs in buds in leaf axils, usually of Q. petraea, these form small spindle shaped Malpighis' galls sticking out of the deformed bud and with an odd 'peg' on the end, green with reddish streaks, the emerging wasps then lay parthenogenetic eggs in the developing male catkins which form Bald-seed galls, very small and inconspicuous as they are yellowish brown from which the wasps emerge to form Malpighis' galls again.

Andricus quercus-radicis / trilineatus / Aphilothrix radicis / Cynips attacks the roots forming Truffle galls, oval swellngs near the base of the trunk containg half a dozen or more larvae, up to several inches across, ovalish, the emerging females then lay unfertilised eggs in young shoots, stems and petioles forming Knot galls which are small swellings hard to find unless the bark is peeled back. The leaves are attacked by Cynips divisa / Diplolepis / Dryophanta / Spathegaster verrucosa, this forms Red-pea galls, glossy, near spherical slightly flattened, hanging by a peduncle from the underside of a rib or vein, a fifth of an inch long and a dozen or so per leaf, starting yellow going orange to reddy brown, the next generation form slightly smaller Red-wart galls of the buds which acquire similar colouring.

The leaf-blade is attacked by Cynips quercus-folii / folii / scutellaris / Diplolepis / Dryophanta / taschenbergi / Spathegaster /giraudi / flosculi, causing Cherry galls, nearly an inch across held by short stalks from the underside veins, brightly coloured, hard ouside spongy inside, these fall to ground as escape capsules, the next generation are from parthenogenetic eggs laid in buds on small twigs and form small Violet-egg galls of dark red, purplish or black with a velvet effect caused by fine hairs.

Cynips longiventris / substituta / Diplolepis / Dryophanta / Spathegaster similis forms Green velvet bud galls in dormant buds, oval pointed grey green to golden brown with numerous white hairs and about a twelth of an inch long, the emerging females lay fertilised eggs in midrib or veins of the underside of leaves which become globular Striped galls, up to half an inch across with blotches or stripes of yellow, red and with whitish hairs, and as many as eight per leaf.

Andricus ostreus / furunculus / Neuroterus schlechtendali fertilised eggs form Oyster galls on the underside of the leaves between the midrib and veins, an eighth of an inch across yellowish green pink or brown (can be affected by sunlight especially as occasionally on upper surface of leaf) the leaf epidermis splits into two flaps to allow the gall to swell then drop, the emerging females lay in terminal or axillary buds making April-bud galls at a surprising speed, these are a third of an inch across, greenish brown and disguised by bud scales making them very difficult to spot as they form and the adult emerges within a week or so!

Neuroterus quercus-baccarum / lenticularis / malpighii / Cynips / Spathegaster / varius / interruptor makes eighty to a hundred Common Spangle galls on the underside of a leaf, these are swollen half spheres that become flat circles, a quarter inch across with a raised centre and slightly hairy, yellowish green turning reddish, and each attached by a short stalk, when mature in autumn they fall to the ground often revealing their pale white or yellow underside, the insects carry on inside protected by fallen leaves till the following spring when they emerge to lay unfertilised eggs in the catkins or young foliage where Currant galls form, looking like bunches of redcurrants, soft spherical a sixth of an inch across going from green to pink and red. Many of the spangles are consumed by game birds.

Silk-button spangle galls are similar, grow on the underside of the leaf in late summer in huge numbers, often a thousand plus per leaf, circles of golden brown an eighth of an inch across with a central depression and covered in fine hairs, pressed up to the leaf surface not on a stalk, these spangles continue to swell after falling, in spring the females lay parthenogenetic eggs in the expanding leaf buds which develop Blister galls of similar size but in the leaf showing as swellings on both side, of a greyish green colour and with narrow ridges on the top surface.

Neuroterus tricolor / fumipennis / Spathegaster / varius forms Cupped Spangle galls, an eighth inch across discs with raised edges forming cups on the underside of the leaf, very similar to common spangles these are smaller and less numerous as well as more cup shaped, greenish yellow with shiny rose red hairs, after over-wintering in the fallen spangles the females lay unfertilised eggs in the leaves to form globular downy Hairy-pea galls, white pale green, yellow about a fifth of an inch across on the underside of midrib or veins, often in dense clusters, with red or brownish hairs.

Neuroterus albipes / laeviusculus / Spathegaster albipes forms the Smooth Spangle gall a sixth of an inch across cream coloured saucer with a tiny cone in the middle, unusually more often found on the upper surface of a leaf, formed in summer this drops in autumn then swells considerably, the females lay unfertilised eggs on the edges of leaves which form solitary tiny Schenck's galls the colour of the leaf and initially hairy becoming smooth, noticeable as the leaf margin becomes indented nearby.

Trigonaspis megaptera / renum / Cynips megaptera forms Pink-bud galls in leaf buds on young trees, roughly spherical, nearly a third of an inch across and reddish, these then in turn give rise to tiny Kidney galls on the leaf underside, glossy, smooth and with a small stalk, yellowish green to purplish brown, starting in late summer these swell quickly and fall in autumn.

There are another dozen and a half or more cynip gall wasps with equally fascinating cycles, most are rare though four not so uncommon are Andricus albopunctatus, A. quadrilineatus, A. solitaries and Neuroterus aprilinus.

Quercus robur, ENGLISH / PEDUNCULATE OAK

Shares very similar co-lives as the sessile oak above and especially as possibly most specimens are hybrids not pure species anymore.

RABBITS

Rabbits eat plants they like and chew down plants they don't like to make space for those they do, thus very few plants escape their damage, especially during periods of snow.
Mixed blessing depending on point of view, edible or cute. Discouraged by yappy dogs, possibly by dusting the area with wood ash or soot. Electric fencing is most effective.

Animal droppings of predators such as weasel or ferret said to repel them. A trip to the zoo could produce some exotic examples that should whiff enough to make the poor creatures leave, and break most health and hygiene codes.

Ranunculus, BUTTERCUPS

Poisonous weeds, fond of wet acid conditions so draining and liming discourages them.
Useful once composted as contain: Phosphorus, Potassium, Cobalt, Copper, Iron and Manganese.
The easy way to get rid of buttercups is to pasture geese on the land.
One of the preferred meals of Agriolimax reticulate slugs. Hosts to Stem Eelworm Tylenchus devastatrix.
Leaf blade and petioles become swollen and coloured yellow to purple by fungus 'Crowfoot smut' Urocystis / Polycistis pompholygodes, the petiole may spiral and the skin eventually splits as black powdery spores are emitted, this smut also found on Anemones making these bad weeds to tolerate near them.

Raphanus sativus, RADISH

Not only grown for the roots, the small seed pods are more delicious.
This crop needs to be grown rapidly to be palatable!

Analysis of dry matter; total crude ash 5.22%, N 1.85, P 0.78, K 1.3, Ca 1.81, Na 0.71.

Most important co-life is the Flea Beetle / Fly / Turnip Flea beetle, Phyllotreta / Haltica atra / nemorum / undulate, small, black or yellow striped, make so many holes in the leaves that this may kill small plants and seedlings. Deterred by damper conditions and presence of tomatoes, the adults are the problem, the larvae live in the soil on plant roots doing little harm.

Cabbage root fly can also bother radish. Erioischia Brassicae / Delia / Anthomyia radicum, eats the roots of all Brassicas, the females consume nectar of Cow parsley Anthriscus sylvestris so are most prevalent when this is flowering, most Brassica plants turn reddish purple once attacked. It is particularly damaging to radish as it tunnels in the swollen edible part. These flies can be lured to traps containing Swede root juice as bait. Interplanting lettuce, clover or Tagetes marigolds reduces infestations. Carefully fitted collars of felt or similar at ground level stop the fly climbing down the stem to the soil and prevent her laying eggs. Heavy attacks of aphids deter this fly and apparently the Garden Pebble moth caterpillar Evergestis forficalis exudes a deterrent chemical in its frass. Rove and Ground beetles also control this by eating the eggs

The roots and more often those of Wild radish R. raphaniastrum, are galled by Coleopteran weevil Ceuthorrhynchus pleurostigma / assimilis / sulcicollis a.k.a. 'Turnip and cabbage gall weevil' which forms marble sized swellings on the roots, this may seriously harm growth in young small plants and older ones may also suffer as the larval exit holes allow in other infections. This can be widespread in an area as it also spreads to Arabis, turnips, cabbages, swedes, and charlock.

Shoot apex galled by Dipteron gall-midge Dasyneura sisymbrii / Cecidomyia barbarea, this arrests normal growth causing glossy swellings and lumps, often cream, pink or reddish, worst in floral parts, serious infestations can form what look much like small raspberries, often spreads to other Cruciferae such as hedge mustard, creeping yellow cress, yellow rocket, cabbage and charlock.

Radish scab Streptomyces scabies makes scabby patches on the skin but seldom does serious harm, attacks may be reduced by mixing grass clippings or other rich organic material into the soil when sowing.

RED SPIDER MITES

Tetranychus telarius are not red and can be a huge problem under cover and outdoors on walls and in hot dry conditions, discouraged by wet and cool conditions, and only easily controlled under cover by releasing predatory mite Phytoseulis persimilis. Controlled on outdoor crops by Capsid bugs, Ladybirds, Lacewings, and pollen eating Typhlodromid mites.

REPLANT disease

Not a disease but apparent effects of poor planting. You must rotate to avoid bad companionship between generations. The old took all suitable nutrients, left unwanted by-products, co-lives and allelopathic compounds and the site needs to recover. Never put back the same genus of tree or shrub where one has stood and especially with roses and apples. Herbaceous plants are often in need of the same consideration and so are most vegetables. Huge applications of compost and or well rotted manure ameliorate the condition. Massive doses of commercially available microbial organisms also help.

REPELLENT plants

Any strong smelling plant might repel some co-life and those with few of their own the more likely so. So strong smells, especially similar ones, do mask the scents of other plants co-lives are looking for. Sprays or just trimmings can be made of such herbs and aromatic foliage to mask the odour of valuable plants rather than having to grow them in situ.

Reseda alba, WHITE MIGNONETTE

Leaf spot Cercospora resedae causes brown patches especially prevalent on plants on damp soil deficient in lime.

Reseda lutea, WILD MIGNONETTE

These flowers specially visited by Prosopis bees.

Reseda luteola, WELD / DYER'S ROCKET

The seeds may remain viable 2,000 years.

Rheum rhaponticum, RHUBARB

An ancient aphicide recipe was boiled rhubarb leaves which contain the poison oxalic acid.
The same spray was used against blackspot on roses and Red spider mites on Aquilegias.
Mice show much distaste to extract of rhubarb root.
Reputed to control clubroot and root flies in Brassicas if piece of stem of rhubarb included in the sowing or planting hole, sadly tests showed only little benefit.
Crown Rot Bacterium rhaponticum although rare is serious, the leaves go pale, the stem bases swell and distort then all goes soft and rotten and needs destroying.
Rhubarb can be attacked by Honey fungus Armillaria mellea with the black bootstraps in the soil, a whitish mycelium and honey coloured toadstools. Grey Mould Botrytis cinerea as found in the greenhouse attacks rhubarb when it's forced in damp dirty conditions.
Brown spots, patchy and irregular are the fungal Leaf Spot Ramularia rhei.

Rhinanthus crista-galli, YELLOW RATTLE

Weed parasitic on grasses and cereals and the seed in grain spoils wheat.

Rhododendron, see also Azaleas

Well known for needing lime free soil Rhododendrons are good at extracting heavy metals from their environment. The big leaved forms generally prefer shade the smaller full sun.

White fly Dialeurodes chittendeni cause leaves to pale and mottle and scales can be seen under the leaves with sooty moulds forming on upper surface of lower leaves from their honeydew.

If there is also chocolate spotting on the underside of leaves then it is more likely the Rhododendron bug Stephanitis rhododendri.

Thrips also cause the leaves to go pale or even brown, their tell tale is little blackish specks on the underside. Often suffer from Vine weevil.

Two fungi Basidiomycetes Exobasidium vaccinii and E. rhododendri causes galls on the underside of the leaf which become powdery with spores.

Rhus typhina, STAGS HORN SUMACH

Very prone to surface running roots suckering everywhere to the point of being a weed, bad choice of plant not suitable for most gardens.

Ribes

Woodland plants, these need mulching and a moist root run.
They often carry aphids which cause leaf curling, usually Aphis schneideri.
They can be damaged by the Clay-colored weevil Otiorhynchus singularis, this is a night feeder like the Red-legged weevil, black with red legs. Both weevils also attack raspberries and are often found on plums. The Clay-coloured is more destructive of the two as it strips bark as well as leaves, it overwinters as the larvae and adult in the ground where the larvae eat roots.
Most Ribes suffer Currant Clearwing Sesia tipuliformis the white with a brown head caterpillar bores in the stems which wilt and the fruit fails.

Ribes grossularia, GOOSEBERRY

Notoriously needy for Potassium often showing this with a blueish green hue and a yellowish brownish margin to the leaf
These also need Magnesium or the leaves can become pale, marbled with a purplish hue.
Occasionally a gooseberry will bear yellow flowers on thornless stems, this is the Buffalo berry rootstock.
They do not like stagnant air.

Giant berry competitors underplanted with chickweed to create cool damp conditions at the roots. I underplant with Limnanthes douglassii for those raised up on a leg with space underneath.

Bullfinches love to strip the buds.

Fruits often sucked dry by wasps with the skin left hanging.

Broad beans may help keep away their sawfly which is their most significant co-life; the Gooseberry Sawfly or apparently sawflies; Pteronidea ribesii, Nematus spp. & Pristiphora pallipes, all of which first appear in late spring early summer. If you keep watch daily one leaf will suddenly have a dozen or two pinhead sized holes; each one being eaten by a wee greeny caterpillar (green spotted with black dots / pale green and black head / dark green and pale head). Having eaten the first leaf they disperse and each munches down its own shoot, rapidly, till all is totally defoliated. Within a month or so they drop to the ground, pupate, and return for up to four generations per year. Oddly the infestation frequently appears in the third or fourth year after planting then often becomes insignificant after the sixth or seventh.

If leaves turn pale yellow and look scorched and drop off check for Gooseberry Red Spider mites Bryobia ribis / praetiosa and B. rubrioculus causing a webbing on the undersurface, these may move onto other trees and shrubs.

Aphids Aphis grossulariae are dark green and feed on the tips crumpling leaves and deforming shoots.

Aphid Eriosoma ulmi lives on the roots where it has a blanket of white woolly webbing to protect it and does serious damage even killing plants.

Big bud mite Cecidophyopsis ribis of blackcurrants does not harm gooseberries much, some buds die and turn brown, but gooseberries do not appear infected by the Reversion virus.

Likewise the Leaf spot can do light damage.

However Capsids can do more crop damage than on the smaller currants through their causing corkiness and splitting the skins of the fewer gooseberry fruits.

Sickly or weak plants may well be suffering from root aphids.

Magpie moth Abraxas grossulariata larvae overwinter in many places especially bark crevices and eat the foliage from early spring, this used to be widespread but seldom seen now.

Gooseberry Leaf Spot Pseudopeziza ribis starts as dark spots on leaves which yellow and drop, the fruit stalks and fruit may also be attacked, bad cases debilitate the bushes.

Another most significant co-life is American Gooseberry mildew Spaerotheca mors-uvae. This appears on the tips, coats the underside of the leaves with a white felting, especially when roots are dry, spreads onto berries which then crack, and also spreads to other Ribes.

European Gooseberry mildew Microsphaera grossulariae is similar but less white, usually only appears on the upper surfaces of the leaves and does not often harm fruits, the spores overwinter on fallen leaves.

Sedges and gooseberries are alternate hosts to the Gooseberry Cluster Cups fungus Puccinia pringsheimiana which cause red and orangey blisters on the leaves and fruits first resembling leaf spots, the fungus spends autumn till summer on the sedges then moves back to the gooseberry and other Ribes.

Gooseberries do not seem to suffer many virus invasions except Vein Banding virus to which the variety Leveller is particularly sensitive.

Ribes nigrum BLACKCURRANTS

These like wet rich conditions, and will even grow in waterlogged soil. Bullfinches love to strip their buds. Undersow with Limmnanthes douglassii to bring in many predatory co-lives.

Significant co-life is an invisible pest causing 'Big bud' making big buds many times size of normal ones, these never open, and are galled by miniscule wind blown acarine gall-mite Cecidophyopsis / Eriophyes / Phytoptus ribis, this destroys fruiting even if not carrying Reversion virus as well, see below. (Variety Foxendown proved resistant to gall mites and so avoided Reversion disease and oddly Golubka and Ben Gairn were not resistant to the mites but were somehow resistant to Reversion.)

Currants commonly carry aphids which cause leaf curling usually Aphis schneideri.

The Currant-sowthistle aphid Hypermyzus lactucae causes currant leaves to curl downwards with stunted growth, these then migrate to their alternate host of sowthistle.

Sudden death or a slow lingering one not otherwise explainable may be Root aphids.

If the tips and leaves wither later in spring then it may be Shoot-borer beetle Lampronia capitella grubs, red turning greenish, which also move into the fruits ruining them, the cocoons are normally hidden in cracks in the bark in winter.

Leaf midges Dasyneura tetensi cause leaves to distort twist and fold similar to aphid attacks but inside are whitish orange grubs, these mature in a month or so and with four generations a year can multiply, they overwinter as pupae in the soil.

Blackcurrants also sometimes get attacked by the Gooseberry sawfly, see above.

All the currants and gooseberries occasionally suffer from Capsid bugs Lygus pabulinus similar to those attacking apples, the leaves are attacked when young and the holes expand with the leaf making them look tatterred, overwinter as eggs on the twigs.

Buds may be destroyed by Leaf and Bud eelworm nematode Aphelencoides / Aphelenchus fragariae and A. ritzemi-bosi, these cause considerable distortions, weakening and stunting and also attack strawberries. Blackcurrants may host Mussel scale, and Red spider mite in hot dry conditions, and Weevil and Looper caterpillars.

Occasionally a Currant Clearwing moth / European Currant Borer Sesia tipuliformis caterpillar, whitish with brown head, may hollow out live and pupate in the stems and branches often killing them. The adult is unusual in having no scales thus clear wings and so resembles a bee. This seems conflated with another or the same grub, the Blackcurrant Crown Borer Bembecia marginata, eggs are laid in summer, the larva overwinters at the base enters a cane, lives inside restricting growth and causing die back, after many months or years pupates then emerges as a clearwing moth.

Old overgrown bushes are often infested with lots of tiny whitish pink pustules to the extent they resemble coral thus Coral Spot Nectria cinnabarina which is sort of decorative in an Addams family way, usually starting on stubs of deadwood or dead shoots this can sometimes spread to ruin the whole plant.

Currants suffer Currant Leaf spot Pseudopeziza / Glaesporium ribis where sticky brown patches, shiny when wet, cause browning and the leaf falls in midsummer with in bad cases a shrivelling of the current currant crop, the spores overwinter on fallen leaves. American Gooseberry mildew Spaerotheca mors-uvae also attacks all the currants and appears on the tips, coats the underside of the leaves with a white felting, especially when roots are dry, spreads onto berries which then crack, become grey, decay and even more Addams family.

European Gooseberry mildew Microsphaera grossulariae is similar, also attacks currants, it is less white than the American, usually only appears on the upper surfaces of the leaves and does not often harm fruits, the spores overwinter on fallen leaves.

Sedges and blackcurrants are alternate hosts for the fungal Gooseberry Cluster Cups little spotty rusts on leaves and fruits, see gooseberries.

Currants must not be grown in some of the American states as they are an alternate host to Blackcurrant rust Cronartium ribicola, which is a.k.a. White Pine Blister rust, which seriously damages Weymouth pines and others with five needles. The rust makes yellow cushions on the underside of the leaves which brown and wither with a woolly hairyness forming and often fall early.

Running Off is when the topmost fruits fall off early, this may be viral, lack of pollination or simply light frost damage.

Blackcurrants suffer many other viruses; Yellows, Variegation, the common Gooseberry Vein Banding and worryingly some strains of Cucumber Mosaic.

The serious problem of Reversion virus infection is normally brought by the Big Bud mite, the leaves become less ornate, more stinging nettle shaped with fewer veins, darker green, and yields drop to never recover, this can be spread on pruning tools.

Ribes rubrum, CURRANTS, RED and WHITE currants

If kept dry and protected the fruits will hang on until early winter in near perfect condition.

Seldom bothered by wasps.

These often suffer massive attacks of Leaf Blistering aphid, Homopteran Cryptomyzus / Capitophorus / Rhopalosiphum / Aphis / Myzus / ribis, causing reddish blisters on upperside though co-life lives below on underside of leaf. This merely 'summer prunes' and seldom depresses yields especially as most of damaged leaves are removed in summer pruning. In summer winged females move to white and red dead nettles and wood woundwort, continue multiplying, and in autumn form males and females, females lay eggs back on the red currants, often on shoot tips.

Although blackcurrants are useless after a decade the red go on longer, even when the top becomes worn out a new one can usually be worked up from the roots, though sometimes these are killed off by Root aphids.

Soft scale Pulvinaria vitis prefers grapevines but moves onto currants where it makes a conspicuous white woolly wad in which the eggs are protected, the larvae move out and form a scale once settled.

The Leaf spot which bothers blackcurrants above can move onto the red and white currants.

Spoon Leaf is a virus symptom caused by Raspberry Ring Spot spread by Longidorus nematode eelworms.

Ricinus communis, CASTOR OIL plant

The oil was used if unpleasant but some other constituents are very poisonous.
One of the many plants reputed but never proved to repel moles. The plants have been used to control nematodes and mosquitos.

Robinia pseudoacacia, LOCUST

An attractive Leguminous tree.
Accumulate Calcium up to three quarters of their mineral content.
The Jew's Ear bracket fungus Hirneola auricula-judae (edible, honestly), brown and hard when dry, gelatinous fresh, may often be found on old trees this also spreads onto elderberry.

RODENTS Rats, mice & voles

Not only do these pesky co-lives eat seeds, fruits and other stores, they nibble and destroy clothes, rubber boots and even your structures. Rats in particular do serious damage to buildings and undermine their foundations. Voles and mice nibble off flower heads and may do weird things such as stack up little piles of strawberries with the seeds chewed off.

You can tell whether you have mice, a problem, or rats, a big problem, by the size of any hole (smaller than a golf ball it's only mice or voles, the droppings (mice are rice sized, rats are raisins), and the teeth marks. Both have small pairs of front chisel teeth leaving pairs of marks but the mice's are tiny while rats' teeth leave broad scrapes. Voles seldom come indoors, are most similar to mice but do more damage in the garden.

(Shrews, these are much smaller with a long snout and a shrill scream, are not rodents, and are one of the gardens most active predators of all sorts of smaller critters.)

ROOTS

In crop rotation these are the rooted vegetables. Most of these are biennials growing one year to save up stores and produce masses of seeds the following. If checked in growth they bolt and flower too early and are useless. Because of this and their physical shape they are rarely transplanted and usually sown in situ.

They can be protected from many soil pests by preceeding green manures of barley, oats, flax or mustard dug in several months before.

ROOT exudations

Plants put things into the soil as well as taking them out and these affect other plants directly and indirectly. Many are utilised by mycorrhizal fungi and bacteria to extract other nutrients from the soil.

ROOT hairs

Extremely fine roots make the bulk of the underground system. The roots in total may measure many miles and even small plants like a beetroot can send roots down and sideways many yards. It is hard to determine where many plants roots stop, the mycorrhizal fungi and bacteria start and the soil as such begins, all are continually in flux. The weight of roots and root hairs left in the soil after a crop is removed will vary with the crop. Legumes and long lived crops leave several tons per acre, potatoes less.

ROOT FLY

A type of common and unwanted co-life especially those of carrots and cabbages. The adults can be excluded with fine netting. For Brassicas a collar protecting each stem prevents the fly laying eggs in the soil near enough the base.

Cabbage root flies may be found dead in great numbers on the underside lip of leaves of Cucurbits especially pumpkins. This may be only coincidence as examination shows they die of an entomophagous fungus attack.

Rorippa sylvestris, YELLOW FIELDCRESS / CREEPING YELLOW-CRESS

A serious weed especially in Japan.
Shoot apex galled by Dipteron gall-midge Dasyneura sisymbrii / Cecidomyia barbarea, this arrests normal growth causing glossy swellings and lumps, often cream, pink or reddish, worst in floral parts, serious infestations can form what look much like small raspberries, often infests other Cruciferae such as hedge mustard, yellow rocket, cabbage, charlock and wild radish.

Rosa, ROSES

A woodland plant so needs moist soil with plenty of organic matter.
Grown everywhere for many years and are natives so many co-lives exist.
Most cultivated rose flowers have no honey only pollen.
Chafer bugs are discouraged away from roses by Petunias and Pelargoniums.

Under-plant with Alliums, especially chives and garlic against Black Spot.

Aphids are also deterred by garlic as are Japanese beetles and chafers.

Aphids, especially Macrosiphum rosae are nearly always present, when massed on the flower buds they may prevent these opening.

The leaves support polyphagous Aphis Macrosiphum euphorbiae which alternate on many plants especially thistles.

Scale insects Diaspis / Aulacaspis rosae are common, small round flat whitish or yellowish discs stuck to the stems.

Seldom seen now is damage by the Red Bud borer, a midge which laid in wounds especially those made when budding roses.

On hot dry walls expect Red Spider mite.

If the leaves are skeletonised or scraped transparent it's one of several sawfly Slug worms.

The Rose Leaf Hopper causes a white mottling on the leaves.

Leaf-cutting bees eat odd, often semi-circular, pieces out of rose leaves with which they construct wee cylinders in which they raise their young.

Clay coloured weevils Otiorrhynchus singularis eat the lower buds, lower leaves and bark even girdling stems of young plants.

Occasionally a Leaf-rolling sawfly will do exactly that, though it might be Tortrix moth caterpillar if the leaves are just drawn together at the tips. Roses get attacked by several other Lepidoptera larvae webbing leaves together, see Volume 2 Really Help Butterflies.

Roses commonly suffer Mildew Sphaerotheca pannosa, a powdery coating on the leaves, stems, buds even thorns, badly affected leaves curl, wither and go purplish and fall, worst in a dry summer.

Likewise they frequently suffer Black Spot Diplocarpon rosae rather defines itself, purplish blotches, mostly on leaves but also on stems, weaken plant and even causes total leaf loss, yellow roses suffer more from this than other strains.

Orange spots and patches are Rust Phragmidium mucronatum, often in leaf joints then it moves to coat the backs of the leaves with little rusty orange pustules which become craters; the leaves drop very soon after, the bush may expire if subject to several serious attacks.

Rosa arvensis, FIELD ROSE

The leaflet is often rolled into a pod by Dipteron gall-midge Wachtiella rosarum / Cecidomyia rosae, under surface of leaflet on outside, thickening and reddish brown, legless larvae.

Also similar pods are formed by Hymenopteran sawfly which pulls upper surface to outside, with some twisting, more withered and untidy aspect with legged caterpillars.

Most aerial parts galled by Hymenopteran gall-wasp Diplolepis eglanteriae to form 'Smooth pea galls' which bulges hide on underside of leaves and may be green turning to rose red.

D. nervosus / rosarum / Rhodites, causes 'Spiked pea galls' similar bulges 1/4 inch size each with up to six spines, also yellowish green to pink and brown.

When the leaflet, rachis or sepal is invaded by Hymenopteran gall-wasp Diplolepis / Rhodites / Cynips rosae / bedeguaris this causes the beautiful Bedeguar gall, Moss gall or Ronins pincushion, like a ball of moss going green through red to brown and often quite large, up to four inches across, blackening in winter in which the eggs and larvae are fed.

The larvae of the last may be joined by gall wasps Periclistus, both being eaten by Chalcid wasps Eurytoma and Oligosthenus. These in turn eaten by hyper-parasites Chalcids Habrocytus bedeguaris and H. periclisti. The Bedeguar gall is also attacked by fungus Phragmidium suncorticum Mayri causes similar galls, less furry, on twigs.

Bedeguar gall was once used as tea to cure diahorrea in cattle.

All these different galls also found on the Dog rose below and sometimes others.

Rosa spinosissima, BURNET ROSE

Diplolepis spinosissimae Hymenopteran gall wasp causes spherical galls inside leaf midrib or petiole, this may also appear on garden roses.

Rosmarinus, ROSEMARY

Perennial not very hardy herb needing dry sunny site. Generally useful as it's scent confuses many pests and good bee plant.

ROTATION

This is vital, change the plants instead of growing more of the same in the same place and unwanted co-lives are handicapped and cannot build up so easily.

Rubus

All have very similar co-lives especially as so many are hybrids.
Probably the best general purpose 'wild-life' plants to fill any site.
May occasionally become infected by Clover Yellow Vein virus; yellow mosaic, necrosis and wilting which spreads most to Legumes: Cajanus, Canavalia, Cassia, Cicer, Crotolaria, Dolichos, Glycine, Hedysarum, Lathyrus, Lens, Lupinus, Medicago, Melilotus, Phaseolus, Trifolium, Trigonella, Vicia, and Vigna, and also to Antirrhinum, Atriplex, Chenopodium, Coriandrum, Cucurbita, Gladiolus, Gomphrena, Nicotiana, Nicandra, Papaver, Petunia, Proboscidea, Spinacia, Tetragonia and Viola.

Rubus caesius, DEWBERRY

Stems are galled by Dipteron gall-midge Lasioptera rubi /
argyrosticta / picta / fusca, which causes swellings on
stems deep within bush, lumpy, rough and reddish brown,
this is an ambrosia gall where fungus introduced at same
time to cause tissues to swell and become food for larvae.
This also attacks most brambles, below.

Rubus fruticosus, and others,

BLACKBERRIES, LOGANBERRIES et al

Remarkably vigorous these remain productive for longer
than most other soft fruits, true blackberries more than
their more raspberry like hybrids.
The former true ones may sometimes crop on side-shoots
off old wood, hybrids rarely do. Thornless varieties
seldom crop as well as thorny forms.
Seeds become inedible as they mature, microscope
reveals they are covered with tiny fish-hooks which
become more indigestible as they ripen!
Their bushes are sanctuaries in nature, small birds and
creatures can hide inside protected by the arching thorns,
the centres are often bone dry and provide a good place
to nest or hibernate.
The late flowering bramble caters for insects in early
autumn when food is getting short and the fruit then
feeds birds till winter.

Corky and dried up parts to fruits with little white maggots are result of Raspberry beetle Byturus tomentosus which commonly does more harm to the fruits of loganberries and similar hybrids than to raspberries.

Capsids Lygus pabulinus suck the foliage which is often badly damaged with large holes formed.

Aphids may do damage similar to that done on currants. Very uneven ripening of the fruits with odd shapes and reddish appearance could be Red-berry disease / Blackberry mite when a gall mite Eriophyes / Aceria essigi attacks blackberries, it overwinters under scales on the shoots and moves to eat flowers and fruit which then stay red without maturing properly.

Blackberry stems are galled by Hymenopteran gall-wasp Diastrophus rubi / Andricus hartigi, this mostly on outside of bush, swollen stems form with less prickles, start green go yellow then pink and purple and old ones become woody and brown, can be large specimens several inches long with hundreds of larvae. Also moves to raspberry. Prosopis bees make small tunnels in bramble stems and frequent the flowers. Osmia bees do similar especially O. leucomelana.

Loganberry is bothered by Cane Spot / Anthracnose Elsinoe veneta which also bothers raspberries, purple spots with white centres on stems, leaves and flower stalks, causes fruit to be small if set at all, generally causes stunting if spots turn to cankers.

Blackberries and loganberries particularly affected by Rubus Stunt virus spread by Leaf-hoppers Aphrodes and Euscelis spp. (These do no other noticeable harm so often not noticed). The leaves distort without mosaic mottling and the stems proliferate as with a witches broom and remain stunted from the viral disease also known as Reversion / Dwarfing.

Rubus idaeus, RASPBERRY

More woodland plants needing rich moist soil, chlorotic leaves with interveinal patterning are probably from too much lime in too dry a soil. Birds are the most associated co-life!

Wasps also damage the fruits leaving them sucked dry. Aphids of two varieties, pale green Rubus aphids Amphorophora rubi, and small greyish green Raspberry aphids Aphis idaei which spread the dreaded Mosaic virus and may also casue leaf curling first.

The infamous raspberry maggot is the grub of the brownish yellow Raspberry beetle Byturus tomentosus and not as often called, a weevil. The overwintering adults lay eggs in the flowers which are then consumed, and the fruits end up with scabby parts and little white grubs.

If there's a lot of damage to leaves with tiny holes, and more on the stems and shoots causing them to wilt or break then it could be the Red Legged Weevil Otiorhynchus clavipes, black with red legs, the damage starts in early spring, and will move onto currants and plums. Similar damage can be by the Clay-colured weevil Otiorhynchus singularis, another night feeder like the Red-legged weevil, these hide in debris during the day. The Clay-coloured is more destructive of the two as it strips bark, shoots as well as leaves, damage appears early summer, it overwinters as the larvae and adult in the ground where the larvae eat roots.

Strawberry Blossom weevils Anthonomus rubi often attack raspberries and lays eggs in the flowerbuds, destroyed by the feeding larvae then the whole fruit and stalk wither, this looks identical with damage by the Strawberry rhyncites Caennorhinus germaicus, both thin the crop so in the end we pick fewer but better berries. Redberry gall mites Aceria essigi are more often found on blackberries and causes poorly ripened berries, it overwinters under scales on the shoots and moves to flowers and fruit which then stay red without maturing. Little pink grubs in cracks in the bark on the canes are Raspberry Cane midges Thomasiniana theobaldi and these often let in disease such as Cane Blight Leptosphaeria coniophyrium, they over-winter in the soil underneath and emerge in early summer when the adults lay their eggs.

Another grub, the Raspberry Cane / Crown Borer Bembecia hylaeiformi eggs are laid in summer, the larva overwinters at the base enters a cane, lives inside restricting growth and causing die back, after several years it pupates then emerges as a clearwing moth about an inch long with four yellow bands on its abdomen so looks like a wasp.

Withered and wilted shoots in spring may have been tunnelled by the reddish grub of the Raspberry moth Lampronia rubiella, this also damages the plug of the fruit, it hibernates in debris.

Verticillium wilt V. dahliae in Dahlias is thought to be cause of Blue Stripe in raspberries where it causes blue stripes on the cane from the base up with leaves dying on the discoloured side, or the whole cane dies if girdled, often overwinters as spores in soil so roots and stem base most often attacked.

Cane Blight Leptosphaeria coniophyrium fungus, often let in by preceeding Cane midge damage, simply kills canes off.

Raspberry Spur blight Didymella applanata fungus starts at nodes and causes purple patches, these may cover the whole cane, buds at the nodes die off and spores are released from whitish patches.

Raspberry Cane spot or Anthracnose Elsinoe veneta causes purple spots with whitish centres on stems, leaves and stalks which sink into cankers or go grey with black dots. These split open cause the leaves to drop, shoots to die and fruits to distort and malform, ripen unevenly and plants do poorly. It overwinters on the old canes, also common on loganberries and other hybrids.

Raspberry Mildew Spaerotheca humili is found in crowded plantations in shade, it makes large white powdery patches on leaves and may sometimes move onto fruits.
Any plants especially old ones are prone to low vigour and yellow mottling from Raspberry Mosaic virus disease.
Raspberry Stunt virus causes the same low vigour without the mottling with numerous spindly dwarf shoots, spread by leaf-hoppers Aphrodes and Euscelis spp. (These do no other noticeable harm so often go unnoticed).
Avoid growing tomatoes nearby as they share a common virus Tomato Black Ring.
Raspberry Ringspot / Leaf Curl virus is spread by Longidorus nematode eelworms and spreads to redcurrants and strawberries, the leaf curling symptom of Ringspot destroyed Lloyd George, Malling Jewel, Malling Enterprise, and Norfolk Giant.
Arabis Mosaic Yellow Dwarf is also spread by nematode eelworms especially Xiphenema and also invades blackcurrants.
Symptoms of dwarfing and stunting could be pollen borne Chlorotic Leaf Spot virus.

Rumex, DOCKS & SORRELS

Mostly wind pollinated, deep rooted weeds.
Famous for relieving nettle stings.
Very rich in vitamin C and oxalates and unpalatable, some species inedible if not poisonous.

Seeds known to remain viable sixty years plus. Large numbers in pasture may indicate horses pastured in past as seeds go through their gut intact.

Docks often attacked by rust fungus Uromyces rumicis, less if plants also attacked by herbivorous insects and vice versa (insects show more mortality and less fecundity on infected plants).

Thought to harbour White Root-rot, Rosellinia radiceperda, and spread Mangold Fly Pegomyia betae, Bean Aphid Aphis rumicis and sawfly Ametastegia glabrata.

Two spot Adalia bipunctata and seven spot coccinella septempunctata ladybirds especially feed on the aphids on docks

All parts of docks are mined by weevils; Apion affine, A. curtirostre, A. frumentarium, A. hydrolapathi, A. marchicum, A. violaceum, and Lixus spp.

Holes initially mined by weevils may become enlarged by small earthworms, woodlice and centipedes.

A fly Contarinia acetosellae larva makes a gall in the flowerhead.

Leaves mined by fly larvae of Norellisoma spinimanum and several Pegomya spp. and these often parasitized by at least 10 species Hymenoptera.

Weevils and fly larvae mostly parasitized by Colastes braconius, Chlorocytus laogore, Eurytoma curculionum, Lamprotarpus splendens, Seladerma breve, Skeloceras truncatum, Chrysocharis nephereus, Entedon rumicis, E. hercyna, Dapsilarthra / Adelurola florimela, Opius rufipes, Biosteres carbonarius, B. impressus, and Lucobracon erraticus.

Leaves and stems attacked by froghopper spittlebugs, these may be (up to 80%) parasitized by a fly Verrallia aucta which attacks the adults rather than the larvae (who are well protected by the spittle).
Much damage caused by green metallic beetles Gastrophysa viridula and yellowish Galerucella nymphaeae larvae and adults, these predated by Anthocorid bugs and hoverfly larvae.

Rumex acetosa, SORREL

Dioecious crop used as spinach more on the continent than UK.
Larvae of the weevil Apion affine form galls in flowerheads and stems, A. cruentatum in base of leaf-stalks, A. frumentarium causes red galls in the petiole and leaf-blade.
Rhinoncus perpendicularis and R. pericarpius feed on the roots.

Rumex acetosella, SHEEP'S SORREL

The numbers increase as a pasture becomes more acid. Accumulates Calcium, Phosphorous, Magnesium and Silica.
Apion rubens weevils eat into leaf stalks and mid-ribs and may cause galls.
A. sanguineum weevils cause galls feeding on roots and stems, adults make circular holes in leaves.

Commonest weevil eating roots is the red A. haematodes.

Rumex crispus, CURLED DOCK

Recognised as a pernicious weed this produces up to 40,000 seeds a year.
Often attacked by Aphis rumicis black-fly.
Chrysomelid beetle Gastrophysa viridula may cause extensive defoliation.
Large red weevil Apion frumentarium / miniatum attacks base of stem and may cause galls the size of walnuts.
Hypera rumicis weevil larvae feed on leaves.

Rumex hydrolapathum, GREAT WATER-DOCK

A Chrysomelid beetle Galerucella nymphaeae may cause extensive defoliation.

Rumex obtusifolius, BROAD-LEAVED DOCK

Accumulates Phosphorus and Nitrogen.
Host to White Root Rot Rosellinia necatrix, and harbours Bean Aphid Aphis rumicis.

Chrysomelid beetle Gastrophysa viridula may cause extensive defoliation.

Large red weevil Apion frumentarium / miniatum attacks base of stem and may cause galls the size of walnuts.

Hypera rumicis weevil larvae feed on leaves.

Rhinoncus perpendicularis and R. pericarpius weevil larvae feed on roots.

Ruta gravaeolens, RUE

Hardy perennial herb, once eaten now considered toxic, attractive blued foliage is very irritant in hot weather. Generally a good influence to other plants and although poisonous was grown near stables to keep away flying pests.

The smell will drive away fleas and Japanese beetles.

SABADILLA dust

This Veratrum lily extract was succesful against grasshoppers, cornworms, cornborers, armyworms, silkworms, melonworm, blister beetle, greenhouse leaf tier, chinch bugs, lygus bug, harlequin bugs, codling moths, webworms, aphids, cabbage loopers and squash bugs since the sixteenth century.

It is now almost unknown, unavailable and illegal in the UK for no obvious reason.

Salix, WILLOWS & SALLOWS

Generally trees of wet places, one best avoids Weeping willow, S. babylonica (intd 1730) in small gardens, it's too big, and no friend to ponds with the leaves polluting the water.

The bark of Salix spp. contains very high levels of salicylic acid and beavers eating the bark have to perspire the excess in their sweat.

The terminal leaves of almost all species are attacked by a Dipteron gall-midge Rhabdophaga rosaria / Cecidomyia / cinerearum which causes 'Camellia gall' or 'Terminal rosette gall' where thirty to sixty leaves are clustered and shortened to make a ball which forms in spring, turns brown and hangs on in autumn, each ball has one pink grub, this matures and pupates inside, sometimes another gall-midge Perrisia iteophila is found with it.

Wood alive and dead is often consumed by the Goat Moth Cossus ligniperda.

The Jew's Ear bracket fungus Hirneola / Auricularia auricula-judae is not only edible but a great Chinese delicacy, brown and hard when dry, the gelatinous fresh, may often be found on dead wood on trees, also on elm, elderberry and false acacias.

The trunks, stumps and large branches, dead and alive, support a semi-circular bracket fungus Polyporus / Polyporellus squamosus, brown scales with white edible flesh smelling of cucumber, this grows quickly can reach many pounds in weight but harms trees causing the wood to decay with timber White rot, also moves onto beech, horse chestnut, lime, poplar and walnut.

Pholiota destruens, inedible, slimy beige to brown caps with numerous whitish scales, brownish gills with ragged edges, bitter with strong mushroom smell, is found on stumps, dead and live wood and also on poplars.
Large decaying willow logs (rejected by a cricket bat factory) used as a low retaining wall resulted some decades later in an annual display of the seldom seen fungal puffballs Rosy Earth Stars Geastrum rufescens.

Salix alba, WHITE WILLOW

The leaf blade of younger near-terminal leaves get attacked by acarine gall mite Eriophyes marginatus causing tiny galls on the margins which rolls inwards on top, seldom more than ten per leaf, starts yellowish going orange, red, purple then brown, each gall has several tiny mites living amongst hairs, this is often found with the Camellia gall midge Rhabdophaga rosaria which also galls terminal foliage.
Leaf-blade also attacked by Hymenopteran sawfly Pontania / Nematus proxima / capreae / gallicola / vallisnieri which causes Bean galls, often several per leaf, sticking out both sides equally, bean shaped and up to half an inch long, usually reddish above greenish yellow below (on crack willows reddish both sides), larvae pupates in yellow cocoon after dropping to ground or hiding in bark, this sawfly can have two broods most years, one of few Hymenopteran gallers which makes hole through which it dumps its excreta instead of letting this remain in leaf.

The leaf-blade is also attacked by Hymenopteran sawfly Pontania vesicator / Nematus crassipes / helicinis / lugunensis causing a pale yellowish green often pinkish oval swelling on underside about half by three quarters of an inch, appearing in early summer to mature by autumn when the larvae drops out on a silk thread to pupate in a silk lined cocoon, often this gall has Melampsora fungal mycelium growing in it.

Salix atrocinerea, GREY SALLOW

The stem is attacked by Dipteron gall-midge Rhabdophaga salicis / Cecidomyia / argyrosticta / de geeri / salicina causing a spindle shaped swelling up to about three quarters an inch long, similarly coloured, with about thirty larvae inside, when they leave each discards its pupal skin projecting from the exit hole.
The stem also attacked by Dipterona gromyzid Agromyza schineri causing cushion galls, up to half an inch or so long swellings in the sides of the stems, often on a spiral or zig-zag pattern, these galls are greenish with faint wavy lines, the larvae leaves to pupate in the soil but the galls perisist, more often found on bushy specimens rather than trees.

Salix babylonica, WEEPING WILLOW

Introduced species, gets too big, often planted near ponds which it then gunges up with dropped leaves and twigs.

Very prone to anthracnose rust attack.

Salix caprea, GOAT WILLOW

Leaf-blade is attacked by Dipteron gall-midge Iteomyia
capreae / Oligotrophus, this forms greenish pouch galls up
to half an inch long in rows between the bigger veins
showing as rounded bumps on the upper side and with a
reddish hole underneath, often found in association with
another gall making causer the bean-gall sawfly Pontania
proxima.

The stem is galled by Coleopteran longhorn beetle
Saperda populnea forming Timberman galls, this the
largest UK gall. The responsible beetle emerges in early
summer, bites a hole through the bark and lays eggs every
few inches, the larvae eat the pith and the tissues swell
around each one, forming spindle shaped galls an inch
long, on aspen the egg entry hole forms raised scars, on
willow a scar depression, it takes two years for the cycle
to complete, the exit hole is often on the opposite side to
the entry.

The stem is attacked by Dipteron gall-midge Rhabdophaga
salicis / Cecidomyia / argyrosticta / de geeri / salicina
causing a spindle shaped swelling up to about three
quarters an inch long, similarly coloured, with about thirty
larvae inside, when they leave each discards its pupal skin
projecting from the exit hole.

The leaf-blade is attacked by acarine gall-mite Eriophyes tetanothorax / Cecidomyia / Phytoptus / salicis forming small spherical slightly hairy galls of yellow green to reddy brown, up to thirty per leaf pushing up through the top surface with a hole underneath, inside is full of hairs, often associated with witches-broom galls, also attacks other Salix.

Leaf-blade is also attacked by Hymenopteran sawfly Pontania viminalis / Nematus viminalis / pedunculi / bellus which makes an half inch long oval gall on the underside (a lump may show on topside) greenish yellow with white hairs, usually near midrib and up to half a dozen per leaf, larvae drops out to pupate.

Salix fragilis, CRACK-WILLOW

Leaf-blade attacked by Hymenopteran sawfly Pontania / Nematus proxima / capreae / gallicola / vallisnieri which causes Bean galls, often several per leaf, sticking out both sides equally, bean shaped and up to half an inch long, usually reddish above greenish yellow below but on crack willows reddish both sides, larvae pupates in yellow cocoon after dropping to ground or hiding in bark, this sawfly can have two broods most years, one of few Hymenopteran gallers which makes hole through which it dumps its excreta instead of letting this remain in leaf.

The leaf-blade is also attacked by Hymenopteran sawfly Pontania vesicator / Nematus crassipes / helicinis / lugunensis causing a pale yellowish green often pinkish oval swelling on underside about half by three quarters of an inch, appearing in early summer to mature by autumn when the larvae drops out on a silk thread to pupate in a silk lined cocoon, often this gall has Melampsora fungal mycelium growing in it.

Salix purpurea, PURPLE WILLOW

The leaf-blade is attacked by Hymenopteran sawfly Pontania vesicator / Nematus crassipes / helicinis / lugunensis causing a pale yellowish green often pinkish oval swelling on underside about half by three quarters of an inch, appearing in early summer to mature by autumn when the larvae drops out on a silk thread to pupate in a silk lined cocoon, often this gall has Melampsora fungal mycelium growing in it.

Salix triandra, FRENCH / ALMOND WILLOW

Leaf-blade attacked by Hymenopteran sawfly Pontania / Nematus proxima / capreae / gallicola / vallisnieri which causes Bean galls, often several per leaf, sticking out both sides equally, bean shaped and up to half an inch long, usually reddish above greenish yellow below (on crack willows reddish both sides), larvae pupates in yellow cocoon after dropping to ground or hiding in bark, this sawfly can have two broods most years, one of few Hymenopteran gallers which makes hole through which it dumps its excreta instead of letting this remain in leaf. Both leaf-bud and catkin attacked by Dipteron gall-midge Rhabdophaga / Cecidomyia heterobia, in spring on some trees many catkins develop a swollen mass on the end up to three quarters of an inch across of greyish down, these catkin galls hang on longer than others and adult midges emerge in early summer to lay eggs in leaf buds where rosette galls form for the next lot of larvae, both galls are usually also infested with Melampsora fungal mycelium. This galler, R. heterobia, also attacks common osiers as well.

Salix viminalis, OSIER

Leaf margin attacked by Dipteron gall-midge Dasyneura /
Cecidomyia / Perissia marginotorquens which lays eggs on
the underside, the feeding larvae roll the leaf edges about
them puckering and turning them blotchy green, yellow
and reddy brown and making a pod several inches long
with many in it, the larvae vacate in autumn to overwinter
in the soil.
Dasyneura / Cecidomyia clausilia does similar causing
separate rolled pods with one larva in each.
Leaf-blade also attacked by Hymenopteran sawfly
Pontania / Nematus viminalis / pedunculi / bellus which
makes an half inch long oval gall on the underside (a lump
may show on topside) greenish yellow with white hairs,
usually near midrib and up to half a dozen per leaf, larvae
drops out to pupate.

Salvia officinalis, SAGE

Smell said to hide Brassicas from many pests.
Leaf-hoppers Erythroneura pallidifrons, pale yellow or
white, eighth inch long, active insects may do some
damage causing bleached areas on leaves, also spread to
Calceolarias, Fushias, Primulas, and Verbenas.
Attacked by Eelworm nematodes causing brown spots and
blackened areas, which also attacks ferns, Begonias,
Coleus, Gloxinias and orchids.

Sambucus ebulis, DWARF ELDER

The foetid vanilla like smell of leaves placed in grain helps protect it from mice, however this also has poisonous berries.

Sambucus nigra, ELDERBERRY

Beloved by small boys for making blowpipes this tree likes rich moist soil. Whole shoots up to six foot long can be snapped off in the green and make excellent bulk compost material.

The berries are a good sacrificial crop to keep birds off other fruit. These make a passable jelly and wine and were once used to add more colour to many wines.

The leaves used to be boiled with soft soap to make an aphicide. This spray was also used against carrot root fly, cucumber beetles, peach tree borers and root maggots. Elderberry is another apocryphal and ineffective mole deterrent.

The blooms are sweet scented but contain no honey, can be battered and fried in moderation.

Masses of black aphids often cover feets of young shoots to the tips.

The Jew's Ear bracket fungus Hirneola / Auricularia auricula-judae is not only edible but a great Chinese delicacy, brown and hard when dry, the gelatinous fresh, may often be found on dead wood on trees, also on elm, willow and false acacias.

The giant edible puffball Calvatia gigantea when found is often near elders and sometimes hazels.

Santolina incana, COTTON LAVENDER

Makes a good edging for paths and the scent may help confuse pests.
Has been made into a spray against corn wireworms and southern rootworms.

Saponaria, SOAPWORT

The flowers are accessible to Lepidoptera only.
Slugs avoided soapwort extracts in trials, contains many saponins which make it a natural cleanser though it may irritate some skins.

SAPONIN

Soapy substance found in many plants particularly in horse chestnut, Aesculus, conkers, which ground up also discourage slugs.

Sarothamnus scoparius / scoparia, BROOM

A Leguminous wild shrub with garden forms useful on poor soil.

Leaf-bud and fruit are galled by Dipteron gall-midge Asphondylia sarothamni / mayri, this is an Ambrosia gall where a fungus also attacks the plant though unusually here the insect does not apparently feed on the distorted material which beomes a pink or reddish oval gall, pointed with a green apex or an elongated pale green swelling on the pod wall.

Sarracenia, PITCHER PLANTS

Surprisingly hardy, carnivorous these are most effective fly catchers, each hollow leaf catches many hundreds and every plant has many such leaves making a large total catch of all sorts of flying insects. S. purpurea is also reputed to catch slugs.

Do remove the flowers or their smell will attract even more flies.

SASSAFRAS oil

This mixed with glacial acetic acid makes bait for codling moths of apples.

Satureia hortensis, SUMMER SAVORY

Annual herb that grows and cooks well with broad beans
and theoretically protects them from blackfly and beetles
though in the UK their seasons barely touch.
Exudates from summer savory significantly reduce
infestations of clubroot fungus of Brassicas.
Winter savory is similar but hardier and less well
flavoured. It's probably this perennial form growing
nearby that helps keep blackfly off broad beans.
Which, summer or winter, is not known but one may
discourage Mexican bean beetles.

SAWDUST

May not be a good material to use as mulch or anywhere
else unless absolutely confident that the wood was
untreated.
If used as mulch add extra nitrogenous material like
seaweed or manure to help prevent the sawdust robbing
the soil as it rots.
Sawdust even at <1%, increases damping off problems,
particularly Pythium, in Brassica and other seedlings.

Scabiosa arvensis, FIELD SCABIOUS

The blooms visited by great number of insects, only
flowers known to be visited by Andrena hattorfiana bees.

Scabiosa columbaria, LESSER / SMALL SCABIOUS

The shoots and associated parts are attacked by acarine gall-mites Eriophyes squalidus / Phytoptus making filzgalls of masses of silky white hairs which resemble fungal growths especially as the attacked parts swell and distort.

SCALE INSECTS AND MEALY BUGS

Scale are hard to spot then you see them everywhere. Small helmet shaped bumps on stems look like buds or indeed scales, when squidged may exude juices or white powder (eggs). More mobile is the other similar pest Mealy bugs, pinkish or greyish white and covered in cottony wax and fluff. Both plague perennial plants under cover and some garden specimens, especially evergreens, such as bay, they may move onto annuals, especially Mealy bug.
Ants often farm Scale and make these far more of a problem than they can achieve by themselves.
Mealy bugs can be lured onto trap plants of sprouting potatoes, tomatoes or cucurbits and then disposed of. The Scale do not oblige so easily.

Under cover when the temperature is above 14°C (5,7°F) use a parasitic nematode Steinernema to parasitise the scales or release a parasitic wasp Metaphycus helvolus. For Mealy bugs introduce the predator Cryptolaemus montrouzieri, a ladybird whose shaggy white larvae control them when the temperature is at least 11°C (52°F).

Both Mealy bug and Scale may also be controlled by Lacewings, and on low growing plants Hypoaspis, which is also used to control Sciarid flies and Thrips.

I have it on good authority that a tropical house at a zoo has controlled mealy bugs, and aphids and baby cockroaches by introducing Flat Tailed Day Geckos, Phelsuma laticauda, which are hand width sized diurnal lizards. Somewhat expensive and impractical for the average greenhouse these are a possibility if you have a large establishment to patrol. I fear my cats would regard them as a legitimate target though!

Scilla nonscripta, BLUEBELL

Native species threatened by imported more vigorous Spanish form.

Scattered brown spots on their leaves is Rust Uromyces scillarum.

Seedlings may be seriously damaged or destroyed by Smut Ustilago vaillantii.

Scorzonera hispanica

Edible crop similar to salsify with long thin carrot like roots.
Attractive flowers beneficial to insects.
This may repel carrot rootfly.
Seldom suffers diseases save White Blister, Cystopus cubicus, which causes small whitish blisters on leaves, seldom serious.

Scrophularia aquatica, WATER FIGWORT / BETONY

The floral parts are attacked by Coleopteran weevils Gymnetron beccabungae which larvae live in and gall the ovary causing the seeds to fail to develop.

Scrophularia nodosa, COMMON / KNOTTED FIGWORT

Has a foetid scent to flowers which attracts wasps.
The floral parts are attacked by Coleopteran weevils Gymnetron villosulum which larvae live in and gall the ovary causing the seeds to fail to develop.

SEAWEED

Typically Scottish farmers applied 25-30 tons per acre, Jersey 45, Isle of Thanet 10-15. When collected fresh the long broad leaf-like deeper water Laminaria has more nitrogenous value than the Fucus bladder-wrack found on the rocks, either have higher potash than the other plants collected with them. Both are richer in spring than autumn. Wet weed contains very approximately 70-80% water, which is drier than many land plants. The 13-25% organic content contains between 0.3-0.5% nitrogen, 0.8-1.8% Potash and 0.02-0.17% Phosphorous (measured as pentoxide).

Whether fresh or processed this renewable resource is one of the best aids to fertility and disease resistance. Use as much as you can get your hands on, spray the diluted extract on everything at least once a month. The smell masks plant smells from co-lives, it stimulates healthy growth and promotes soil activity. Contains every trace element in appropriate proportion thus immediately corrects for nutrient deficiencies. Seaweed solution sprayed on plants nutritionally out of balance has an effect noticeable over-night and I am convinced many problems are avoided by the health doses of seaweed induces. Probably as good for us as well.

Secale cereale, RYE

This makes excellent cover for winter green manure producing great bulk by most springs.

Sedum spectabile, Autumn Joy

Succulent garden flower extrememly prone to vine weevils eating roots.

Sempervivum, HOUSELEEKS

These need full exposure and little else.
Clumps can be pulled to bits by birds searching for lunch.
The leaves become covered with yellowish brown spots of Rust Endophyllum sempervivi.

Senecio greyi

A tough ever-grey shrub, in the same genus are several herbaceous plants below, all are subject to the Rust Coleosporium senecionis, this causes bright yellow waxy patches which are seldom noticed as these occur only on the underside of the leaves of the shrubs.

Senecio jacobaea, RAGWORT

Several other related weeds resemble ragwort, including groundsel, but the real Ragwort is commonly much larger than any contenders.

It is dangerous to stock and is considered a weed despite its wildlife value.

The blooms have been recorded visited by 49 different species predominantly bees and flies, another reference gave 40 species: 3 butterflies and moths, 16 species bee, 18 species Diptera flies and 3 other.

Flowers certainly attract Colletes fodiens bees, these are there preyed upon by Cuckoo bee Epeolus rufipes.

Ragwort is an alternate host for the common leaf-hopper Eupteryx aurata shared with hogweed, hemp agrimony, mint, and stinging nettles.

The stems support agromyzid stem-borer Melanagromyza aeneoventris.

Senecio sylvaticus, HEATH GROUNDSEL, S. aquaticus, MARSH RAGWORT, and S. erucifolius, HOARY RAGWORT

The latter pair and Common Ragwort are attacked by Dipteron gall-midge Contarina jacobaeae / Diplosis which lays an egg in the flowerhead, a larva eats out the inside of the base which swells and becomes pear shaped, the bracts may become wine coloured and twisted together, this gall may reach an inch across, and up to a quarter of all flowerheads may be galled in a large clump, the larvae drop to pupate and overwinter in the ground.

Senecio vulgaris, GROUNDSEL

This will germinate even in winter months.
Accumulates Iron and Nitrogen.
Blooms seldom visited by any insects.
Host for many plant co-lives over-winter especially of Peach-potato aphid, Myzus persiceae, which also attacks lettuces and other crops and nematodes that likewise attack many other crop and ornamental plants. Also subject to Wilt fungus, Powdery Mildew, Downy Mildew, Petal Blight, several Rusts and Pine Cluster-cups Peridermium pini.

Most parts galled by rust fungus Basidiomycete Coleosporium secionis which spends part of its life on Scots and Austrian pines alternating with groundsel and cultivated Cinerarias.
Lettuce Mosaic and Cabbage Black Ringspot viruses

SENESCENCE

In old age most plants look poorly and eventually die, annuals do so in one year. The symptoms of senescence may resemble disease or nutrient disorders for the very reason that the plant is withdrawing material from some parts for use or storage elsewhere. I am frequently asked to look at allegedly blighted potatoes which have only died back naturally as the crop matured!

Sequoiadendron / Sequoia gigantea / Wellingtonia, WELLINGTONIA, MAMMOTH TREE

A huge very long living evergreen trees with remarkably deeply fissured, remarkably soft and spongy, bark full of cracks and crevices. Only introduced to the UK in 1853 and not common except in the larger parks and gardens it has become adopted by Tree Creepers Certhia familiaris britannica. They have discovered they can wriggle into fissures in the bark. These are THE perfect fit, really well insulated, and camouflaged, roosting places for them. The numerous niches in this tree are so appealing these birds have inadvertantly congregated; perforce becoming more social. It will be interesting to see where this leads and it seems likely their plumage will be moving to match the same distinctive reddy brown of this tree.

SEX

Some plants are dioecious and have their male and female parts on separate plants. They need pollinating agents and must have, not just a suitable pollinating companion, but one of the right sex, and flowering at the same time. Common dioecious plants are; asparagus, kiwi vines, some old grapevines, butcher's broom, campion, holly, Pernettya, sea buckthorn, Skimmia and some willows.

Sida spinosa and S. rhombifolia

Warm country weeds which are especially dangerous as white fly Bemesia tabaci spreads Bean Dwarf mosaic; yellow mosaic and stunting, to beans from these.

Sidalcea

These garden flowers prone to Hollyhock rust, Puccinia malvacearum which infests many hosts but does not alternate between them at different stages, however be warned that it will spread to common mallows, tree mallows, Abutilons and hollyhocks, in all of them it infests the leaves and petioles forming yellow to brown pustules on the undersides often causing swelling and distortion.

SILICA

Much undervalued trace element essential for tough healthy plants. Teas made from nettles and Equisetum containing Silica have fungicidal properties.
High percentages occur in Polygonum aviculare, the common knotweed and couch grass which makes these especially valuable for compost, after wilting or drowning!

SILVER foliage

Most plants with this are sun lovers and dislike shade and damp situations. Silvering usually caused by fine hairs covering surface, reduce water loss, decrease sunlight and handicap insects but may also trap moisture and be more prone to rots and moulds.

Sinapsis alba, WHITE MUSTARD

This carries most of the co-lives of Brassicas but thus also the predators that control them. Host in particular of Turnip Flea Beetle or Fly, Phyllotreta / Haltica nemorum, this makes so many holes in leaves that it can kill smaller plants and seedlings
and of course Brassica Clubroot Plasmodiphora Brassicae and another fungal problem Peronospora parasitica.

Sinapsis alba / arvensis, CHARLOCK / WILD MUSTARD

Similar to cultivated form above and to wild radish, a problem weed tough to kill.

The roots are galled by Coleopteran weevil Ceuthorrhynchus pleurostigma / assimilis / sulcicollis 'Turnip and cabbage gall weevil' which forms marble sized swellings on the roots, this may seriously harm growth in young small plants and older ones may also suffer as the larval exit holes foster other infections. This can be widespread in an area as it also attacks Arabis, turnips, cabbages, swedes and wild radish.

Shoot apex attacked by Dipteron gall-midge Dasyneura sisymbrii / Cecidomyia barbarea, this arrests normal growth causing glossy swellings and lumps, often cream, pink or reddish, worst in floral parts, serious infestations can form what look much like small raspberries, often infests other Cruciferae such as hedge mustard, creeping yellow cress, cabbage, yellow rocket and wild radish.

Sisymbrium officinale, HEDGE MUSTARD

Host in US to Colorado beetle Doryphora decemlineata.

Sisymbrium sophia, FLIXWEED

Shoot apex galled by Dipteron gall-midge Dasyneura sisymbrii / Cecidomyia barbarea, this arrests normal growth causing glossy swellings and lumps, often cream, pink or reddish, worst in floral parts, serious infestations can form what look much like small raspberries, often infests other Cruciferae such as yellow rocket, creeping yellow-cress, cabbage, charlock and wild radish.

Sium latifolium, GREATER WATER PARSNIP

Blooms visited by 32 insect species: 0 butterflies and moths, 0 species bee, but 20 species Diptera flies and 12 other.

SLIME MOULDS / FUNGUS

Odd slimy foamy masses appearing overnight, usually where there is plentiful organic material, most often Mucilago / Spumaria spp. later the foam dries to blackish mass of spores.

SLUGS & SNAILS, mollusc gastropods

Well known co-lives found almost everywhere. Many different species are native to the UK, 80 land snails, 40 water snails and 20 slugs. There is even a carnivorous cannabilistic Shelled slug Pestacella / Testacella haliotidea, pale yellowish and up to three inches long, identifiable by the small vestigial shell like a fingernail on its tail, this mostly predates worms.

Most snails are hermaphrodite and are right-handed, dextral with seldom a sinistral left hander occurring. However Clausilia bidentata a small snail found on mossy tree trunks and masonry is normally sinistral.

The Edible or Roman snail Helix pomatia is only found in lime rich soil areas and is indeed edible, as are the eggs (which are farmed as a caviar like food). These eggs are spherical whitish transparent laid in masses in the soil usually under some debris and hatch in approx. three weeks in warm conditions.

The commonest snails that cause major plant losses are the Large / Garden Helix aspersa which is very common with a grey brown shell with paler markings, this does much damage especially when it gets into trays of seedlings and so on.

The small Strawberry snail Hygromia striolata also does a lot of damage.

The Banded snail has a variable colour from white through yellow pink and brown with one to five spiral darker bands and is more of a farm than a garden inhabitant.

Although snails do some harm most are often recycling dead and decaying material or grazing algae off surfaces when they become useful. By far and away it is slugs who do the more serious damage in most gardens.

The commonest slugs are; the Large Black Arion ater which may actually be any shade of black to chestnut brown, and the Great Grey Limax maximus. Both do relatively little damage despite their size (up to 8 inches long) as they eat predominantly decaying material.

The nearly as big Red slug Arion rufus is seldom seen in any number.

The Garden slug Arion hortensis is usually smaller but may reach over an inch, dark with a most distinctive yellowish orange sole and has tougher skin than others.

The White-soled slug is flattened, greyish with a white sole.

The Netted slug Agriolimax reticulatus is pale and mottled and particularly troublesome as it 'climbs' up plants and gets inside many especially lettuces and cauliflowers.

The Field slug mottled grey, reddish or yellow tinged, is very common and very voracious.

The Keeled slug is brown or greyish brown with a ribbed keel along its back and is particularly fond of roots and potatoes.

A new super sized Spanish slug is supposedly invading the UK, however few have ever seen our own giant, the woodland Ash Black slug Limax cinereoniger which can reach 15inches (38cm).

The symptoms are too well known; bits missing; whole trays of seedlings gone, holes on edges and also in middles of leaves, in roots, round stems, in tubers, especially prone are freshly planted thus wilting plants, most seedlings and of course fallen fruits. These ubiquitous co-lives eat by rasping with file like tongues so holes in solid surfaces tend to be rounded not angular. Their description needs no describing. In their absence the confirmation of their guilt is the slime trail. This slime is also harmful to vegetation as it promotes the germination of grey mould spores, Botrytis cinerea. Slugs generally prefer to eat dandelion, shepherd's purse, fat hen and clover before wheat so no weeds at all in the wheat means losses first from slugs and then from botrytis.

Thorny, prickly and evergreen plants with dusty dry soil underneath and strong smelling herbs such as rosemary, wormwood and oak leaves may dissuade them proceeding. Traps of saucers of beer, milk or juice lure them to drown. Twigs must be put in for beetles to escape on. Any cool, dark moist place attracts them so marrow shells, hollowed out carrots, apples, spuds and flat bits of rotten wood make excellent traps.

Can be lured to leaves of creeping buttercup and stinging nettles - a use for these weeds. In trials slugs could find most easily cut potato, carrot, lettuce and germinating wheat. Slugs and snails have been shown to avoid crushed tubers of Cyclamen purpurascens and will not cross a barrier made of them. Slugs most avoided ginger and soapwort extracts in trials, followed by herb Robert and marjoram. Slugs also avoided ground up horse chestnuts, cocoa shells and raw wool (a pelleted form is now available commercially).

Slugs and snails were killed by extract of Euphorbia splendens. Pine needles make it harder for snails to detect their food. Boiled potatoes, and possibly the water, consumed by slugs, allegedly removes their responses to light and so they may more easily be caught by birds.

One simple but expensive solution is the commercially available parasitic eelworm nematodes. When the soil is moist and the temperature above 5°C (41°F) water on Phasmarhabditis hermaphrodita, a microscopic worm, repeating this every 6 weeks or so will almost eradicate slugs. These parasitic eelworms are not so effective on snails which are harder to get at being protected by their shell and also by living away out of the soil. However the nematodes may still work on snails if watered on the surfaces the molluscs crawl across.

Ducks, especially Khaki Campbells and Indian Runners, love slugs and snails and do much less damage than hens, in the East they rent flocks to clean the crops.

Then there are nature's predatory co-lives, Song birds being especially useful. Their encouragement is so important especially as they give us so much pleasure too. Do remember to make sure there are a few big stones about to serve as anvils for the thrushes to shatter their snail's shells upon.

Ponds and pools particularly those with muddy edges and marginal areas help breed up Marsh Sciarid flies which attack slugs and snails. And of course those wet areas also help the frogs, newts and toads all of which will keep the mollusc population down.

Ground beetles of many families eat the odd slug or snail but more importantly massacre their eggs. And of course though falling in numbers all over the UK there are still many hedgehogs well known for their nightly foraging of all sorts of pests (and beneficial creatures too, indeed they eat anything smaller than them that moves).

I decided rather than kill so many so often I would make them atone for their damage and made a moated snailcatraz where these are confined along with the larger slugs. The cage has water, soil, fresh food and cardboard (they like this) and spaced stacks of tile and pot to hide in. Every few weeks I wash this through to extract their manure which I give to my crops- as natural and 'expected' as worm droppings.

Solanum dulcamara, BITTERSWEET

Poisonous plant.
Host in US to Colorado beetle Doryphora decemlineata.

Susceptible to wart disease / black scab / potato cancer /
Synchytrium endobioticum / Chrysophlyctis endobiotica /
Oedomyces leproides of potatoes.

Solanum melongena, EGGPLANT / AUBERGINE

Related to tomatoes, potatoes and peppers it is often
grown with the last as they like same warm rich
conditions but should be kept away from the first two as
sharing too many co-lives.
Can be hidden in US from Colorado beetles by
interplanting with beans.

Solanum nigrum, BLACK NIGHTSHADE

Black berried weed often confused with other
nightshades, bittersweet and deadly nightshade.
This is considered poisonous in all parts, however it
appears to be identical with the fruit known as a type of
(non-vaccinium) Huckleberry in the USA and the same
plant is eaten as a spinach in the Caribbean, it seems likely
different strains have been selected!
These have long lived seed as flushes appear when old soil
is newly uncovered. This is also said to appear where too
many hoed crops have been grown.
Potential host in US to Colorado beetle Doryphora
decemlineata though also rumoured to poison them.

Host to Black Bean aphid overwinter.
Also susceptible to Wart disease of potatoes, see.

Solanum sarrachoides, GREEN NIGHTSHADE

Another poisonous species, also host in US to Colorado beetle Doryphora decemlineata.

Solanum sisymbrifolium, LYCHEE / LITCHI TOMATO

A thorny straggly plant resembling a tomato crossed with a thistle this blue flowered relative planted out in infested soil awakens potato cyst nematodes which cannot actually live on it and are thus starved. In trials it's shown extremely effective at reducing levels, by 80%, and more if repeated. Can be regularly kept cut back for comfort, the haulm does not need to be dug in and as it's very thorny I suggest burn rather than compost everything above ground level.
Note- in trials with Nicotiana tabacum as a comparison the year before, the following potato plants were late and stunted by both precursors. And following peas were much more stunted by Solanum than Nicotiana precursors.

Solanum tuberosum, POTATOES

Dried potato contains 4% ashes.

Potato juice made by cold extraction from the tubers, especially after the tubers have sprouted, is extremely toxic to bacteria, yet breaks down quickly in light or with heat.

Being highly bred and much grown these are very prey to pests and disease, keep them well away from their relations tomatoes.

Onions and other Alliums going before in rotation will prevent Rhizoctonia infections.

Raspberries are not good with or near potatoes as suspected of promoting blight AND the raspberries share a Ring spot virus with tomatoes so are doubly suspect.

The bird-dropping-like slug of the Lily beetle Lilloceris lilli, a bright reddy orange rather smart looking beastie, destroys the leaves also eats lilies, lily of the valley, hollyhocks, Hostas, Solomon's seal and tobacco.

In the USA aubergine plants can be used amongst potatoes as sacrificial crops to their devastating Colorado beetle Leptinotarsa / Doryphora decemlineata, a yellow and black striped ladybird like beetle with reddish orange grubs with small legs. Overwinters as adult, which eats young potato foliage, lays up to four hundred eggs in batches of two dozen on the underside of leaves, these hatch into the grubs which eat even more foliage and having two or more generations soon reach plague proportions.

This last co-life and several potato eelworms are harboured by black and woody nightshade so these should be kept weeded out, especially as they may be spurred into germination by potatoes.

Potato nematode eelworms Heterodera rostochiensis are microscopic, survive as cysts in soil for years, activated by root exudates they invade the potato destroying vigour, stunting the plant which yellows, new cysts form on roots which can just be seen by naked eye. Incorporating fresh compost and growing Tagetes whose exudates reduce populations of eelworm nematodes helps, as can green manures of mustard, barley or oats grown and dug in beforehand. For a possible way to eliminate Potato cyst nematode, see S. sisymbrifolium above.

The Green Capsid bug Lygus pabulinus is commonly found on potatoes as it has so many other common host plants, the adults are only a fifth of an inch long, green with long legs, these and their similar but smaller nymph larvae suck sap causing leaf crinkling and a loss of vigour in extreme infestations, later when the causers have left this damage may be confused with several diseases.

Spreading virus diseases are green aphid Myzus persicae and Potato aphid Macrosiphon solani which also steal sap and reduce vigour.

Occasionally potatoes are attacked by Anthomyia tuberosa root flies particularly when following a poorly rotated cabbage family crops.

Tubers may develop faults predominantly caused by incorrect growing or storing conditions;

Tuber Blackening is caused by unbalanced and excessive feeding.

Black Heart in tubers is mostly caused by poor anaerobic storage.

Erratic watering, insufficient humus in the soil and initial pest damage can encourage self explanatory Hollow Heart, Jelly End rot, Cracking and Secondary growths (small tubers on bigger tubers).

Sudden heatwaves cause Sunstroke / Heat canker.

And poor storage causes Soft tubers and Premature Sprouting.

Common Potato scab Streptomyces / Actinomyces scabies causes raised rough patches on tubers, often only if weather is dry when flowers seen and small tubers forming, scabby patches just affect appearance not food value, made much worse by excess lime in soil. Scab can be reduced by mixing grass clippings, oak and or comfrey leaves in with the soil about the sets, and also by digging in a green manure of soya beans beforehand.

Corky or Powdery scab Spongospora subterranea is similar, causes more distortion and some wartiness, rare in UK, most commonly found where rotation not practised.

Tubers are attacked in store by similar looking fungus disease Dry Rot, Fusarium caeruleum where end of tubers become mummified.

Black Speck / Scurf / Collar rot, Corticium solani, may be seen as white incrustation on base of stem, can cause haulms to die, causes black scurf on skins of tubers, these are sclerotia, mostly cause poor appearance and tubers still edible.

Skin Spots Oospora pustulans are tiny pimples, turn darker if wetted, mostly superficial damage, tubers still edible but do not replant.

Silver Scurf Spondylocladium atrovirens are tiny black specks with a silvery sheen most easily seen on greening tubers while chitting, may kill eyes and so do not replant affected tubers.

Sclerotinia Rot / Stalk Break / Sclerotinia sclerotiorum, more common in wetter cooler districts where often more of a problem on carrots, other root crops and artichokes, white patches on stems, tops die or rot, sclerotia up to the size of peas formed on and in stems, these remain in soil so affected plants must be pulled and burnt.

Wart disease / Black scab / Potato Cancer / Synchytrium / Synchitrium endobioticum / Chrysophlyctis endobiotica / Oedomyces leproides is a serious and notifiable fungal disease, over-wintering sporangium of golden yellow release zoo-spores which get into potato tubers especially through the eyes, the shoots wrinkle and brown, the galled tuber develops huge cauliflower like warts, most modern varieties are resistant if not immune, no cure, burn everything, never use 'suspicious source' seed potatoes!

Potato Late Blight Phytophthora infestans first attacks leaves with blotches, then streaks run down stems, everything rots, infected tubers redden under skin, some varieties partly resistant. If you cut off tops as soon as see first infection then tubers may be saved. (Do not confuse this with the natural dying back of the haulm of early varieties in early summer, or with Blackleg, see below.) Blight also attacks tomato plants so keep separate.

Violet Root Rot, Helicobasidium purpureum / Rhizoctonia crocorum, web of loose violet / purplish threads on surface of tubers, also affects other root crops especially carrots, turnips, seakale, asparagus, no cure, burn all parts.

Pink Rot, Phytophthora erythroseptica, rare fungal disease causing pink colouration of tubers which when cut turns to purplish black, burn all parts.

Blackleg, Bacterium phytophthorum, carried in on tubers, base of stem rots and tops die, infects the new tubers so do not replant your own, infested tuber may rot to slime and then infect good tubers in store especially if damp. In the field Blackleg withers odd plants here and there whereas Blight is usually more widespread and spreading.

Leaf-Drop Streak, small brown patches on leaves getting bigger, leaves wither and hang on not dropping off, do not replant tubers.

Many viruses trouble potatoes, most are spread by green Peach aphid Myzus persicae and also by Potato aphid Macrosiphon solani. However our habit of saving tubers can perpetuate the attacks.

Potato Leaf Roll / Leaf Curl virus disease, affected leaves curl upwards, are not limp as with most diseases but thick and crisp and may even rattle, infection reduces size of both crop and tubers.

Potato Mosaic Y virus has more deleterious effects than Leaf Roll as the leaves mottle and the plant becomes weak and stunted.

Crinkle virus is similar to Leaf Roll without the roll, the leaves thicken, pucker and crinkle.

Aucuba virus causes mottling of leaves from faint to strongly yellowed spots or patches.

Many other viruses occur worldwide.

Solidago virgaurea, GOLDENROD

A good host flower late in year to hoverflies and wasps.

Sonchus, SOW-THISTLES

These will germinate even in winter months. Edible. Good hen food.

Accumulate Copper, Nitrogen. Crude ash 14.95 %: N 2.39, P 0.88, K 4.77, Ca 1.94, Na 2.16.

These harbour Mangold Fly Pegomyia betae and Stem Eelworm Tylenchus devastatrix.

Sonchus arvensis, PERENNIAL / FIELD MILK / CORN SOW-THISTLE

This and S. oleraceus have their leaves galled by Dipteron gall-midges Cystiphora sonchi which cause up to twenty glossy circular pustules pointed above the leaf and concave underneath, each about a sixth of an inch across, the centre pale and the area around dark purple with a reddish stain beyond.

Sorbus aria, WHITEBEAM

Leaf-blade gets leaf blistering caused by acarine gall-mite Eriophyes / Phytoptus / Typhlodromus, small swellings on both sides of leaf, yellowish green to red and purple, brown at maturity, unless a very heavy infestation does little damage to established trees but can weaken poor ones, also attacks mountain ash below.

Sorbus aucuparia, ROWAN / MOUNTAIN ASH

Juniper stem galls caused by rust fungi Gymmnosporangium juniperi moves to mountain ash where it causes orange yellow below red on top galls on foliage.

Sorghum halepense, JOHNSON GRASS

A weed in US where a spray made from it kills willamette mites (sic).

Sparaxis

A bulbous garden flower which may be infected by Bean Yellow mosaic; dark and yellow patches with bright yellow spots which can spread to most Leguminous plants: Cajanus, Canavalia, Cassia, Cicer, Cladrastis, Crotolaria, Dolichos, Glycine, Hedysarum, Lathyrus, Lens, Lupinus, Medicago, Melilotus, Phaseolus, Pisum, Robinia, Trifolium, Trigonella, Vicia and Vigna, and also Alpinia, Chenopodium, Gladiolus, Freesia, Babiana and Tritonia.

Spergula arvensis, SPURRY

Sprays of this have been used against aphids, cutworms, caterpillars and rootworms.
Analysis of dry matter, crude ash 10.12% - N 2.36, P 1.08, K 4.21, Ca 1.52, Na 1.91.
Host to Stem Eelworm Tylenchus devastatrix.

SPIDERS, Arachnida

Many people fear them but they are almost all totally beneficial. An acre of healthy, hedged meadowland contains several millions. The true Spiders, and the very similar Harvestmen, are all predators and do nothing but good in our garden (well they will occasionally eat another predator, or even another spider but apart from that).

SPIDER MITES especially Red Spider Mites

These are not spiders and cause a great deal of damage. Red Spider mites are not red either but sort of grey green with a couple of brown blobs inside, they become rusty brown in autumn when they disappear to hide over winter. Most mites are just visible, the sharp naked eye perceives them as tiny specks, more often we notice the fine webbing like gossamer that covers the younger shoots and tips. They turn leaves yellow and leave them desiccated with tens of thousands of tiny pinpricks. The under surfaces of leaves become bronzed; older leaves become withered or crisp. The fine webbing protects these pests from many predators, sprays and dusts. And they also carry some diseases.
Usually a greenhouse pest these may attack soft fruits outdoors in hot weather and are common and serious on plants under any cover and especially on dry walls.

The commercially available predator Phytoseulis persimilis are just bigger than the spider mites and control them but only if introduced early enough in the season. Otherwise keeping the air humid and spraying water on the underside of leaves discourages them, seaweed, and soft soap solutions the more so. They can be thinned by attracting them onto melon or broad bean plants in pots which are then taken away and composted. Rhubarb nearby is said to keep them off Aquilegias. Garlic, chilli pepper and soap sprays have some effect, seaweed sprays reduce their number. 2% coriander oil apparently kills them.

Spinacia oleracea, SPINACH

Can be used as a green manure with benefit to almost all crops except cauliflower. It should be much more widely used as so easily killed and incorporated and aids humus formation being rich in saponins.
Round seeded spinaches do best in summer but for winter and early spring sow prickly seeded spinaches.
Spinach may get attacked by the Mangold fly which also attacks beetroot.
If the leaves have yellow spots and a violet or grey mould it's Downy Mildew Peronospora farinosa / effusa which causes younger leaves to thicken with spots and a greyish mat on the underside, they then yellow, brown and blacken with loss of growth, this is spread both on the seed and from debris and litter and favoured by damp conditions.

Virus Yellows is spread by the aphids Myzus persicae and Aphis fabae, the leaves develop patches of yellow turning orangey red, these mostly on the edge of leaves, these then become brittle and break up on handling, the growth is poor so are resultant crops.

Can be infected by virus Broad Bean Wilt; yellow mosaic and distortion which spreads to lettuce, pea, broad bean and other Legumes.

May also become infected by Clover Yellow Vein virus; yellow mosaic, necrosis and wilting which spreads to most Legumes: Cajanus, Canavalia, Cassia, Cicer, Crotolaria, Dolichos, Glycine, Hedysarum, Lathyrus, Lens, Lupinus, Medicago, Melilotus, Phaseolus, Trifolium, Trigonella, Vicia, and Vigna, and also Antirrhinum, Atriplex, Chenopodium, Coriandrum, Cucurbita, Gladiolus, Gomphrena, Nicotiana, Nicandra, Papaver, Petunia, Proboscidea, Rubus, Tetragonia, and Viola.

Spiraea ulmaria, MEADOW-SWEET, see Filipendula

Stachys sylvatica, HEDGE / WOOD

In summer supports Homopteran aphid Capitophorus / Rhopalosiphum / Aphis / Myzus ribis which spreads to and causes leaf blistering galls on redcurrants.

Stellaria media, CHICKWEED, see also Cerastium spp.

Chickweed will germinate even in winter months. Edible. Employed by giant gooseberry competitors who grow it underneath to keep the fruits cool and moist.
Accumulates Copper, Iron, Manganese, Nitrogen and Potassium.
Host of plant pests and diseases over-winter especially of Peach-potato aphid, Myzus persiceae, which also attacks lettuces and other crops and of Lettuce Mosaic and Cabbage Black Ringspot viruses, and source of nematodes that attack many crop and ornamental plants.

SUCCESSION

Replacement of one species by another in nature. For example if you stop cutting your lawn the grass becomes long. The different conditions favour different plants so grasses are replaced by clovers. This also changes the conditions and the area becomes covered in nettles and brambles. These change the conditions again and are replaced with saplings and so on.

SYMBIOSIS

Two or more forms of life gaining mutual benefit from each other. Examples range from insects and flowers exchanging food for pollination to lichens where neither the fungus nor algae could thrive or even exist without the other.

SYMPHALIDS

These are white slender grubs quarter inch long, often confused with nematode eelworms but are much bigger, hugely so, indeed up to as long as your fingernail. Prevalent in soils rich in organic matter these can attack beans, cucumbers, lettuce, tomatoes and other greenhouse crops, often at ground level at night leaving exposed roots looking corky and gnarled, and rots may then get in.

Symphytum officinale, COMFREY

Used for poultices, ointments for skin conditions and internally against arthritis though discouraged officially (I suspect they would rather you only have official treatments for their profit!).
The dried leaves give 15% ash, Potassium 3-7%, Calcium 1-2.5%, Phosphorus 0. 7-1.25%, Iron 0.1-0.5% and Manganese 85-200ppm.

Potentially most usefully comfrey is one of the few plants that accumulates any Cobalt.

Comfrey has very high protein levels, and one of the highest production rates per acre at seven times that of Soya. One acre can annually yield fifty tons wet containing two and a half percent ash, a ton and a quarter of dry matter with four thousand pounds of crude protein three or four hundred pounds of oil and over two tons of carbohydrate. Crops of over a hundred tons per acre have been grown in warmer countries.

Durable in wet spots comfrey extracts nutrients from foul water that would kill many other plants.

Comfrey can reduce scab on potatoes if handfuls of the wilted leaf are put in with the sets.

Comfrey leaves rotted in a barrel make an excellent concentrated liquid feed. This smells awful. Diluted down at least 20:1 it is ideal for tomatoes, potatoes, gooseberries and pot plants requiring high potash levels (However too much can cause chlorosis in those plants that do not like much potash.)

Comfrey also either manufactures or extracts vitamin B12 from the soil, the only garden plant source, with three to twelve nanograms per gram whereas dried yeast has only one.

Syringa vulgaris, LILAC

The leaves get tunnelled by Leaf Miners Gracilaria, same ones also attack privet causing blisters and curling.

Tagetes, MARIGOLDS, FRENCH, AFRICAN, MEXICAN

All from S. America, all are tender and must be started off under protection and planted out.
The flowers are hosts to hover flies.
Well known for keeping whitefly out of greenhouses they will not drive them out once in though! Their strong scent should be used to hide valuable plants from pests in every garden, most useful amongst the tomatoes and beans and they are cheerful to look at as well.
In trials at University of Hohenheim including Tagetes in crop rotations reduced nematode populations by 85%. African and Mexican forms kill nematodes, and deter Mexican bean beetles.

Tagetes erecta

This grown with tomatoes protected them from soil fungal disease Alternaria solani.

Tagetes patula

Has root exudates toxic to plants, bacteria and numerous soil organisms.

Tamarix gallica, TAMARISK

Capable of surviving in salt laden water containing up to twenty percent salt.

Tanacetum vulgare, TANSY

A strongly scented plant traditionally used to repel ants, maybe it was originally called Antsy (butterflies were apparently first called flutter-bys).
The dried herb is useful against clothes moths and other household pests.
Accumulates Potassium.
Tansy is a host to ladybirds and blooms are visited by at least twenty seven different insect species: 5 butterflies and moths, 7 species bee, 7 species Diptera flies and 8 other.
Tansy spray has been used against aphids, cabbage worms, Colorado beetles, Japanese beetles, striped cucumber beetles and squash bugs.

Taraxacum officinale, DANDELION

A well known edible and health giving weed though consumption said to cause bed-wetting.
Much liked by geese and hens.
Flowers open at 7am and close at 5pm and during rain.
Accumulates Calcium, Copper, Iron and some Silica.

Smell allegedly deters Colorado beetles.
Blooms attract predatory wasps and at least 93 different insect species: 7 butterflies and moths, 58 species bee, 21 species Diptera flies and 7 other. Unfortunately including the Mangold Fly, Pegomyia betae.
Shoots get attacked by bacterium Corynebacterium fascians which causes fasciation, stems become broad, flattened and ribbed, splayed and curved, this spreads to jasmine, plantains, Chrysanthemums, dogwood, Cotoneaster, Euphorbias, Forsythia, Hibiscus, holly and Inula.

Taxus baccata, YEW

Foliage and seeds deadly poisonous, the ripe red aril has been eaten safely.
Yew scale is similar to Peach scale but flatter and paler. Apex of shoots galled by Dipteron gall-midge Taxomyia / Cecidomyia taxi, this forms an 'artichoke gall' which persists for a year or more.

TEA leaves

These have been used as a house plant feed successfully. They keep hydrangeas blue and have been mixed with seeds to prevent maggots.

Tetragonia, NEW ZEALAND SPINACH

May become infected by Clover Yellow Vein virus; yellow
mosaic, necrosis and wilting which infects most Legumes:
Cajanus, Canavalia, Cassia, Cicer, Crotolaria, Dolichos,
Glycine, Hedysarum, Lathyrus, Lens, Lupinus, Medicago,
Melilotus, Phaseolus, Trifolium, Trigonella, Vicia and
Vigna, and also Antirrhinum, Atriplex, Chenopodium,
Coriandrum, Cucurbita, Gladiolus, Gomphrena, Nicotiana,
Nicandra, Papaver, Petunia, Proboscidea, Rubus, Spinacia
and Viola.

Thlaspi arvense, FIELD PENNYCRESS

Edible. This germinates even in winter months.
Accumulates Zinc and near old mines shown to have 13%
Zinc oxide in leaves.
Host for plant pests over-winter.

THRIPS and SCIARID MARSH FLIES

Heliothrips haemorrhoidalis the Common thrip and Thrips
tabaci the Tobacco thrip are tiny just visible insect pests
causing speckling, dessication, distortion and damage to
many plants especially under cover. Little tiny black things
jumping about indoors are probably Thrips especially if
they are on African violets or Chrysanthemums. Thrips do
occur outside but mostly in hotter drier seasons.

They cause all sorts of problems considering their small size; mottling, distortion, leaf blistering, loss of growing points, and damage flowers. Look for small whitish areas of damage surrounded by black dots. Thrips are worst in hot dry years.

Can be trapped by sticky plants such as Nicotianas and are thought to be discouraged by Tagetes marigolds. Brushing young plants (gently, 20 times, twice daily) significantly reduces later thrip populations. Controlled under cover by releasing the commercially available predatory control Ambleysius.

Very similar to Thrips are Sciarid, Marsh or Compost flies; these tend to indicate a sour wet acid compost and are not usually a problem except on some young bedding noticeably Busy lizzies (Impatiens) where they eat the roots. Improving the compost's drainage, adding lime if possible, and vacuum cleaning the area help. Releasing the commercially available Hypoaspis predatory mite when the temperature is above 11°C (52°F) will control them, and can help control the Thrips as well.

On a few crops such as peas and flowers Thrips can be a problem outdoors but more often little black jumping things outdoors will be Flea beetles, see.

Thymus, THYMES

Very short lived herbs with lovely seldom grown varieties such as caraway scented Herba barona and golden Anderson's gold.

Very good in the kitchen thyme is also wonderful for bees as so rich in nectar.

Exudates from thyme significantly reduce infestations of clubroot fungus of Brassicas and extracted oil controls Botrytis, Grey mould.

Thyme teas have been used to deter cabbage loopers, cabbage worms and whiteflies.

Terminal leaves are attacked by acarine gall-mites Eriophyes thomasi / Phytoptus which appear as tufts of cotton wool or mould as the leaves become clustered in filzgalls, gobular masses a third of an inch or so across covered in white hairs.

Tilia europaea, LIMES

These trees get very big.

They shade plants underneath and aphid attacks cause a continuous dripping of honeydew, this damages plants as sooty moulds grow on it.

Their insignificant flowers are full of nectar and one tree may fill a beehive with honey.

Rarely set seed in UK, the seed was once made into a 'chocolate'.

The leaves have special hidden pockets, domatia, underneath a fringe of hairs at the forks of the ribs, these provide shelter for mites who help control fungi and bacteria by eating them.

Leaf-blade often galled by acarine gall-mites Eriophyes spp. These are many in variety, the commonest are Nail or Bugle galls, pouch galls formed by E. tiliae typicus, up to 150 per leaf protruding through the top surface, yellow, red or brown, nail or tack shaped each filled with tiny hairs.

E. t. exilis galls are less in number, maybe 50 per leaf, and restricted to the angles between larger veins, more rounded though sometimes elongated, similarly coloured but less shiny and covered with hairs which form tawny coloured patches underneath.

E. tetrastichus forms roll galls along the leaf margin, greeny to reddy brown and hairy more so inside the roll, sometimes a flat pouch may form on the leaf blade instead.

 E. leiosoma forms just a rough patch hairy, initially whitish this turns reddy brown with age.

The trunks, stumps and large branches, dead and alive, support a semi-circular bracket fungus Polyporus / Polyporellus squamosus, brown scales with white edible flesh smelling of cucumber, this grows quickly can reach many pounds in weight but harms trees causing the wood to decay with timber White rot, also spreads to beech, horse chestnut, poplar, willow and walnut.

The litter grows the highly poisonous Boletus satanus with a light grey to brown cap, pale blue flesh, most often found on calcerous soils.

Tilia x vulgaris, COMMON LIME

The lime tree most often found is usually this hybrid.
The leaf-blade is galled by Dipterous gall-midge Dasyneura tiliamvolvens and D. thomasina, these form rolled galls on the leaf margins which turn purplish brown, the gall is hairy inside and out with D. thomasina but not more than the rest of the leaf with tiliamvolvens.

The leaf-blade is also galled by a Dipteron gall-midge Didymomyia reanuriana, many, up to fifty, may cluster together each a pustule usually rounded underneath and cone shaped above, greeny yellow but forming a pool of red staining the leaf around them, the galls spring off as 'escape capsules' when the larvae are mature to lie on the ground and leaving a crater in the leaf which fades from red to brown.

The petiole or midrib or even stem or flower may be galled by Dipteron gall-midge Contarinia tillarum / Cecidomyia tiliae / excavans / floricola / limbivolens / Sciara tilicola, this makes a globular swelling up to half an inch across, bright red turning black, often found on young shoots suckering round base of trees, the leaf beyond may be inhibited and often becomes hairy and thus a refuge for other mites.

TIMING

This is everything. Plants sown on the 'best' day do far better than those a few days earlier or later. The best day is hard to spot, some employ astrology or lunar cycle, and varies with all the microclimatic factors to be taken into account on top. Correct timing can reduce pest and disease damage by avoiding their peak periods, help co-life continuity, and pollination.

TOADS

One of our best friends and they eat more pests than you can believe possible. Encourage them all you can with nice cold damp nests made of buried flowerpots and make a pool, pond or refuge.

Torilis, HEDGE / BUR PARSLEY

Blooms visited by nine different species of insect.

Tragopogon porrifolius, SALSIFY

A long thin carrot like vegetable similar to carrots and used to discourage carrot root-fly.
Attractive flowers beneficial to insects.

May get White Blister, Cystopus cubicus, which causes small whitish blisters on leaves, seldom serious.
Rust, Puccinia hysterium, causes orange to brown spots on leaves, seldom serious but best burn all affected plants.
Very occasionally may get Powdery mildew but seldom badly unless growing conditions are poor.

Tragopogon pratensis, GOATSBEARDS / JOHN GO TO BED AT NOON

Blooms open at 4am and close before midday.
May be galled by Hymenopteran gall-wasp Aulacidea tragopogonis, eggs are laid in the base of the stem, the larvae over-winter in the gall.

Trichoderma virides

This predatory fungus can be used as a pruning compound and inoculation to stop fungal attacks to woody plants. Likewise treatment with this preserves fence posts et al. Added to dirty water it may prevent damping off disease in seedlings.

Trifolium, CLOVERS & TREFOILS

Leguminous low growing plants that attract many insects especially bees, and red clover also attracts many butterflies.

One of the best short term ground covers and green manures if you can dig it in or kill it in situ with light excluding mulch.

A mixture of red clover and alsike is more effective than either alone at improving yields of hay.

Clovers provide cover to ground beetles, are hosts to predators of Woolly Aphis and help deter Cabbage Root Fly if sown underneath.

After some years land may get 'Clover sick' the plants being weakened by Clover Rot Sclerotinia trifoliorum and/or Stem Eelworm Tylenchus devastatrix. This last has alternate host of oats and especially of the old tulip-rooted oats, never follow or precede these with clovers.

The Burnet moth caterpillars seek Birdsfoot trefoil plants with higher cyanide levels as this then protects them.

Can suffer fungal Violet root rot / Copper-web Helicobasidium purpureum which also attacks asparagus, beet, carrot, parsnip, potatoes and even alfalfa, also harboured by several weeds.

Clovers are main alternate host for Clover Yellow Vein virus; yellow mosaic, necrosis and wilting which spreads amongst most other Legumes: Cajanus, Canavalia, Cassia, Cicer, Crotolaria, Dolichos, Glycine, Hedysarum, Lathyrus, Lens, Lupinus, Medicago, Melilotus, Phaseolus, Trigonella, Vicia, and Vigna, and also Antirrhinum, Atriplex, Chenopodium, Coriandrum, Gladiolus, Gomphrena, Nicotiana, Nicandra, Papaver, Petunia, Proboscidea, Rubus, Spinacia, Tetragonia, Viola and some cucurbits especially squash.

Thrips tabaci and Frankliniella occidentalis spread Tobacco Streak virus (aka Bean Red Node); red nodes, necrosis and red spots, also seed borne this also affects alfalfa, chickpea, fenugreek, Datura, soybean, Nicotiana, beans and many other plants.

Trifolium pratense, RED / PURPLE CLOVER

Once known as Bee Bread as particularly good for humble and bumble bees.

May be parasitised by Dodder and Broom-rape.

Foliage contains from 6-11% mineral ash.

Attacked by Clover 'Pear-shaped' / Purple Clover Weevils Apion apricans / flavifemoratum which feed on seeds turning blossoms rusty and withering flowerheads.

Trifolium repens, WHITE / DUTCH CLOVER

This is the one for honeybees as the flower suits their short tongues.

Contains over 9% ash with lime 3% and phosphoric acid 0.6%.

Roots colonised by Rhizobium / Bacillus radicicola Leguminous partner.

Flowers galled by acarine gall- mites, this may cause phyllody where floral parts become leafy.

Leaflets galled by Dipteron gall-midge, Dasyneura / Cecidomyia trifolii which rolls them up to form a pod of yellow to reddy brown.

May become infected by Clover Yellow Vein virus; yellow mosaic, necrosis and wilting which infects most other Legumes and also Antirrhinum, Atriplex, Chenopodium, Coriandrum, Cucurbita, Gladiolus, Gomphrena, Nicotiana, Nicandra, Papaver, Petunia, Proboscidea, Rubus, Spinacia, Tetragonia and Viola.

Trigonella foenum-graecum, FENUGREEK

Legume, the seed is the spice, as with garlic fenugreek can be smelt in the perspiration of those eating much of it.

May become infected by Clover Yellow Vein virus; yellow mosaic, necrosis and wilting which spreads to most other Legumes: Cajanus, Canavalia, Cassia, Cicer, Crotolaria, Dolichos, Glycine, Hedysarum, Lathyrus, Lens, Lupinus, Medicago, Melilotus, Phaseolus, Trifolium, Vicia and Vigna, and also Antirrhinum, Atriplex, Chenopodium, Coriandrum, Cucurbita, Gladiolus, Gomphrena, Nicotiana, Nicandra, Papaver, Petunia, Proboscidea, Rubus, Spinacia, Tetragonia and Viola.

Triticum aestivum / turgidum / vulgare, WHEAT

Reduces to 2.4% ashes which contain 22% potash, 16% soda, 2% lime, 10% magnesia, 1.4% iron oxide, negligible manganese oxide, 49% phosphoric acid, 0.2% sulphuric acid, a little silica and a little chlorine.
The flower of wheat is galled by a nematode eelworm Tylenchus tritici / scandens causing 'corn cockle', 'purples', 'false ergot', 'peppercorn gall' when the ovary fails to set seeds but swells and turns purple to brown or black, this falls to release up to fifteen thousand new nematodes, these may survive twenty years, and worse, the nematodes carry a fungus Dilophospora alopecuri which causes 'Twist disease'.

Berberis, especially the wild form over-winters rust and should be kept well away from wheat as Berberis is galled by 'Black rust of wheat' fungi Puccinia graminis forming yellow brown spots and orange cluster-cups underneath the leaves, after infesting the wheaty this rust lies dormant through winter then erupts basidospores which reinfest the Berberis.

Tritonia

Another bulbous garden flower which may carry infections of Bean Yellow mosaic; dark and yellow patches with bright yellow spots which spreads to many Leguminous plants: Cajanus, Canavalia, Cassia, Cicer, Cladrastis, Crotolaria, Dolichos, Glycine, Hedysarum, Lathyrus, Lens, Lupinus, Medicago, Melilotus, Phaseolus, Pisum, Robinia, Trifolium, Trigonella, Vicia, Vigna and also Alpinia, Chenopodium, Gladiolus, Freesia, Babiana and Sparaxis).

Tropaeolum majus, NASTURTIUMS

These flower best on poor soil.
Entirely edible, flowers and leaves enliven salads, pickled seeds are excellent.
Allegedly eating them is good for the lungs.
Their strong smell drives woolly Aphis off apple trees and keeps aphids and bugs away from broccoli and squash.

They are themselves attacked by black aphids and
cabbage caterpillars so can be used as sacrificials
especially to tomatoes and beans.
Their smell said to keep whitefly out of greenhouses and
off Bassicas.
Yellow Sawfly caterpillars may eat the leaves from
underneath.

Tulipa, TULIPS

Edible if not palatable, mice and voles can be prevented
from eating them by mixing in poisonous bulbs like scillas.
Bulbs and flowers also eaten by pigeons, pheasants and
peacocks.
Aphids may make a mess of blooms but worse carry the
virus causing Break.
Shanking Phytophora cryptogea rots the base of the
flower stem which falls and withers.
Fire disease looks like a rust but is Botrytis tulipae causing
scorched spots of brownish grey on every part, the
flowers get pitted spots, worst in wet conditions.
Sometimes bulbs decay away from Grey Bulb rot
Sclerotium tuliparum which also affects Narcissus and
Gladioli amongst others.
The Break virus brought by aphids stunts the plants which
perform badly with mottled leaves and small streaked and
speckled flowers.

TURPENTINE

A paint thinner somewhat like paraffin but derived from distilling pine trees and one of the more useful smells for discouraging insects but unfortunately taints food crops.

Tussilago farfara, COLTSFOOT

A pernicious weed, good for consolidating sandy slopes and often found on Eastern UK sea cliffs.
Accumulates Potassium, Calcium, Copper, Iron, Magnesium and Sulphur.

TYPHLODROMID MITES

These feed on pollen but are also very beneficial friends to the gardener as these are one of the natural predators of Red Spider Mites.

Ulex europaeus, FURZE / GORSE

Leguminous, found on poor soils, overwinters Aphis rumicis black fly. Always has some flowers so excellent pit stop for errant insects.

Ulmus, ELMS

Seldom grow above 1,500ft.

Dutch elm disease spread by beetles has destroyed most trees.

Seldom set seed in UK but suckers and many live on in hedges and maintain the genes.

Bark varies from mildly acidic to just alkaline side of neutral- ph 4.7-7.1.

Foliage was once dried for winter forage.

Suffers from Nut scale which is similar to Peach scale except the base of each is widened just above junction, which spreads to pears, hazels, hawthorns and Pyracantha.

Wood consumed by Goat Moth Cossus ligniperda.

The Jew's Ear bracket fungus Hirneola / Auricularia auricula-judae is not only edible but a great Chinese delicacy, brown and hard when dry, the gelatinous fresh, may often be found on dead wood on trees, also on elderberry, willow and false acacias.

Ulmus campestris / procera, COMMON ELM

Leaf-blade galled by Homopteran aphid Schizoneura languinosa which makes it into a pouch, grey at first turning red and purple, puckering and containing many aphids, these in turn eaten by Pipiza hoverflies.

Also galled by Homopteran aphid Tetraneura ulmi / Byrsocrypta / Aphis gallarum-ulmi, this casues the 'Fig gall' when a smooth urn or cone shaped pouch develops on top of the leaf, this turns reddish later, only six per leaf on average but thousands per tree.

Ulmus glabra, WYCH ELM

Leaf-blade galled by Homopteran aphid Erisoma / Schizoneura / Aphis / ulmi / foliorum, one half of leaf becomes swollen and puckered then rolled over going through yellowish green to pink to grey, this aphid also lives on the roots of redcurrants where it does not form galls. These are predated by Anthocoris gallarum-ulmi 'Elm gall bug', and by syrphid hoverfly Pipiza. These galls may also form on other species of elm.

Urtica dioica, STINGING NETTLES

Blooms, male and female on different plants, wind pollinated.
The soil left by stinging nettles is very rich in humus and Iron, they are also hungry for phosphates and exceptionally successful stands in poor soil may indicate sites of old human middens, stock pens or rabbit warrens. Nettles make a spray rich in Nitrogen, Potassium, Calcium, Copper, Iron, and Silica used for invigorating plants and for fungicidal properties and alone or mixed with comfrey they are rotted down to make an excellent liquid feed.

These aid composting, help fruit to ripen yet stop it going mouldy.

Dried nettles are good for all livestock, cooked they are good for us, try passing young shoots through a flame which burns off stingers then eat as Barbecued.

The seeds are given to horses to make them brisk and have a good skin.

The remedy for stings of rubbing in dock juice is nearly always to hand as the plants usually occur together.

Scavenge your surroundings for nettles to add to the compost but leave some in the sun for butterfly caterpillars.

Birds, Whitethroats feed on insects on nettles, as may Great tits.

Snails are lured to stinging nettles, cut and leave pieces around new transplants etc. Includes Copse snail Arianta arbustorum, Silky snail Ashfordia granulate, Garden snail Cepaea hortensis, Grove or Brown-lipped snail Cepaea nemoralis, Kentish snail Monarcha cantiana, Hairy snail Trichia hispida, and most commonly the Strawberry snail Trichia striolata.

Spiders living on nettles include Araneus cucurbitinus, Clubiona reclusa & other spp. Dictyna arundinacea, Enoplognatha ovate, Lyniphia clathrata, L. peltata, L. triangularis, Meta mengei, Philodromus spp. Tetragnatha Montana, Theridion pictum, T. sisyphium & other spp. Xisticus cristataus.

Nettles are a food source for many other insect families, either on plant itself, or on other creatures on the plants. Indeed nettles are such a good source there are numerous insects which are only associated with nettles so * indicates unique to nettles.

Nettles support earwigs Forficula auricularia, Thrips urticae*, crickets Pholidoptera griseoaptera, Lacewings Chrysopa carnea, and scorpion flies Panorpa spp. and many Hymenoptera and Diptera parasites. 6 Diptera flies are solely dependent, some sustained as larvae eating other insects, Gall or Nettle midge Dasineura urticae*, found in galls and mines in leaves and stems, also Agromyza anthracyna*, A. pseudoreptans*, A. reptans, Melanagromyza aenea* and Phytomyza flavicornis*.

Nettles support 26 varieties of Heteroptera bugs with 3 solely sustained; Adults may be partly predatory, larvae may eat nettles; Ant damsel bug Aptus mirmicoides, Marsh damsel bug Dolichonabis limbatus, Common damsel bug Nabis rugosus, Orius spp. Common flower bug Anthocoris nemorum, A. nemoralis & other spp. Nettle ground bug Heterogaster urticae, Scolopostethus affinis & S. Thomsoni. Capsid bugs Deraeocoris ruber, Calocoris alpestris, Potato capsid C. norvegicus, Common green capsid Lygocoris pabulinusa & L. spinolai, L. lucorum. European tarnished plant-bug Lygus rugilipennis & L. wagneri, Calocoris fulvomaculatus & C. sexguttatus, Heterotoma planicornis, Common nettle capsid Liocoris tripustulatus*, Dicyphus errans, Orthotylus ochrotrichus, Orthonotus rufifrons*, Plagiognathus chrysanthemi & P. arbustorum.

Nettles support 23 varieties of Homotera frog and leaf-hoppers and plant lice Psyllids & Aphis, with 6 solely sustained* or with but one other sustainer**. Includes Cuckoo-spit Philaenus spumarius, Aphrodes bicinctus, Aphrophora alni, Cixius nervosus, Cercopis vulnerata, Empoasca decipiens, Eupteryx aurata (shared with hogweed, hemp agrimony, mint and ragwort), E. Cyclops* & E. urticae*, Javasella spp. Macropsis scutellata*, Macrosteles sexnotatus & M. variatus, Macustus grisescens. Psyllids Trioza urticae*, Bean aphid Aphis fabae, Bulb and potato aphid Rhopalosiphoninus latysiphon, Hop aphid Phoroon humuli, Large nettle aphid Microlophium carnosum**, Peach potato aphid Myzus persicae & M. ascalonicus, M. cymbalariae, Small nettle aphid Aphis urticata*.

Nettles also have 15 sorts of beetles eating foliage and pollen with 5 solely sustained, 12 as larvae, some hoverflies, Lacewings and Rove beetles eating other larvae. Includes at least five ladybirds; Seven-spot ladybird Coccinella 7-punctata, Eleven-spot C. 11-punctata, Two-spot Adalia bipunctata, Ten-spot A. 10-punctata and Fourteen-spot Propylea 14-punctata. Weevils; Ceutorhynchus pollinarius*, Cidnorhinus quadrimaculatus**, Phyllobius pomaceus*, Apion urticarium*. Flea beetle Crepidodera ferruginea, Flower beetle Brachypterus glaber & B. urticae**. Rove beetles Tachyporus spp. Click beetles Elateridae spp. Soldier beetle Rhagonycha fulva. And ? beetle Demetrias atricapillus.

Leaves are thickened, curled or pocketed and eventually turn brown when attacked by Homopteran Psyllid Trioza urticae.

Most aerial parts attacked by Dipteron gall-midge Dasyneura / Perrisia / Cecidomyia urticae 'Nettle gnat' which has different gall shapes on each part; the galls are generally small round swellings, yellowish green through red to brown.

Vaccinium

Lime haters. Most have edible berries.

Our native Bilberry, V. myrtillus and Cranberry, V. oxycoccus have recently been superceded in the garden by the more productive American versions of Blueberry, V. corymbosum hybrids and Cranberry, V. macrocarpon, these may well soon exhibit similar associates as the natives.

Certainly Blueberries are subject to Scale insects.

Russula paludosa with a rose or strawberry coloured to orangey yellow cap is considered edible, it prefers damp pine or spruce forests, peat bogs and the company of bilberries.

Cortinarius / Dermocybe cinnamomeoluteus is edible but risky as hard to tell from poisonous species, has a yellowish brownish olive cap with radial markings, gills start yellow going to brown and the yellow stipe has little fibrils spread over it, the yellowish flesh smells of beetroot, this is also very common in coniferous forests on acid soil.

Vaccinium myrtillus, BILBERRY

Richer in nectar than V. uliginosum

Vaccinium vitis-idaea, COWBERRY / RED WHORTLEBERRY

Shoots are attacked by fungi Calyptospora goeppertiana / Melampsorella causing them to increase in height, proliferate and develop smooth glossy spindle shaped galls up to three inches long, yellowish green going to red then brown, this fungus has it's other stage on Silver fir making these bad neighbours.
Another fungi Exobasidium vaccinii causes large oval or domed smooth succulent galls on the underside of the leaf which becomes powdery with spores, and may also cause reddish spindle shaped swellings in stems.

Valeriana officinalis, VALERIAN

One of the generally helpful beneficial plants good for insect friends, cats and earthworms.
Stimulates composting and accumulates Phosphorus.
Flowers secrete nectar easy for insects to get at.

Valerianella, CORN SALAD

Edible crop, will grow in winter making useful green manure /fodder for hens.

VARIEGATED plants

Many of these need shade or they burn. Some are variegated because of virus problems, care should be taken not to transmit these unwittingly. Reverted growth should be removed or it predominates.

Veratrum

A poisonous lily once used to make 'hellebore' powder for killing gooseberry sawfly caterpillars.

Verbascum, MULLEINS

The flowers poor in nectar but rich in pollen attract wide range of insects.

Verbena

Leaf-hoppers Erythroneura pallidifrons, pale yellow or white, eighth inch long, active insects may do some damage causing bleached areas on leaves, also found on Calceolarias, Fuchsias, Primulas and Salvias.

Veronica anagallis-aquatica, WATER SPEEDWELL, and V. beccabunga, BROOKLIME

Floral parts are attacked by Coleopteran weevils Gymnetron villosulum which live in and gall the ovary causing the seeds to fail to develop.

Veronica chamaedrys, GERMANDER SPEEDWELL

This is pollinated by small flies.

Alternate summer host for Myzus cerasi aphids which cause galled leaves on many of cherry family so these are not good neighbours.

The leaves are attacked by acarine gall-mite Eriophyes anceps / Phytoptus causing them to twist and form a hairy whitish to yellowish brown gall in midsummer.

The terminal leaves are also attacked by Dipteron gall-midge Jaapella veronicae / Perrisia / Cecidomyia / chamaedrys, in this two leaves are caused to swell and curve together to form a globular gall often red or purple, woolly and about a quarter of an inch across.

VERTICILLIUM albo atrum, V. WILT

A fungal disease that strikes down plants in full growth, especially if on cold side, if the stems are cut through a dark stain greenish brown can be seen in the tissues. This often gets in though minor damage, it overwinters in the soil, on debris and in tubers, can be spread on pruning tools and by cuttings.

Predominantly attacks Asters, Antirrhinums, carnations, Chrysanthemums, Dahlias, lupins, paeonies and poppies.

Viburnum lantana, WAYFARING-TREE

The leaf-blade is attacked by acarine gall-mites Eriophyes viburni / Phytoptus / Cephaloneon pubescens causing one eighth inch high and wide pouch galls mostly on the upper side of leaves in shade, these may be green, pink, red or purple and have velvet appearance from fine hairs.

Vicia, BROAD / FAVA / FIELD BEANS & VETCHES

Accumulate Cobalt, Copper, Nitrogen, Phosphorous and Potassium.
Will germinate even in winter months.
These are Legumes so enrich the soil.
Field crops of small beans known as Tick or Horse beans, smell sweet and provide a lot of nectar for bees, the haulm makes a good base for bedding and sheet composts.
Tick beans are heavy croppers with typically a ton and a half per acre giving eight hundred or so pounds of protein and nearly a ton and a half of carbohydrate but little oil with only forty pounds or so per acre. Beans may be grown with cereals as mixed feed for animals when both crops benefit from pest and disease protection producing more in total fodder than either alone. Once used for food but now more for fodder, and as cover and green manure crops.
Many have gland stipules at base of leaves.

Aphids on vetches are preferred food of some ladybirds enabling them to multiply.

May be infected by Clover Yellow Vein virus; yellow mosaic, necrosis and wilting which infects most other Legumes: Cajanus, Canavalia, Cassia, Cicer, Crotolaria, Dolichos, Glycine, Hedysarum, Lathyrus, Lens, Lupinus, Medicago, Melilotus, Phaseolus, Trifolium, Trigonella, Vigna, and also Antirrhinum, Atriplex, Chenopodium, Coriandrum, Cucurbita, Gladiolus, Gomphrena, Nicotiana, Nicandra, Papaver, Petunia, Proboscidea, Rubus, Spinacia, Tetragonia and Viola.

Also infected by Bean Curly Dwarf mosaic; mosaic, stunting and rugosity, also infects Phaseolus species, soybean, pea, chickpea, lentil, mung bean and Leguminous weeds,

Vicia cracca, TUFTED VETCH

Bombus terrestris bites hole in side of flower to steal nectar.

Vicia faba, BEANS, BROAD

Ashes contain 21% potash, 19% soda, 7% lime, 9% magnesia, 1% iron oxide, negligible manganese oxide, 38% phosphoric acid, 13% sulphuric acid, 3% silica and 1.5% chlorine.

The flowers are often cut into by buff-tailed and small earth humble bees whose tongues are too short to reach the nectar by legitimate means, this results in reduced pollination of the seeds and many flowers produce pods with fewer seeds than the standard or just abort.

Beans are often autumn sown to avoid the Black Bean aphid a.k.a Black Fly, Dolphin and Collier, Aphis rumicis / fabae which also attacks other beans but not as frequently, this may be discouraged by growing summer savory nearby which also cooks well with beans, nipping out the bean tips above the flowers is more effective.

Black bean aphids overwinter on the wild spindle tree, furze, fat hen and black nightshade and also attack beetroot and spinach. (These aphids often killed en masse in humid warm weather by fungal disease Entomophthora spp.)

Seeds may be damaged by Bean beetle Bruchus granarius / rufimanus, the Pea beetle B. pisorum and the Broad Bean beetle Acanthoscelides obtectus all cause holes and transparent patches in the seeds, the adults lay eggs on the pods and the larvae eat into the seeds, the pupae may not be noticed in saved seed and then sown with the next crop.

Planted with gooseberries they discourage sawfly caterpillars.

Chocolate Spot, Botrytis cinerea / fabae, instead of the more usual grey fluffy mould plants get dark chocalate coloured spots on leaves and streaks on stems and may defoliate even die, pods and seeds may also suffer, worse in wet soils and unbalanced conditions, this also attacks many other plants and overwinters on debris.

Other leaf spots caused by Acochyta fabae, Cercospora fabae etc. often just damaging to appearance rarely fatal, indeed frost damage and aphid bites may also cause similar spots to no great detriment.

Rust, Uromyces fabae, typical spotty rust fungus attack, improve conditions but in general more of a problem with appearance than growth.

Broad Bean wilt virus, yellow mosaic and distortion, spread by aphids, invades large number of crops and other plants including lettuce, pea, spinach and other Legumes.

Vicia sativa, COMMON VETCH

Flower and more often leaf-bud galled by Dipteron gall-midge Contarinia / Diplosis / Cecidomyia loti, flower distorted fails to open and becomes downy, yellow, pink or reddish brown. When the leaf is galled it forms a miniature bunch of bananas greenish yellow or brown. This also attacks Bush vetch below.

Vicia sepium, BUSH VETCH

The flowers designed to exclude smaller insects and common Humble bee Bombus terrestris bites hole through side to get at nectar.

Vigna, MUNG BEANS

Warm climate Legumes
May be infected by Bean Curly Dwarf mosaic; mosaic,
stunting and rugosity, also infects Phaseolus species,
soybean, pea, chickpea, lentil, broad bean, and
Leguminous weeds.
Also may be infected by Clover Yellow Vein virus; yellow
mosaic, necrosis and wilting which infects most other
Legumes: Cajanus, Canavalia, Cassia, Cicer, Crotolaria,
Dolichos, Glycine, Hedysarum, Lathyrus, Lens, Lupinus,
Medicago, Melilotus, Phaseolus, Trifolium, Trigonella and
Vicia, and also Antirrhinum, Atriplex, Chenopodium,
Coriandrum, Cucurbita, Gladiolus, Gomphrena, Nicotiana,
Nicandra, Papaver, Petunia, Proboscidea, Rubus, Spinacia,
Tetragonia,and Viola.

Viola

Many violets have two sets of flowers, the normal we
observe and hidden, cleistogamous, flowers in autumn
without petals or stamens that set seed unnoticed.
Flowers visited by Plusia moths, humble bees and the fly
Rhyngia rostrata.
Plants often attacked by aphids and eelworms.
In dry conditions they suffer Red Spider mite curling and
puckering foliage.
Rust Puccinia viola starts as yellow spots on leaves and
stems which become fruiting cups of brown spores.

Often have minor infestations of Leaf spots and Smut.
May be infected Clover Yellow Vein virus; yellow mosaic,
necrosis and wilting which infects most Legumes: Cajanus,
Canavalia, Cassia, Cicer, Crotolaria, Dolichos, Glycine,
Hedysarum, Lathyrus, Lens, Lupinus, Medicago, Melilotus,
Phaseolus, Trifolium, Trigonella, Vicia and Vigna, and also
Antirrhinum, Atriplex, Chenopodium, Coriandrum,
Cucurbita, Gladiolus, Gomphrena, Nicotiana, Nicandra,
Papaver, Petunia, Proboscidea, Rubus, Spinacia and
Tetragonia.

Viola odorata, SWEET VIOLET

All aerial parts galled by nematode eelworm Aphelenchus
olesistus longicollis, this causes considerable distortions,
weakening and stunting.

VINE WEEVIL

Two things occur, apparently independently. Pencil sized holes appear clipped out the edges of leaves, and some plants weaken and suddenly die. These are both due to small beetle like weevils with long snouts which can be caught out at night. There are several similar varieties but all do the same damage; adults chew at the edges of leaves doing little harm, but in the soil their larvae, whitish grubs about fingernail length, with dark heads, eat the roots and corms of plants destroying them. Especially attacked are Begonias, Cyclamens, Primulas, Fuschias, grapevines, strawberries and evergreen ornamentals. The adults can be caught if you surround suspected plants with newspaper and visit it at night, a shake and any weevils will fall to be dealt with. They hide in dry cracks between pot and soil and can be trapped in bundles of rolled up corrugated cardboard. Running chickens or ducks in an area controls them though this is only a suitable method for certain areas such as vineyards or fruit cages. The adults can be kept away from pot plants by rings of non setting glue or by standing them in double saucers with a moat between of, preferably salty, water, or oil. Large tubs can be stood on feet in trays of similar. Any suspected plants in pots should be evicted and inspected. In the open ground the grubs are obviously harder to find though all dead plants should be disinterred and their soil inspected.

When the soil temperature is over 12°C (54°F), and the soil must be moist, water on the biological controls Heterorhabditis megidis or Steinernema carpocapsae, microscopic pathogenic nematodes that swim in the soil moisture searching out the vine weevil grubs to parasitise. These nematodes are also most effective used on the compost of plants in pots and tubs and the greenhouse border.

VIRUSES

A major but often going unnoticed problematic co-life with many of our plants; often spread by cutting tool damage, and pests such as aphids and nematodes. Sometimes brought in on seed but most commonly spread by vegetative propagation.

Viscum album, MISTLETOE

Classic example of parasitism with long mystical associations so rather surprisingly there are no recorded companion or co-life effects. It is said that birds, mostly thrushes and blackbirds, eat the sticky berries and wipe the seeds off onto the trees, others say they wipe their backsides as the seeds come through intact.

Vitis vinifera, GRAPEVINE

Do not overfeed vines! Ancient instructions to bury a dead horse / sheep / cow under a vine is hardly easy or hygienic, and is foolish.

Grapes most powerful associated co-life is the birds who rob you.

Vine Weevil can weaken and kill vines.

Under cover Mealy Bug, Tortrix moths and Thrips do their worst.

In the UK we are lucky as we can grow grapes on their own roots (ie we can grow new plants from rooted cuttings) as we have no Phylloxera aphids eating them here but on the Continent and with most bought vines they are grown on resistant rootstocks. The American Vitis labrusca hybrid varieties seem naturally resistant.

Scale Lecanium persicae which also attacks peaches and nectarines is yellowish greenish brown and a quarter inch by a sixth ovals.

Soft scale Pulvinaria vitis prefers grapevines but will move onto currants, it makes a conspicuous white woolly wad in which the eggs are protected, the larvae move out and form a scale once settled.

Vine Powdery mildew Uncinula necator attacks leaves and fruits and the latter split once it has hardened their skin, most often a problem in dull weather or shade, disappears in hot bright conditions.

Downy mildew Plasmopara viticola attacks only the leaves but can seriously reduce growth. Both are made worse by sudden changes in atmosphere, dryness at the roots and fluctuating humidity.

Black rot Guignardia bidwellii causes brown irregular patches on young leaves, resembles scald but black specks can be seen, then fungus moves to berries which dry up and shrivel.

Ripe Rot Glomerella cingulata causes swollen oblong patches on the fruits which exude stickiness and become purple, highly infectious.

Shanking is similar where the stem of the bunch of fruits dies turning brown and shrivelling, the fruits stop developing normally and even if near ripe tend to be bitter.

WASABI

A tender plant needing wet acid semi-shady conditions. Japanese condiment, mustard like compounds in stem effective against major Japanese food poisoning bacteria Vibrio parahaemolyticus and also E. coli, Staphylococcus aureus and Helicobacter pylori, this last being cause of tooth decay.

WASPS

Friends when they eat other insects but real pests when they turn to our fruits.

They can be helped by providing rotting wood for them to rasp off to make the paper for their nests.

Although undoubtedly vicious when cornered thay seldom defend their nests in the way honey bees do and if you must destroy a nest wait till the queens have left in late summer to ensure a fresh crop next year.

Underground nests often cohabited by Volucella pellucens fly larvae eating wasp grubs excrements.

Hornets are much like larger wasps found most often in woodland and are quite scarce, they often have a beetle Velleius dilatatus living in their nests.

WEEDS

Plants in the wrong place. They can help by accumulating nutrients that would be leached away or can be providing shelter, nectar and pollen. Often they are just hangers on sapping away air, light and water. The effects of weed competition are serious to many crops especially if the weeds grow from the start or before the crop. May also be carriers of pests and diseases, and also of their controls.

WEEVILS

Small beetles, usually with long snouts, have been deterred by aromatic herbs, their oils and garlic but in trials were repelled best with an extract of Bugle, Ajuga reptans.

WHITEFLY

Tiny white moths, really tiny. Under cover you rarely go long before Whitefly appear, often in clouds. The flying adults lay their eggs on the underside of leaves, their attacks soon weaken plants. They can be thinned with a vacuum cleaner. Or by introducing Sweet tobacco plants in pots and removing them once the whiteflies have settled on them (they can be held in place with sugar syrup or 'hair' spray). They can be choked with soft soap sprays, yellow sticky traps are not effective traps but good indicators of the pests presence.

You can introduce the commercially available biological control Encarsia formosa. These are small parasitic wasps that have been used with phenomenal effectiveness since the 1920s. They reduce whitefly populations by attacking their whitish scales, which turn black once parasitised by the wasps. Under warm cover with year round plantings I find having plants such as Lippia dulcis and Salvia coccinea act as bankers, always carrying some whitefly these also keep some of the parasites alive and so the pest stays permanently under control without new introductions.

Most often a problem in the greenhouse, whitefly can be discouraged from ever coming in with Tagetes marigolds, Nicandra physaloides, nasturtiums or burning oak leaves. They are more prevalent on tomatoes when these suffer Phosphorus or Magnesium deficiency.

Brassiccas are often bothered by another different whitefly, actually a moth, in the open and again marigolds and nasturtiums are good deterrents.

WIND

An enemy of plants, a gentle breeze is fine but strong winds sap moisture and warmth. A wind of only a few mph can seriously reduce growth. Draughts are as bad for indoor plants. Windbreaks improve the microclimate and increase growth as do nurse crops for seedlings.

WIREWORMS

Agriotes lineatus, A. obscurus and Athous haemorrhoidalis.
Wireworms are long thin hard yellowish grubs, with three pairs of tiny legs too small to readily notice. Rather difficult to squidge, these are the larvae of the Click beetle. (Click as in the adult, if placed on it's back, can spring up the right way emitting a click.) Wireworms are pests of grass roots but long lived and after their first year may move off the grass onto plants nearby damaging their roots for the next four or five years! These may be killed when a green manure crop of flax or mustard is incorporated and suppressed by white mustard, buckwheat and woad, or trapped with hollowed out potatoes or roots.

WOOD ashes

A rich source of potash these should be sprinkled on the ground, ideally in spring, before they're wetted or the goodness washes out. These have been used to discourage pests and are effective against many fungus diseases. Wood ashes are most appreciated by gooseberries and culinary apples.

WOODLICE / SLATERS / PILLBUGS / PEA BUGS

Lucasius spp. Apparently edible if not palatable relation of lobster and crab, 37 species in UK.
Most common predation (40% of population is eaten) by centipedes.
These do similar damage to slugs and snails leaving trails of destruction behind them. However whilst molluscs rasp these pests have different and smaller mouthparts and chew at the edges of leaves and petals and through and around small stems. They are often the real culprit when slugs and snails are thought the guilty ones. Coming out mostly at night they may attack en masse when they do considerable damage, I've seen a pack of woodlice chewing down a potato plant. They also predate other smaller pests and their eggs and are processors of dead material such as decaying wood so have their part to play in the garden ecology being useful snacks to bigger creatures.

Good food for chickens or wild birds they are easily caught with a portable vacuum cleaner as they're too quick to catch by hand. Trap woodlice under bits of decaying old wood or bark, in hollowed out potatoes or roots and in stacks of tiles, bricks or saucers.

Several species of woodlice live in ants nests; Lucasius myrmecophilus, L. pallidus, L. tardas and L. pauper. One wood louse Platyarthrus hoffmanseggi, is associated with ants all over Europe. It has been living in their nests so long it has evolved to an eyeless white form found only in ants nests.

WOOLLY APHID / AMERICAN BLIGHT

Eriosoma lanigerum is a particular problem on apples, some more than others, Allington Pippin and Blenheim Orange especially so. Growing nasturtiums under and up through the trees takes several seasons to reduce the infestation.

Predated by Ladybird larvae, Hoverflies and a minute wasp-like parasite Aphelinus mali.

WORMS

These are probably the most important animals on the planet. It is due to their efforts that most soils are fertile and they should be encouraged. Grass clippings and seaweed meal feed them, valerian is beneficial and they may like onion wastes. The big worms we wish to encourage need lime in the soil to thrive. Their main predators are many birds, moles, foxes and badgers, and they're currently being wiped out by Flatworms.

Yucca, ADAM'S NEEDLES

American plant there pollinated by small white moth, this makes a ball of pollen, deliberately inserts this into a special hollow in the top of the stigma of the next flower and lays eggs in the ovary, the larvae consume some of the resultant seed but seldom all.

Zea mays, CORN, MAIZE, SWEET CORN

Maize as grown worldwide are varieties for animal fodder and are not good eating whereas Sweet Corn are varieties chosen for their soft sweet kernels. Pop corn is a special variety and Mealies are the African forms of maize.

Maize may produce up to fifty tons per acre with a dry matter yield of five tons containing three hundred pounds of oil and five hundred pounds of ash.

Sweet corn and maize was traditionally grown in hillocks covering a dead fish. Incorporating fishmeal, seaweed meal or compost is the modern alternative as they need very rich soil.

The dried stems, leaves and all, tied in bundles and secreted in dry places such as inside evergreens and under eaves make remarkably popular homes for over-wintering ladybirds.

The Frit fly Oscinis frit can ruin maize plants, also attacks oats, the eggs laid in spring hatch to tiny legless larvae which eat into the growing point and the plant is stunted even killed, new leaves are stunted and crops suffer, there can be up to three generations in a year, then larvae overwinter in grasses.

Smut Ustilago maydis causes large boils which ooze on any part of the plant especially the cobs, the infection is purely local with boils forming wherever spores land, it does not progress through the whole plant though yields drop because of infected cobs and the plant may become distorted, commoner in warm wet years when temperature is approx. 86°F. Chlamydospores overwinter on debris and remain viable for up to five years. Oddly the infected cob is considered an esculental delicacy in some countries.

Zinnia.

These easy garden flowers have been observed to attract a very wide range of different insect species.

Glossary

English common names and their Latin genus.

ABELE Populus
ACRID LETTUCE Lactuca
ADAM'S NEEDLES Yucca
AGRIMONY Agrimonia
ALDER Alnus
ALDER-BUCKTHORN Rhamnus
ALFALFA Medicago
ALGERIAN IRIS Iris
ALPINE CURRANT Ribes
ALPINE LADY'S MANTLE Alchemilla
ALPINE MEADOW-GRASS Poa
ALPINE SAXIFRAGE Saxifragas
ALSIKE CLOVER Trifolium
AMARANTH Amaranthus
AMPHIBIOUS BISTORT Polygonum
ANISE Pimpinella
ANISEED Anise
ANISE HYSSOP Agastache
ANNUAL MEADOW-GRASS Poa
APPLE Malus
APRICOT Prunus
ARCTIC SAXIFRAGE Saxifraga
ASPARAGUS BEAN Vigna
ASTER Callistephus

AUTUMN GENTIAN Gentiana
AUTUMN HAWKBIT Leontodon

BABY BLUE EYES Nemophila
BABY'S BREATH Gypsophila
BAJRA Pennisetum
BALSAM Impatiens
BANEBERRY Actaea
BARNYARD GRASS Echinochloa
BARLEY Hordeum
BASIL Ocimum
BASTARD BALM Melittis
BAY Laurus
BEANS Phaseolus & Vicia
BEARBERRY Arctostaphylos
BEAR'S BREECHES Acanthus
BEAUTY BUSH Kolkwitzia
BEE BALM Monarda
BEECH Fagus
BEET Beta
BEETROOT Beta
BELL HEATHER Erica
BENT GRASS Agrostis
BERGAMOT Monarda
BERMUDA GRASS Cynodon
BERSEEM CLOVER Trifolium
BETONY Betonica / Stachys
BILBERRY Vaccinium
BINDWEED Convolvulus
BIRCH Betula
BIRCH BRACKET FUNGUS Polyporus

BIRD CHERRY Prunus
BIRD'S-FOOT Ornithopus
BIRD'S FOOT TREFOIL Lotus
BIRTHWORT Aristolochia
BITING STONECROP Sedum
BITTERCRESS Cardamine
BITTER SNEEZEWEED Helenium
BITTERSWEET Solanum
BLACK BINDWEED Bilderdykia / Polygonum
BLACK BRYONY Tamus
BLACK GRAM Phaseolus
BLACK HOREHOUND Ballota
BLACK MEDICK Medicago
BLACK MULLEIN Verbascum
BLACK NIGHTSHADE Solanum
BLACKBERRIES Rubus
BLACKTHORN Prunus
BLADDER CAMPION Silene
BLADDER SEDGE Carex
BLADDER SENNA Colutea
BLANKET FLOWER Gaillardia
BLAZING STAR Liatris
BLUEBELL Scilla
BLUEGRASS Poa
BOGBEAN Menyanthes
BOG MYRTLE Myrica
BOX Buxus
BOX ELDER Acer
BRACKEN Pteris
BRAKE Pteris
BRANCHED BUR-REED Sparganium

BRANDY-BOTTLE Nuphar
BRISTLY OX-TONGUE Picris
BROAD BEANS Vicia
BROAD-LEAVED WILLOW-HERB Epilobium
BROME GRASS Brachypodium & Bromus
BROOKLIME Veronica
BROOM Cytisus /Sarothamnus
BROOM-RAPES Orobanche
BROWN BENT-GRASS Agrostis
BROWN BRACKET FUNGUS Polyporus
BROWN-RIBBED BRACKET FUNGUS Paxillus
BUCKBEAN Menyanthes
BUCKTHORN Rhamnus
BUCKWHEAT Fagopyrum
BUGLE Ajuga
BUGLOSS Anchusa
BULLACE Prunus
BULBOUS BUTTERCUP Ranunculus
BULRUSH Scirpus
BURDOCK Arctium
BURNET ROSE Rosa
BURNET-SAXIFRAGE Pimpinella
BURNING BUSH Dictamnus
BURR CHERVIL Chaerophyllum
BUSH-GRASS Calamagrostis
BUSH VETCH Vicia
BUTCHER'S BROOM Ruscus
BUTTERBUR Petasites
BUTTERCUPS Ranunculus
BUTTERFLY BUSH Buddleia
BUTTERWORTS Pinguicula

CABBAGE Brassica
CALIFORNIAN POPPY Eschsolzia
CANARY GRASS, Phalaris
CANDYTUFT Iberis
CANOLA Brassica
CAPER SPURGE Euphorbia
CAPE HYACINTH Galtonia
CARAWAY Carum
CARDINAL FLOWER Lobelia
CARDOON Cynara
CARLINE THISTLE Carlina
CARNATION SEDGE Carex
CARROT Daucus
CASTOR Ricinus
CATCHWEED Galium
CATNIP Nepeta
CAT'S-EAR Hypochaeris
CAT'S TAIL GRASS Phleum
CAULIFLOWER Brassica
CEDAR Cedrus
CELERY Apium
CENTAURY Erythraea
CHAMOMILE, CORN Anthemis
CHAMOMILE, GERMAN Matricaria
CHAMOMILE, ROMAN Anthemis
CHAMOMILE, STINKING Anthemis
CHARLOCK Brassica & Sinapsis
CHERRY Prunus
CHERRY LAUREL Prunus
CHERVIL Anthriscus

CHESTNUT, HORSE Aesculus
CHESTNUT, SWEET Castanea
CHICKWEEDS Cerastium & Stellaria
CHICKPEA Cicer
CHICORY Cichorium
CHILEAN GLORY FLOWER Eccremocarpus
CHILEAN POTATO TREE Solanum
CHINA ASTER Callistephus
CHINESE CABBAGE / GREENS Brassica
CHIVES Alliums
CHRISTMAS ROSE Hellebore
CINQUEFOIL Potentilla
CLEAVERS Galium
CLIMBING BITTERSWEET Celastrus
CLOVER Trifoliums
CLUSTER BEANS Cyamopis
CLUSTERED BELLFLOWER Campanula
COCK'S-FOOT GRASS Dactylis
COCKSPUR Panicum
COGONGRASS Imperata
COLLARDS Brassicas
COLTSFOOT Tussilago
COLUMBINE Aquilegia
COMFREY Symphytum
CONEFLOWERS Rudbeckia
CONFLUENT LICHEN Lecidea
CORAL FLOWER Heuchara
CORAL-ROOT Cardamine
CORIANDER Coriandrum
CORN CHAMOMILE Anthemis
CORN COCKLE Agrostemma

CORN GROMWELL Lithospermum
CORN MARIGOLD Chrysanthemum
CORN MINT Mentha
CORN SOW-THISTLE Sonchus
CORNEL Cornus
CORNELIAN CHERRY Cornus
CORNFLOWER Centaurea
CORN SALAD Valerianella
COTTON Gossypium.
COTTON-GRASS Eriophorum
COTTON LAVENDER Santolina
COTTON THISTLE Onopordum
COUCH Agropyron
COURGETTE Cucurbita
COWBANE Cicuta
COWBERRY Vaccinium
COW PARSNIP Heracleum
COWSLIP Primula
COW-WHEAT Melampyrum
CRABGRASS Digitaria
CRACK WILLOW Salix
CRANE'S-BILL Geranium
CREEPING CLUB-RUSH Scirpus
CREEPING CROWFOOT Ranunculus
CREEPING SOFT-GRASS Holcus
CREEPING YELLOW-CRESS Rorippa
CRESS Lepidium
CRESTED DOG'S-TAIL GRASS Cynosurus
CRIMSON CLOVER Trifolium
CROSS-LEAVED HEATH Erica
CROWBERRY Empetrum

CUBAN SPINACH Claytonia
CUCKOO-FLOWER Cardamine
CUCKOO PINT Arum
CUCUMBER Cucumis
CUDWEED Filago / Gnaphalium
CURLED DOCK Rumex
CURRANTS Ribes
CYPRESS Chaemaecyparis
CYPRESS SPURGE Euphorbia

DAFFODIL Narcissus
DAISIES Bellis
DAISY BUSH Olearia
DAME'S VIOLET Hesperis
DANDELION Taraxacum
DARNEL Lolium
DAYLILY Hemerocallis
DEADLY NIGHTSHADE Atropa
DEAD NETTLE Lamium
DEPTFORD PINK Dianthus
DEVIL'S-BIT SCABIOUS Scabiosa
DEVIL'S CLAW Proboscidea
DEWBERRY Rubus
DILL Antheum
DOCK Rumex
DODDER Cuscuta
DOG LICHEN Peltigera
DOG ROSE Rosa
DOGWOOD Cornus
DOUGLAS FIR Pseudotsuga
DUCKWEED LEMNA

DUKE OF ARGYLL'S TEA PLANT Lycium
DUSTY MILLER Cineraria
DWALE Atropa
DWARF ELDER Sambucus
DWARF JUNIPER Juniperus
DWARF MALLOW Malva
DYER'S GREENWEED Genista
DYER'S ROCKET Reseda

EARTHNUT Conopodium
EGGPLANT Solanum
ELDERBERRY Sambucus
ELMS Ulnus.
ENCHANTER'S NIGHTSHADE Circaea
ENGLISH CATCHFLY Silene
ESPARSETTE Onobrychis
EUROPEAN SILVER FIR Abies
EVENING PRIMROSE Oenothera
EVERGREEN OAK Quercus
EVERLASTING PEA Lathyrus
EYEBRIGHT Euphrasia

FALSE ACACIA Robinia
FALSE-OAT Arrhenatherum
FALSE VALERIAN Centranthus
FAT HEN Chenopodium
FENNEL Foeniculum
FEN-SEDGE Cladium
FENUGREEK Trigonella
FESCUES Festuca
FEVERFEW Chrysanthemum / Matricaria

FIELD BINDWEED Convolvolus
FIELD BROME-GRASS Bromus
FIELD GENTIAN Gentiana
FIELD MAPLE Acer
FIELD MELILOT Melilotus
FIELD MOUSE-EAR CHICKWEED Cerastium
FIELD FORGET-ME-NOT Myosotis
FIELD SCABIOUS Knautia
FIELD SOUTHERNWOOD Artemesia
FIELD WOOD-RUSH Luzula
FIELD WOUNDWORT Stachys
FIG Ficus
FIGWORT Scrophularia
FIORIN Agrostis
FINE BENT Agrostis
FIRS Abies
FIRETHORN Pyracantha
FLAX Linum
FLEABANE Inula & Erigeron
FLIXWEED Sisymbrium
FLOWERING CURRANT Ribes
FLY AGARIC Agaricus
FOXGLOVE Digitalis
FORGET-ME-NOT Myosotis
FRENCH BEANS Phaseolus
FRENCH MARIGOLD Tagetes
FRENCH WILLOW Salix
FROSTED ORACHE Atriplex
FUMITORY Fumaria

GALINGALE Cyperus

GARLIC Allium
GARLIC MUSTARD Alliaria
GAY FEATHER Liatris
GERANIUM (tender) Pelargonium
GERMAN MILLET Setaria
GIPSYWORT Lycopus
GLADDON IRIS Iris
GLAUCOUS SEDGE Carex
GLOBE ARTICHOKE Cynara
GLOBE-FLOWER Trollius
GLOBE THISTLE Echinops
GOJI Lycium
GOLDENROD Solidago
GOATSBEARDS Tragopogon
GOLDEN RAIN TREE Koelreuteria
GOLDEN SAMPHIRE Inula
GOOSEBERRY Ribes
GOOSEFOOT Chenopodium
GOOSEGRASS Galium
GRAM Cicer
GRAIN SORGHUM Sorghum
GRAPE HYACINTH Muscari
GRAPEVINE Vitis
GREATER PERIWINKLE Vinca
GREAT MULLEIN Verbascum
GREAT WOOD-RUSH Luzula
GREATER BURNET-SAXIFRAGE Pimpinella
GREATER FLEABANE Inula
GREATER KNAPWEED Centaurea
GREATER MEADOW-RUE Thalictrum
GREATER REED-MACE Typha

GREATER STITCHWORT Stellaria
GREATER WATER PARSNIP Sium
GREEN ALKANET Pentaglottis
GREEN AMARANTH Amaranthus
GREENLEAF Desmodium
GREEN NIGHTSHADE Solanum
GROUND ELDER Aegopodium
GROUND IVY Glechoma
GROUNDNUT Apios
GROUNDSEL Senecio
GUELDER ROSE Viburnum

HAGBERRY Prunus
HAIR- GRASS Aira
HAIRY BIRCH Betula
HAIRY NIGHTSHADE Solanum
HAIRY VETCH Vicia
HAIRY WOOD-RUSH Luzula
HAIRY WILLOW-HERB Epilobium
HAREBELL Campanula
HARE'S-TAIL COTTON-GRASS Eriophorum
HAWKWEEDS Hieracium
HAWKWEED OX TONGUE Picris
HAWTHORN Crataegus
HAZELS Corylus
HEARTSEASE Viola
HEATHER Erica
HEATH FALSE-BROME GRASS Brachypodium
HEATH BEDSTRAW Galium
HEDGE BEDSTRAW Galium
HEDGE OR BUR PARSLEY Torilis

HEDGE WOUNDWORT Stachys
HEDGE MUSTARD Sisymbrium
HEATH RUSH Juncus
HELIOTROPE Heliotropium
HELLEBORINES Epipactis
HEMLOCK STORK'S-BILL Erodium
HEMP Cannabis
HEMP AGRIMONY Eupatorium
HEMP-NETTLE Galeopsis
HENBANE Hyoscyamus
HERB ROBERT Geranium
HIMALAYAN BALSAM Impatiens
HOARY MULLEIN Verbascum
HOG'S FENNEL Peucedanum
HOGWEED Heracleum
HOLLY Ilex
HOLLYHOCK Alcea & Althaea
HONEYSUCKLES Lonicera
HOLM OAK Quercus
HONESTY Lunaria
HOP Humulus.
HORSE CHESTNUT Aesculus
HOREHOUND Marrubium
HORNBEAM Carpinus
HORSERADISH Armoracia
HORSESHOE VETCH Hippocrepis
HORSETAIL Equisetum
HOUND'S-TONGUE Cynoglossum
HUNGARIAN GRAZING RYE Lolium
HYSSOP Hyssopus

INDIAN BEAN Catalpa
ITALIAN RYEGRASS Lolium
IVY Hedera
IVY-LEAVED TOADFLAX Cymbalaria

JACOBS LADDER Polemonium
JAPANESE ANGELICA TREE Aralia
JAPANESE KNOTWEED Fallopia / Reynoutria
JAPONICA Chaenomeles
JERUSALEM ARTICHOKE Helianthus
JOHNSON GRASS Sorghum
JOINTED RUSH Juncus
JUDAS TREE Cercis
JUNIPER Juniperus
JUTE Corchorus

KALE Brassica
KEMPTON'S WEED Stevia
KIDNEY VETCH Anthyllis
KIWI Actinidia
KNAPWEED Centaurea
KNOTGRASS Polygonum
KNOTTED FIGWORT Scrophularia
KOHL-RABI Brassicas

LABLAB BEANS Lablab
LADY'S BEDSTRAW Galium
LADY'S-MANTLE Alchemilla
LADY'S SMOCK Cardamine
LAMB'S EARS Stachys
LAMBSQUARTERS Chenopodium

LARKSPUR Delphinium
LAURUSTINUS Viburnum
LAVENDER Lavendula
LEAF BEET Beta
LEAFY SPURGE, Euphorbia
LEOPARDS-BANE Doronicum
LEAST LETTUCE Lactuca
LEEKS Allium
LEMON Citrus
LEMON BALM Melissa
LENT ROSE Hellebore
LENTIL Lens
LESSER MEADOW-RUE Thalictrum
LESSER QUAKING-GRASS Briza
LESSER REED-MACE Typha
LESSER SCABIOUS Scabiosa
LESSER STITCHWORT Stellaria
LESSER YELLOW TREFOIL Trifolium
LETTUCE Lactuca
LILAC Syringa
LILY OF THE VALLEY Convallaria
LIME Tillia.
LIMPOGRASS Hemarthria
LING Calluna
LITTLE MOUSE-EAR CHICKWEED Cerastium
LOCUST Robinia
LOOSESTRIFE Lythrum
LORDS AND LADIES Arum
LOTUS Lotus
LOUSEWORT Pedicularis
LOVAGE Levisticum

LOVE IN A MIST Nigella
LUCERNE Medicago
LUNGWORT Pulmonaria
LUPINS Lupinus
LYCHEE TOMATO Solanum
LYME GASS Elymus

MADAGASCAR PRIMROSE Caltharanthus
MADWORT Alyssum
MAIZE Zea
MALE FERN Aspidium
MALLOW Malva
MANY-COLOURED BRACKET FUNGUS Polystictus
MAPLE Acer
MARAM GRASS Psamma
MARJORAM Oreganum.
MARRAM-GRASS Ammophila
MARROW Cucurbita
MARSH BEDSTRAW Galium
MARSH LOUSEWORT Pedicularis
MARSH MARIGOLDS Caltha
MARSH PEA Lathyrus
MARSH SEDGE Carex
MARSH SOW-THISTLE Sonchus
MARSH ST JOHN'S WORT Hypericum
MARSH THISTLE Carduus
MARSH WILLOW-HERB Epilobium
MAT-GRASS Nardus
MAYWEEDS Matricaria & Anthemis
MEADOW BUTTERCUP Ranunuculus
MEADOW CAT'S-TAIL Phleum

MEADOW FESCUE-GRASS Festuca
MEADOW FOX-TAIL Alopecuris
MEADOW GRASSES Poa
MEADOW SAFFRON Colchicum
MEADOW SAXIFRAGE Saxifraga
MEADOW-SWEET Spiraea / Filipendula
MEADOW VETCHLING Lathyrus
MEDLAR Mespilus
MELILOT Melilotus
MELON Cucumis
MEXICAN COCKROACH PLANT Haplophyton
MEZEREON Daphne
MICHAELMAS DAISY Aster
MIGNONETTE Reseda
MILK THISTLE Silybum
MILK-VETCH Astragalus
MILKWEEDS Asclepias
MILKWEED VINE Morrenia
MILKWORT Polygala
MINTS Mentha
MISCANTHUS Miscanthus
MISTLETOE Viscum
MONKSHOOD Aconitum
MORNING GLORY Ipomea
MOSS CAMPION Silene
MOSSY SAXIFRAGE Saxifraga
MOTH BEAN Vigna
MOTHERWORT Leonurus
MOUNTAIN CRANBERRY Vaccinium
MOUNTAIN EVERLASTING Antennaria
MOUNTAIN SAXIFRAGE Saxifraga

MOUSE-EAR CHICKWEED Cerastium
MOUSE-EAR HAWKWEED Hieracium
MUGWORT Artemesia
MULBERRY Morus
MUNG BEAN Vigna
MUSTARD Brassica

NAKED LADIES Colchicum
NARROW-LEAVED RAGWORT Senecio
NASTURTIUMS Tropaeolum
NAVELWORT Cotyledon
NEEDLE-FURZE Genista
NETTLE-LEAVED BELLFLOWER Campanula
NIGHTSHADES Solanum
NOTTINGHAM CATCHFLY Silene

OAKS Quercus
OAT-GRASS Avena / Arrhenatherum
OATS Avena
OKRA Hibiscus/Abelmoschus
OLEANDER Nerium
ONIONS Allium
ORACHE Atriplex
ORANGE Citrus
ORANGE WALL LICHEN Xanthoria
OREGANO Oreganum
OREGON GRAPE Mahonia
ORPINE Sedum
OX EYE DAISY Chrysanthemum
OX TONGUE Picris

PAK CHOI Brassica
PALMER AMARANTH Amaranthus
PANSY Viola
PARSLEY Petroselinum
PARSNIP Pastinaca
PASSION FLOWER Passiflora
PEA Pisum
PEA TREE Caragana
PEACH Prunus
PEAR Pyrus
PEARL MILLET Pennisetum
PELLITORY Parietaria
PENNYCRESS Thlaspi
PENNYROYAL Mentha
PEPPERMINT Mentha
PEPPERS Capsicum
PERPETUAL SPINACH Beta
PERENNIAL RYEGRASS Lolium
PERENNIAL SOW-THISTLE Sonchus
PERFORATED St. JOHN'S WORT Hypericum
PERIWINKLE Vinca
PERUVIAN CHERRY Nicandra.
PETTY SPURGE Euphorbia
PIGEON PEA Cajanus
PIGWEED, Amaranthus retroflexus
PINE Pinus
PINE BRACKET FUNGUS Polystictus
PITCHER PLANT Sarracenia
PLANES Platanus
PLANTAINS Plantago
PLOUGHMANS SPIKENARD Inula

PLUM Prunus
POACHED EGG PLANT Limnanthes
POKEWEED Phytolacca
POPLAR Populus
POPPY Papaver
PORTLAND SPURGE Euphorbia
PORTUGESE LAUREL Prunus
POT MARIGOLD Calendula
POTATOES Solanum
PRICKLY LETTUCE Lactuca
PRICKLY SALTWORT Salsola
PRIMROSE Primula
PRIVET Ligustrum
PROSO MILLET Panicum
PUMPKIN Cucurbita
PURPLE COW-WHEAT Melampyrum
PURPLE NUTSEDGE Cyperus
PURPLE SANDWORT Spergularia
PURPLE SAXIFRAGE Saxifraga
PURPLE SMALL-REED Calamagrostis
PURPLE VIPERS BUGLOSS Echium
PURPLE WILLOW Salix
PURSLANE Portulaca
PYRAMID ORCHID Anacamptis

QUACK GRASS Agropyrum
QUAKING-GRASS Briza
QUICKTHORN Crataegus
QUINCE Chaenomeles / Cydonia

RADISH Raphanus

RAGGED ROBIN Lychnis
RAGWEED Ambrosia / Senecio
RAGWORT Senecio.
RAMSONS Allium
RASPBERRY Rubus.
RAULI Nothofagus
RED BEET Beta
RED BRYONY Bryonia
RED CAMPION Lychnis
RED CLOVER Trifolium
RED DEAD NETTLE Lamium
RED GOOSEFOOT Chenopodium
RED GRASS DigrAphis
RED HEMP-NETTLE Galeopsis
RED MILLET Panicum
RED OSIER Cornus
RED RATTLE Pedicularis
REDROOT PIGWEED Amaranthus
REDSHANK Polygonum
RED SPURREY Spergularia
RED WHORTLEBERRY Vaccinium
REED Arundo
REED-GRASS DigrAphis
REED MEADOW-GRASS Poa
REFLEXED MEADOW-GRASS Poa
REST-HARROW Ononis
RHUBARB Rheum
RICE Oryza
ROCKET Barbarea
ROCK-ROSE Helianthemum & Cistus
ROSE BAY WILLOWHERB Epilobium

ROSEMARY Rosmarinus
ROSES Rosa
ROUGH BROME-GRASS Bromus
ROUGH CHERVIL Chaerophyllum
ROUND-HEADED RAMPION Phyteuma
ROWAN Sorbus
RUBBER PLANT Ficus
RUE Ruta
RUNNER BEANS Phaseolus
RUSH Juncus
RUSSIAN LAVENDER Perovskia
RYE Secale
RYEGRASS Lolium

SAFFLOWER Carthamnus
SAGE Salvia
SAINFOIN Onobrychis
SAINT JOHN'S WORT Hypericum
SAINT PATRICKS CABBAGE Saxifraga
SALAD BURNET Poterium
SALSIFY Tragopogon
SANDBUR Cenchrus
SAND QUITCH Agropyrum
SANDWORT Arenaria / Alsine
SAND-SPURREY Spergularia
SAVORY Satureia
SAWWORT Serratula
SCABIOUS Scabiosa
SCARLET PIMPERNEL Anagallis
SCENTLESS MAYWEED Tripleurospermum
SEA ASTER Aster

SEA BINDWEED Convolvulus
SEA BLITE Sueda
SEA BUCKTHORN Hippophae
SEA CAMPION Silene
SEA CLUB-RUSH Scirpus
SEA FESCUE-GRASS Festuca
SEA HARD-GRASS Lepturus
SEA HOLLY Eryngium
SEAKALE Crambe
SEA LAVENDER Limonium
SEA MEADOW-GRASS Poa
SEA MILKWORT Glaux
SEA ORACHE Atriplex
SEA ROCKET Cakile
SEA SANDWORT Arenaria
SEA SPURGE Euphorbia
SEA SPURREY Spergularia
SEA WORMWOOD Artemesia
SEDGES Carex
SELF-HEAL Prunella
SERVICE Sorbus
SHALLOTS Allium
SHASTA DAISY Chrysanthemum
SHEEP'S FESCUE Festuca
SHEEP"S SORREL Rumex
SHEPHERD'S PURSE Capsella
SHINING BLACK BRACKET FUNGUS Daldinia
SHINING CRANE'S-BILL Geranium
SHOOFLY Nicandra
SICKLE MEDICK Medicago
SILVERWEED Potentilla

SIMPLE BUR-REED Sparganium
SLENDER FALSE-BROME GRASS Brachypodium
SLENDER St. JOHN'S WORT Hypericum
SLOE Prunus
SMOKE TREE Cotinus
SMOOTH HAWKSBEARD Crepis
SMOOTH MEADOW-GRASS Poa
SMOOTH-PEEL FUNGUS Corticum
SMOOTH SOWTHISTLE Sonchus
SNAKES HEAD FRITILLARY Fritillaria
SNAPDRAGON Antirrhinum
SNEEZEWEED Helenium
SNOWBERRY Symphoricarpus
SNOWDROP Galanthus
SNOWFLAKE Leucojum
SNOWY MESPILUS Amelanchier
SOAPWORT Saponaria
SOLOMONS SEAL Polygonatum
SORGHUM Sorghum
SORREL Rumex
SOUTHERNWOOD Artemesia
SOWBREADS Cyclamen
SOWTHISTLES Sonchus
SOYA Glycine
SPANISH BROOM Spartium
SPANISH CATCHFLY Silene
SPEEDWELL Veronica
SPIDER PLANT Chlorophytum
SPINACH Spinacia
SPINDLE Euonymous
SPOTTED PERSICARY Polygonum

SPREADING MILLET-GRASS Milium
SPRING SANDWORT Minuartia
SPRUCE Picea
SPURGES Euphorbia
SPURRY Spergula
SQUARE-STEMMED WILLOW-HERB Epilobium
SQUASHES Cucurbita
STAGS HORN SUMACH Rhus
STAR LICHEN Physcia
STARWORT Aster
STATICE Limonium
STRAWBERRY TREE Arbutus
STRAWBERRIES Fragaria
STINGING NETTLE Urtica
STINKING GOOSEFOOT Chenopodium
STINKING GROUNDSEL Senecio
STINKING IRIS Iris
STINKING MAYWEED Anthemis
STINKWEED Diplotaxis
STOCKS Matthiola
SUCCORY Cichorium
SUGAR BEET Beta
SUGAR MAPLE Acer
SUMMER HYACINTH Galtonia
SUMMER SAVORY Satureija
SUNFLOWER Helianthus
SUN ROSE Cistus
SUN SPURGE Euphorbia
SUPERB LILY Gloriosa
SWAMP BEDSTRAW Galium
SWEDE Brassica

SWEDISH COFFEE Astragalus
SWEET ALYSSUM Alyssum
SWEET CHESTNUT Castanea
SWEET CICELY Myrrhis
SWEET FLAG Acorus
SWEET GALE Myrica
SWEET GUM Liquidamabr
SWEET PEA Lathyrus
SWEET ROCKET Hesperis
SWEET-SCENTED VERNAL GRASS, Anthoxanthum
SWEET TOBACCO Nicotiana
SWEET WILLIAM Dianthus
SWINE CRESS Coronopus
SWISS CHARD Beta
SYCAMORE Acer
SYRIAN SAGE Salvia

TALL FESCUE Festuca
TAMARISK Tamarix
TANSY Tanacetum / Chrysanthemum
TARES Vicia
TARO Colocasia
TARRAGON Artemesia
TEA-LEAVED WILLOW Salix
TEASELS Dipsacus
THISTLES Carduus and Cirsium
THORNAPPLE Datura
THRIFT Armeria
THYME Thymus
TIGER FLOWER Tigridia
TIL Sesamum

TIMOTHY Phleum
TOADFLAX Linaria
TOBACCO Nicotiana
TOMATO Lycopersicon
TOOTHWORT Lathraea
TORMENTIL Potentilla
TOWER MUSTARD Arabis
TRAVELLER'S JOY Clematis
TREACLE MUSTARD Erysimum
TREE MALLOW Lavatera
TREE OF HEAVEN Ailanthus
TREFOIL Trifolium
TUBEROUS PEA Lathyrus
TUFTED DEER'S-GRASS Scirpa
TUFTED HAIR-GRASS Aira
TUFTED SEDGE Carex
TUFTED VETCH Vicia
TULIP TREE Liriodendron
TURNIP Brassica
TWAYBLADE Listera
TWITCH, Agropyrum

UDU Aralia
UNICORN Proboscidea

VALERIAN Valeriana
VIRGINIA CREEPER Parthenocissus
VELVETLEAF Abutilon
VERVAIN Verbena
VETCHES Vicia
VIOLETS Viola

VIPER'S BUGLOSS Echium
VISCID MOUSE-EAR CHICKWEED Cerastium

WALLFLOWERS Cheiranthus
WALL HAWKWEED Hieracium
WALL PENNYWORT Cotyledon (sic)
WALNUTS Juglans
WATER AVENS Geum
WATER BETONY Scrophularia
WATERCRESS Nasturtium
WATER FIGWORT Scrophularia
WATERMELON Citrullus
WATER-MINT Mentha
WATER PLANTAIN Alisma
WATER SPEEDWELL Veronica
WATER STITCHWORT Stellaria
WAYFARING-TREE Viburnum
WEEPING LOVEGRASS Eragrostis
WELD Reseda
WHEAT Triticum
WHITE BEAK-SEDGE Rhynchospora
WHITEBEAM Sorbus
WHITE BRYONY Bryonia
WHITE CAMPION Lychnis
WHITE CHARLOCK Raphanus
WHITE CLOVER Trifolium
WHITE DRYAS Dryas
WHITE MIGNONETTE Reseda
WHITE STONECROP Sedum
WHITE WATERLILY Nymphaea
WHORL FLOWERED CLARY Salvia

WILD BEET Beta
WILD MADDER Rubia
WILD MUSTARD Brassica & Sinapsis
WILD PEA Lathyrus
WILD RADISH Raphanus
WILLOWHERB Epilobium
WILLOW LETTUCE Lactuca
WILLOWS Salix
WINGED SPINDLE Euonymous
WINTER ACONITE Eranthis
WINTERCRESS Barbarea
WINTER HELIOTROPE Petasites
WINTER PURSLANE Claytonia
WITCH Agropyrum
WITCH HAZEL Hamamelis
WOAD Isatis
WOLF'S-BANE Aconitum
WOOD AVENS Geum
WOOD BETONY Stachys
WOODBINE Lonicera
WOODRUFF Asperula
WOOD SORREL Oxalis
WOOD SPURGE Euphorbia
WOOD VETCH Vicia
WOOD WOUNDWORT Stachys
WOODY NIGHTSHADE Solanum
WORMWOOD Artemisia

YARROW Achillea
YELLOW ARCHANGEL Lamiastrum
YELLOW BALSAM Impatiens

YELLOW FIELDRESS Rorippa
YELLOW FIGWORT Scrophularia
YELLOW FLAG Iris
YELLOW FOXTAIL Setaria
YELLOW HORN Xanthocerus
YELLOW LOOSESTRIFE Lysimachia
YELLOW MEADOW-RUE Thalictrum
YELLOW MELILOT Melilotus
YELLOW RATTLE Rhinanthus
YELLOW-RIBBED BRACKET FUNGUS Stereum
YELLOW ROCKET Barbarea
YELLOW WATERLILY Nuphar
YEW Taxus
YORKSHIRE FOG Holcus

Printed in Great Britain
by Amazon

36381976R00280